Marketing Massage

How to Build Your Dream Practice

Dedication

To my parents, Floyd and Beverly Roseberry, for their boundless love and unwavering support.

Marketing Massage

How to Build Your Dream Practice

Monica Roseberry

DELMAR

TM

THOMSON LEARNING

Australia • Canada • Mexico • Singapore • Spain • United Kingdom • United States

Marketing Massage
How to Build Your Dream Practice
by Monica Roseberry

MILADY STAFF:

President:
Susan L. Simpfenderfer

Publisher:
Marlene McHugh Pratt

Acquisitions Editor:
Pamela B. Lappies

Developmental Editor:
Judy A. Roberts

Executive Production Manager:
Wendy A. Troeger

Production Editor:
Eileen M. Clawson

Executive Marketing Manager:
Donna J. Lewis

Channel Manager:
Wendy E. Mapstone

Cover Design: Dutton and Sherman Design   Composition: Type Shoppe II Productions

Printed in Canada

2 3 4 5 6 7 8 9 10   XXX 06 05 04 03 02

For more information contact Milady, 3 Columbia Circle, PO Box 15015, Albany, NY 12212-5015

Or find us on the World Wide Web at http://www.Milady.com

Library of Congress Cataloging-in-Publication Data

Roseberry, Monica.
        Marketing massage : how to build your dream practice / by Monica Roseberry
            p. cm.
        ISBN 1-56253-746-6
        1. Massage--Practice. I. Title

    RA780.5 .R674 2001
    615.8'22'068--dc21

                                                                2001045696

NOTICE TO THE READER

Contents

SECTION II
Muscle Marketing—Reaching, Rebooking, and Referrals 97

Preface

Who This Book Is For

This book is written for anyone who wants fast, effective, safe, proactive, low/no-cost, hope-free marketing to build a long-term career in massage. Whether you are a massage student still in school, a recent graduate just starting out, a part-time therapist trying to go full time, or you're tired of just getting by financially and want to grow your practice, this book is for you. If you are an experienced therapist moving to a new area and need to start a practice from scratch, this book can take months off your rebuilding process. If you are changing the emphasis of your practice to a new bodywork modality that will draw from a different market than you are familiar with, or if you want to make the leap from employee status to owning your own practice, this book will give you the marketing tools to help make your dream a reality. Whatever your situation, if you would rather spend your time working on your clients than doing traditional marketing, this book is definitely for you!

Massage in the New Century

Massage is growing at an unprecedented rate and is enjoying a surge in popularity with people from every walk of life. No longer just a luxury for the rich and famous, massage is making its way into the mainstream culture, and prospective clients everywhere are searching for professional massage therapists to help them with a host of needs. The current state of the profession is exciting, and for those of us who have worked for years to improve the stature, legitimacy, and acceptance of massage, it is gratifying to see the public embracing massage so eagerly.

However, massage is still an emerging profession, and we have much work ahead of us in continuing to define our profession, and educate the public about who we are and what we do. Massage has undergone continuous transformation over many centuries in many countries, revealing the fascinating and ever-changing cycles of how humans deal with their bodies and feel about touch. Now at the dawn of a new century, massage emerges again with practitioners facing opportunities and obstacles unique to this time, place, and profession. Marketing massage in the 21st century will take skills practiced by our forerunners in ancient Rome, Greece, Europe, and Asia, but it also will take reaching and serving clients with methods totally unique to our current circumstances. No other service industry faces such tremendous advantages or challenges as modern-day massage, and understanding how to market during this time can mean the difference between failure and success.

How This Book Got Started

To build your dream practice in the current environment of massage, you need to know two things: what successful massage professionals across the country have in common so you can learn from them, and what unsuccessful massage professionals have in common so you can avoid the mistakes that have cost countless practitioners their dreams. Discovering what it takes to succeed in this profession has been my passion, both for my own practice as well as for the thousands of students I have taught.

However, I never intended to extend that passion to writing a book about marketing massage. I never planned on doing years of research or traveling thousands of miles to learn what it takes to build and maintain a practice, but a single incident changed the course of my life and led to the long circuitous path that eventually culminated in this book. The incident lasted but a few moments and was fairly uneventful. I was standing in line at a coffee shop, laughing with a friend, waiting for my mocha, when I heard a voice calling my name over the hiss of frothing foam. I looked over the counter toward the voice, and my life was never the same again.

Her name came to me quickly, but the recognition wasn't a joyful one. The woman making my mocha was one of my former massage students, a woman who had gifted hands, who had struggled through numerous hardships to stay in massage school, and for whom I had high hopes when she graduated.

"What are you doing here?" I asked as casually as I could, fighting back my stab of fear of what her answer would be. "Oh, I tried to get a practice going after I graduated," she shrugged, "but I just couldn't get enough clients to make a living. You gotta eat, you know, so here I am."

I didn't cry then, since that's not the sort of thing I prefer to do in a coffee shop, but I did later. I had talked to other former students who hadn't quite made it in massage, but somehow this one really hurt. What had gone wrong? How could someone with gift and heart and a great education still not be able make a living in massage? What more could we have taught her? What else did she need to know to get her through those first stages of building a practice?

I had no answers to my questions, and since at that point I had left the massage school where I worked and taught for seven years, I had no forum to work within, so I took my questions and frustrations and shelved them. However, not too long after that, destiny stepped in. I got a call from a former massage student who had been in my business classes. "Would you be willing," she asked "to teach a seminar on marketing at a convention for the California Chapter of the American Massage Therapy Association?" I laughed. I asked her why I would want to teach a marketing class when it seemed to me that much of what I had taught before didn't work. "Besides," I confessed, "I've never really done the type of traditional marketing people would think they should hear about in a marketing seminar, so I don't think I should teach a class on it." My caller, Marcia, persisted. "But you've had a practice for years," she exclaimed. "How did you do that?" She was right. I'd had a successful practice since 1984, and since clients don't fall out of the sky, I must have been marketing, though not in the way most people would define as marketing.

I was about to say "no" again when I thought about the woman in the coffee shop. This was my chance to help her and others like her. This was my golden opportunity to sit down, think hard, read everything about marketing I could get my hands on, listen to every tape I could find, and create a marketing training program to answer the questions that had nagged me since I had seen her. I said "yes" to the seminar, not knowing what I was going to say or how much work I had ahead of me.

After months of gathering ideas about how to build a practice, especially in California where obstacles to success were so numerous, I came up with a marketing strategy that was a hit. My seminar students loved it and were eager to implement their new tools to build their practices. I was pleased with the seminar and gave it numerous times to other audiences, but deep in my heart I still felt there was something unthought of and unsaid that cut to the core of true success in the field of massage. I decided to broaden my search and began calling industry leaders, massage school owners, and teachers across the country, hoping to expand my perspective on what was nagging at me about marketing massage. But I was still unsatisfied.

What I really wanted was a formula for success, a kind of marketing massage formula that professionals could use to build their practices no matter where they lived and no matter what obstacles they faced. Did such a formula even exist, I wondered, and if it did, how would I find it? Finally, in the summer of 1999, I went on the ultimate quest for answers about marketing massage. I got a trailer, hitched it up to my truck, and drove 15,988 miles through 24 states over the span of five months conducting countless interviews with massage professionals, massage school owners, and the general public in search of what it takes to truly market massage.

What I found, especially from the general public, shocked, amazed, pleased and dismayed me, and eventually forced me to reconsider totally what I believed about marketing. More than anything, I was surprised because during my search, here's what I found: successful professionals with only a simple business card for advertising, skilled therapists whose primary marketing was wearing a T-shirt that mentioned massage, and person after person who could not tell me how they had marketed their way to a full practice beyond "just talking to everybody." From the mountain peaks of Idaho to the shores of Georgia, I came across therapists who had done little of what experts would consider to be marketing, yet they were thriving in their practices. On the other hand, I also met therapists with all of what I thought were the right marketing ingredients but who weren't making it financially. One woman in particular blew up my last shred of preconceived notions as she was closing up shop in spite of her fancy office with a receptionist, professionally designed cards and brochures, coupons, impressive website, and medical referral and insurance reimbursement setup.

I was stunned! Could marketing massage be so basic yet successful? I realized I'd have to start this formula for marketing success from scratch and identify a new set of common ingredients beyond the standard definition of marketing and more consistent with my field research. After sifting through my interview notes and memory bank, I found what I was looking for. I found what I believe to be the bare bones basics of what successful therapists have in common in virtually every type of practice anywhere in the country.

How to Use This Book

The book you hold in your hands is the result of my years of searching for how to market massage. After 17 years in private practice, thousands of hours of teaching and writing classes, and hundreds of hours of research, personal interviews, thinking, and rethinking to find real solutions for the real problems that massage therapists and bodyworkers face in building their practices, I think what I have learned can help you. For you as a massage student or professional aiming to make a living with massage, I hope what follows will start you on your way and keep you on the road to helping yourself while helping others by building a successful practice. For that student in the coffee shop, this is what I would have told her if I knew then what I know now.

The lessons I have gathered are recorded in two sections in this book.

The first section, Bare Bones Marketing, covers the fundamentals of basic marketing starting with the personal and professional attributes that are at the heart of marketing the personal service of massage. Combining these attributes with key marketing skills and tools covered in the Bare Bones section should give many professionals the foundation on which to build a flourishing practice. The formula for the first section is simple: Marketing Attributes + Skills + Tools = Success.

Please be forewarned, however, before reading the first section. My goal is to help you become a successful therapist with as many clients as you want for as many years as you choose to practice. Not everything I say may be comfortable, politically correct, or to everyone's liking. Some of the material may seem simplistic and mundane, or perhaps even strongly opinionated, but after interviewing hundreds of people who have received a professional massage or hired therapists as employees, I realized that I can take no skill for granted. I apologize up front if these basic but crucial skills of communication and human interaction seem obvious. However, after listening bug-eyed to an onslaught of horror stories of unprofessional behavior by purportedly professional therapists, I would be remiss if I did not do whatever possible to make an impact on my readers about what is bottom-line necessary to make it in this field. Every venture, whether it be learning a martial art, playing basketball, or building a massage practice requires practice and mastery of the fundamentals. Finally, you can learn what those fundamentals are.

The second section, Muscle Marketing, covers what virtually every successful practitioner has in common, or what I call the Three Rs of marketing. The Three Rs thoroughly cover numerous way to reach new clients, rebook those clients, and get personal referrals from them. Muscle Marketing builds on the Bare Bones, adding advanced skills, tools, and concepts designed to help practitioners grow a practice quickly, survive in a highly competitive market, or reach a very select clientele. However, I have found from my research that advanced marketing skills and tools are useless if the basic attributes are not in place, so master the attributes in the first section before you spend your time, energy, and money on the more advanced marketing in the later chapters.

These two sections will give you a solid foundation for beginning and operating your practice, and will provide many more ideas about growing your dream practice into reality. Take the time to read it and practice what you've learned. Then watch your practice grow!

About the Author

Monica Roseberry is a speaker, teacher, author, and massage therapist since 1984. A self-described "touch activist," she has reached thousands of massage therapists with the intention of helping each one succeed, driven by her belief that massage and bodywork professionals can change the culture of touch one massage at a time. Ms. Roseberry has written for *Massage Therapy Journal* and *Massage Magazine*, was an Item Writer for the National Certification Exam for Therapeutic Massage and Body Work, and is the author of an upcoming book on massage for The Body Shop, International. She lives in Walnut Creek, California.

Acknowledgments

This book would not have been possible without the help and support of numerous people. Special acknowledgment and undying gratitude goes to Jeannine Karafotas for her unflagging love and support; to Vav and Tatay for more than I can ever repay; to Susan Koenig who gave me a true love for massage; to Mack Terry who made becoming an author possible; to Dr. CJ Kalin, Karen Smith, and Ted Frey for conversation and feedback; and to my clients and friends who put up with my disappearance while writing. A special "thank you" to David Lauterstein of Austin, Texas, whose one-hour interview changed the course of this book; and many thanks to the many school directors, teachers, therapists, and countless strangers who gave me their time and told me their stories that made this book unfold. Additional thanks go to Lydia Wagner, copyeditor extraordinaire, and to Pamela Lappies, Judy Roberts, and the team at Delmar Thomson Learning for believing in me, this book, and the value of massage.

To contact the author, call 800-707-3462, or write to her online at Monica@MarketingMassage.com.

Bare Bones Marketing
Attributes, Skills, and Tools

Marketing Attributes

After reading this chapter, you should be able to:
- identify the four personal and professional attributes of successful massage professionals.
- identify your personal definition of success.
- describe the elements of your dream practice.
- identify common obstacles to success.
- explain the importance of setting boundaries.

The Definition of Marketing

What is marketing? There are many definitions, but for massage therapists, marketing, simply, is anything you do that affects your ability to get and keep clients. Marketing is a way of being; it is representing yourself, your work, and your profession in thousands of tangible and intangible ways. With this definition in mind, marketing can range from what topics you discuss with clients, to what types of oils you use or how you write press releases. Marketing can be the message you leave on your telephone answering machine, the television ad you create, or the extra five minutes you give listening to a lonely client. Essentially, everything you are and do is marketing. Marketing is the foundation on which your dream practice is built. We are going to delve deeply and specifically into what it takes for you, as a touch professional, to get and keep the clients you need to build your dream practice.

Without marketing, people will not consider massage as an option in their health, wellness, or recreation strategy. They also will not find therapists, even if they want massage, and they will not know to choose you to help them with their needs. Without marketing to get and keep clients, massage professionals will not be able to make a living in their chosen profession. Time and again, I have met therapists with good hands and caring hearts, but no understanding of marketing, who had to give up their dream of a career in massage.

Ultimately, then, at the heart of each therapist's professional success, is marketing. Even our personal satisfaction that comes from making a contribution of massage to so many lives is affected by our understanding of and ability to market. Marketing can help you reach your personal and professional dreams by building and maintaining a practice that serves you and your clients, and which, in turn, can make this world a better place to live. Touch professionals have the power in their hands to change the world and marketing is what it takes to get clients under your hands.

The Attributes of a Successful Professional

The first step in marketing massage is to recognize that massage therapy, unlike some professions, is often driven by the personality and attributes of the practitioner. Massage is a very personal service, and for lack of a better way to describe it, most therapists who have Swedish-based practices basically touch naked people for a living. This one fact alone separates us from virtually every other service profession, and it is why traditional marketing has not been very effective in our field. Since we touch naked people, how we comport ourselves and how we behave makes all the difference in the world in our ability to make a living. Plumbers and electricians can be rude or late, interior decorators can be brusque or condescending, web designers can be surly and unkempt, and landscapers do not have to make conversation as long as they do their jobs well. Even medical professionals who also deal with naked bodies can have poor bedside manner, but patients have little choice because medical care for illnesses or injuries is necessary, not optional in the way massage is.

Compared to most other professions, massage therapists are often judged by who we are, not just by what we do. Quite simply, if potential clients do not trust us or like us, we often will not get the chance to demonstrate our hands-on skills, no matter how good they are.

Therefore, the most important factors for marketing that I have found are personal attributes that build trust and maintain it at every step of the client/therapist relationship. During my research for this book, I saw that there were a few key attributes that successful practitioners had in common and that unsuccessful practitioners were missing. I discovered that if these key attributes were in place, therapists could make a living no matter what working environment they practiced in and regardless of their competition, regulatory laws, local economy, or education level. While these attributes are more about human nature than traditional marketing, they are a mandatory foundation for the function of marketing, which is to get and keep clients.

Marketing Attribute #1: A Desire to Serve

A desire to serve people may sound corny and simplistic, but it is not. Visiting a fraction of the more than 1,000 massage schools that have sprouted up across the country, I have found many filled with students who yearn to serve, mixed in with students lured primarily by dreams of easy money and high per-hour fees. While money is a crucial factor in success, long-term financial rewards are earned through years of work, sustained and motivated through the normal ups and downs by the unflagging desire to serve.

Clients, whether they can verbalize it or not, know when their massage therapist genuinely cares about them, or when they are in it for the fast buck

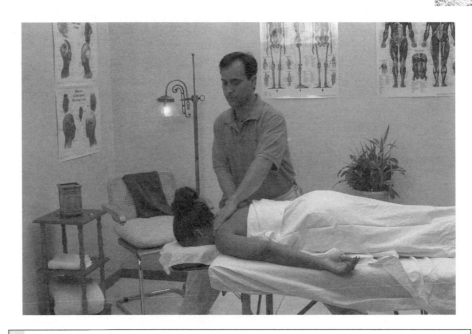

Figure 1–1   The desire to serve others is your key to success.

or other primarily personal reasons. Due to the very personal nature of massage, most private practices have been, and will continue to be, successful because of repeat clients and referrals. So let's face it. Unless therapists can love clients in spite of their often imperfect bodies and all-too-human personalities, repeats and referrals probably will not occur. While other professions may be able to skate by with lip service to genuine caring, the factor of touch in massage gives away true intentions. Like it or not, your desire to serve or not can be felt directly by your clients. Short-term success may be achieved without this attribute, but every massage therapist I've met who has achieved long-term success, carries in his or her heart and hands a genuine desire to serve.

I do not know if the desire to serve can be taught or learned. Some people seem to gravitate naturally toward a life of service while others would never dream of it. If you are somewhere in between and want to strengthen your ability to care for others so that you can market more effectively, I'll let you in on a secret: successful massage therapists serve others because it feels good. True service brings them a life of joy and satisfaction. At my most honest, I serve others for both altruistic and selfish reasons. When I help other people feel good or relieve their pain, I am happy, engaged with life, present, and fulfilled. When given the responsibility of touching other people's lives, and their bodies, I must grow and learn. This is one of the core factors to human happiness.

Serving others has a great payoff, but it is also fraught with risk. Caring about others opens us up to being hurt. We can be abandoned, or have our serving and caring rejected. We can have our attempts to help rebuffed. I can spend two years writing this book with the earnest desire to help my field and no one may read it. Really, serving others is not for wimps. Having a passion for helping others in a culture that is veering dangerously toward apathy and jadedness may not be cool, but it is great for succeeding in massage.

Building a dream practice demands a foundation of the desire to serve. That desire may come easily or take some effort, but without it, your practice will collapse with the tremors that eventually shake every business. If you don't have the desire to serve, cut your losses now. Put this book down, re-think your career, and consider other work options. It will save you time, money, and great frustration because long-term success is not possible without the drive fed by the desire to serve. However, if joy, happiness, financial reward, and fulfillment are part of what you envision in your dream practice, keep reading. If you are willing to explore the adventure of serving others, then you have what it takes to embark on a journey of self-discovery, life lessons, and a career in massage therapy.

EXERCISE: The Desire to Serve

- Write down 10 things that you hope to gain by serving others. Consider rewards that are mental, emotional, physical, spiritual, financial, and relational.

Marketing Attribute #2: The Commitment to Succeed

The commitment to succeed is a much more complex attribute than the desire to serve. While most professionals in this field have a genuine and unfettered desire to serve, the subject of success becomes a bit cloudier. First off, every person has his or her own unique definition of success. Second, many people do not know what it truly takes to succeed in massage. Third, many massage therapists have very mixed feelings about the consequences of being successful.

The Definition of Success

Before we get to what it takes to succeed, you first have to know what it is that you think success is. So, what is success to you? Do you have a clear and ready answer, or are you not all that sure? Have you made up your own definition, or has it been handed to you by someone else such as your parents, teachers, or friends? Take a minute to think about what success is to you.

Is success a feeling you have or is it based on what money can buy? Is it a big house on the hill or is it making a contribution to humanity? Is it making the world a better place or is it raising good children? Or is it all of these?

No answer is right or wrong. No answer is "better" than another. Your definition of success can be a powerful motivator for you and you should not edit it just because someone else has a different definition.

Is your definition of success easy to gain or are you making it too difficult? I suggest that you make it easy to feel successful. Success breeds success, so start easy; set and reach small, short-term goals; and get used to success and build up to the big stuff. Some people make it too difficult to feel successful. The challenge may drive them, but after a while, they get discouraged. If you decide that you are going to wait until you have a million dollars to finally be happy, that may take too long. Frankly, success can be as simple as the fact you woke up this morning. After all, a lot of people who were alive yesterday never woke up this morning, so just being alive may be a good enough measure of success.

As for a successful practice, that is yours to define as well. If you want a part-time practice operated out of your home while you pursue your acting career, that's fine. If you want to own a chain of massage franchises or a retreat center on 100 acres of wilderness, and have 20 healing arts practitioners from different disciplines working there, that's great too. If you want to work with dancers, infants, or homeless people, that is your prerogative to include them in your dream practice. This is your life and your practice that we are going to spend the rest of this book trying to make real, so think about it now and define your own success.

EXERCISE: Your Definition of Success

■   Write down your definition of success.

■   Write down 10 factors that would describe your successful dream practice.

What It Takes

Of all the attributes that I studied among massage therapists, what I found brought success to long-term therapists was this: a determined commitment to succeed. This may sound kind of obvious, but many people confuse hoping and wishing with commitment. If hoping and wishing worked, we would all have ponies, or motorcycles, or be great guitarists in a rock-and-roll band. Hoping and wishing have their place, but they don't get results. Commitment does. Resolve, determination, and doing what it takes is what gets you your success. It isn't always pretty and it isn't always fun, but if you want to strengthen your commitment to succeed so that you can reach your goals, keep reading.

The commitment to succeed became very clear to me when I met a woman who began her practice in the 1970s. At that time, she did not have a massage table, a car, or a telephone. No telephone? Most people would consider those items the bare necessities of building a practice, but to get started, she rode her bicycle to her clients' homes, put pillows on the floor, and gave massages for $5. When I interviewed this woman in March of 2000, her practice was still going strong. While her life is easier now that she has a table and a car and a telephone, I know that she can be successful no matter what her circumstances. She knows the secrets of true marketing, and her commitment to succeed supersedes any excuses, leaving her with what matters: results.

The first step in building your commitment to succeed is to work on your ability and willingness to manage and overcome obstacles. These can be external obstacles such as punitive licensing laws, or internal obstacles such as the fear of rejection. People end up with one of two things when facing the inevitable obstacles to building a practice: they get good excuses or good results. The successful therapists I met have worked through internal obstacles such as anger, and frustration and resentment of external obstacles such as unfair treatment by authorities, establishments, employers, or building owners. They overcame hostile environments, competitors with major advantages, or being forced to practice without a license because the city where they worked refused to give business permits to massage therapists. Regardless of their circumstances, successful therapists used their determination to work their way around whomever or whatever got in their way.

Professionals that I spoke with across the country who were "making it" had slogged through internal obstacles such as low self-esteem, flagging confidence, fear of the unknown, a sense of inadequacy, and weak boundary skills. Not surprisingly, many of them also had grappled with taking money for their caring touch. Issues such as these face most every massage therapist I have met or taught. While one may not consider confidence or self-esteem to be part of marketing, lack of either definitely can make it more difficult to get and keep clients. The commitment to succeed calls for dealing with difficult internal and external barriers of all types: it makes the difference between a happy and satisfying massage career or just working on a few friends and family members.

The unsuccessful therapists I met complained about everything imaginable. It was as if they were guided by a powerful belief that anything painful, disruptive or inconvenient was a personal affront to them, and was a valid reason to quit. Whether their friends and relations sympathized with their struggles, or they felt self-righteous in blaming the environment, their school, or the ever-popular "saturated market" for their woes, their commitment was to being right about their excuses, not about doing whatever it took to succeed. Unfortunately, their seemingly credible excuses nonetheless kept them from their dream of making a living with massage.

It is perfectly normal to feel fear, balk at change, or be resistant to new ideas. However, when these come out in the form of complaining or blaming, the commitment to succeed has to kick in, otherwise it is all over but the loan payments on an expensive education. When I was a massage teacher, a group of students got up in arms because the school where I worked had not yet put in a bicycle rack. Mind you, only one student actually rode a bike at that time, but you would think the school was on fire, given the outpouring of energy and group focus. All I could do was once again marvel that the normal fear that comes with growth and change came out as misdirected anger over something so trivial. Unfortunately, I had seen this pattern before with other groups of students. Somehow, just when they were reaching stages of major growth and change, something minor became the group's obsession and they backed away from the brink of their own success. For this particular group, some students were so wrapped up in being upset about the inconsequential bike rack that they damaged a significant portion of their learning experience, and very likely harmed their careers.

If you catch yourself getting angry or upset at seeming injustices and obstacles, that's normal and okay. It is when you get stuck in anger and frustration that the commitment to succeed and to serve must come to the fore to move you past the latest obstacle. If you have a "bike rack" obstacle that looks like a big deal but probably really isn't, consider the possibility that it is a smoke screen for internal fears. It is crucial that you treat those fears with respect and deal with them. If you don't, you will be likely to generate so many smoke screens that you will never get around to the actual work of getting and keeping clients.

Unfortunately, marketing and all that it represents in taking steps to meeting people, telling them about your work, and booking an appointment can set off alarm bells and push all the buttons human beings have. If your commitment is to being safe and comfortable, or to never feeling rejected or afraid, then you cannot grow the amount necessary to run a long-term practice. Growth can be scary, but it can also be exhilarating and life changing. If you want to succeed, you must grow and move past your fears and obstacles. It is part of maturing as a human being and, quite honestly, the process is one of the best benefits of being a massage therapist.

From Fear to Growth

Fear is a subject that most people do not seem eager to talk about. After all, it isn't very hip to admit that you are afraid of something. On the other hand, millions of people pay good money to get scared watching horror movies, reading creepy novels, or riding harrowing amusement park rides. Kids love ghost stories and getting scared about the monsters under their beds. Television shows that cause great fear and anxiety are considered grand entertainment. We do not like to admit that we are afraid of things, but we seem to enjoy the sensations of fear. What is wrong with this picture? Personally, I think that fear is a big seller because most people are bored out of their minds with their safe, predictable lives. Or maybe it is easier to deal with fantastical fears than with our own basic human fears. After all, which is scarier to deal with: being attacked by a giant python in the Amazon jungle, or facing the criticizing voice in your head that tells you you're not good enough or that you're not wanted? Anyone opt for the snake?

While I do not want to make light of fear, I do want to at least make you curious about it. If fear can be stimulating, engaging, and exciting in the movie theater, why not make it that way in your own life? Since fear seems to be a natural part of being human, perhaps we can approach fear, not with the intention of eliminating it, but with the intention of using it for our own purposes. Fear can be very motivating or very debilitating, depending on how you approach it. If we are experiencing fear, lets make the most of it and use it to strengthen our commitment to succeed.

Turning Fear into Success

Fear can be transformed into growth and success in countless ways. Let's focus on three very helpful methods for turning fear into success.

1. Name and embrace your fears.
2. Visualize what scares you about success and practice different scenarios with the images until your fear changes.
3. Change your mountains into molehills with a personal mission.

The act of naming, acknowledging, and embracing fears is a huge leap toward success. The first step in the process is to verbalize what you are actually afraid of. It can be something as basic as "I'm afraid to do outcall massage because I always get lost," not liking to talk about money, or being afraid your work isn't good enough. Once you recognize a fear, don't try to banish it; somehow, it doesn't seem to work very well anyway. Instead, do the opposite and embrace the fear. Thank your fear for protecting you from the harm it imagines will befall you. Then explain to your fear that it will not hurt you to get lost once in a while, talk to a new client about your rates, or pick up a telephone and call a new referral. It may feel scary, but once you do what you were afraid of, the exhilaration is wonderful and freeing. Your hands may shake for a half-hour, but then many people pay $3 for a double espresso to get the same feeling.

The next time you face the necessity of repeating this stress-causing behavior, your brain will remember that you have done this before. This time, however, the behavior will not be totally new, and your defense system will not go on red alert. Now it may just go on yellow alert. You may experience discomfort or anxiety, but most likely you will not have the same reaction as the first time. The third time, you may only feel a twinge of doubt, and after that, you can enjoy reaching new clients or whatever it was that brought up some form of fear or stress in the past.

EXERCISE: Managing Common Fears

Reviewing all the fears that can block your path to your dream practice is beyond the scope of this book. However, after listening to my students over the years, there are a few fears that seemed to show up more frequently than others. Take a moment and look at the following list. See if any ring a bell for you. Even an acknowledgment of a fear puts you leaps and bounds ahead because you will know to consider fear as a possible source of trouble if you suddenly find yourself doing things that undermine your commitment to succeed.

On a scale of 1–10, with 1 low and 10 high, rank each common fear by how much it possibly may affect your practice.

Common Fears

Failure	_____
Success	_____
Ridicule	_____
Looking bad or foolish	_____
Being wrong about your decision	_____
Making other people wrong by becoming successful	_____
Rejection	_____
Abandonment	_____
Loss of love from those you care about	_____
Disappointing yourself or others	_____
Criticism	_____
Making mistakes	_____
Not being good enough	_____
Not being wanted	_____
Other _____	_____

For any fear that scored above a five, give it the respect and attention it is due. Some fears are deep-seated and take hard work to overcome; and some will vanish with being named and recognized. Remember, you do not have to eliminate a fear to move forward. Many successful massage therapists pushed forward toward goals with fears in full and glorious bloom. Do not wait for fear to go away before you build or grow your practice. Push on in the face of it and learn to succeed regardless of what comes up.

Visualization
Of the fears we have just covered, some are learned and some are instinctive. This may sound a bit paradoxical, but many pains and fears are actually good for us. They are crucial for our survival and, in fact, without them, most of us would die at a very young age. Pain and fear are deeply wired into our nervous systems to protect us from what can hurt us. However, sometimes that protective mechanism can spread too far and tell us that things are dangerous to us when they aren't. This is especially true of fear of the unknown, which can come up when we face something new or different. To build a practice will require doing many things that are new and different, and while some people are engaged with the adventure of getting and keeping clients, others may be stopped by it. To override this protective mechanism, we must somehow notify the nervous system that the new activity we are about to engage in is not life-threatening and does not require the fight-or-flight response to save us.

If you find yourself suddenly trimming the hedges, dusting the hall closet, or deciding it is really crucial to change the vacuum bag right now, you may be showing signs of avoidance, one of the favorite methods of coping with fear of the unknown. If that is the case, it may be time to pull out

Figure 1–2	Visualize your dream practice becoming a reality.

one of our most powerful fear-busting tools: visualization. Quite simply, visualization is using your imagination for a specific reason. Since many fears are based on the unfamiliar, one way to deal with them is to make them familiar and safe in your imagination before you do them in reality. Visualization can let you do a mental walk-through of new experiences before you actually become involved in them. By seeing, feeling, and experiencing situations that are new or frightening to you, you can monitor your own reactions, and practice the visualization over and over until all your physical and emotional responses are what you would want them to be in a real setting.

If, for example, you have a businesswoman in mind with whom you would like to work, visualize your first interaction with her. Imagine how you would introduce yourself, what you would say to make her excited about getting massage from you, and how you would respond to a number of different reactions she might have. See her face, hear her words, and see yourself writing her name down in your appointment book. Then imagine that she has a large circle of friends she would love to refer to you! Imagine your telephone ringing off the hook as all her friends call you, eager to get a massage and ready with waiting checkbooks.

It is helpful to practice a number of scenarios, including a worst-case scenario, where you have different ways of handling it or ending it until you can run through it without feeling fear. You even can practice handling the scary situation and turning it around so that you have a great ending. Now that can be a lot of fun!

Some fears of success are valid, but most are not. Typical fears of success include not being able to fulfill others' expectations, having people "discover" that you don't really know what you're talking about, or worrying that your success will come at too high a price. All of these may be valid fears and they need to be dealt with accordingly. However, if these fears are taken out into the light of day, you can examine them closely and see that you have ways to handle each of them. If you are afraid of not meeting people's expectations, it may be helpful to realize that your work often can get results where other medical techniques cannot. If you are afraid of not knowing enough, realize that while you may not know everything, you probably know more than enough to help people.

Most of all, you need to know you are capable of managing success without hurting your body, your relationships, your soul, or anything else you might fear that success could conceivably damage. If you find yourself in a moment of doubt, put down the dust pan or car polish and do a quick visualization. Imagine yourself quickly and effectively handling the situation with confidence, skill, or whatever you need to turn that fear into preparedness. If you are generally anxious, imagine yourself in a quiet and beautiful place where you can be still long enough to figure out what is getting to you. Bring in a wise person to talk to, perhaps a mentor or teacher. Take advantage of the moment and train your brain for success. You can imagine things such as seeing yourself healthy and strong, enjoying the love and support of family and friends, helping people, growing your bank account, or whatever motivates you. Visualization is a wonderful tool, and you can use it to move yourself toward success with remarkable speed.

EXERCISE: Visualization

- Write down a visualization scenario that you can use when you are afraid of something concerning your practice. It may be a quiet, beautiful place you can visit in your imagination where you can relax and think clearly, or it can be a full "mind movie" featuring you, living your dream life with your dream practice. Choose images, sounds, and other sensations that make your "mind movie" powerful and compelling so that you can use it to motivate you anytime.

Self-sabotage

Understanding and planning how you will handle success is important because in the face of fear and change, many people sabotage themselves or their careers. It is not uncommon for therapists to feel that they do not deserve success. Some have been told they would never amount to anything, or they have some unrecognized belief that runs contrary to what they are working toward. For example, if a woman was raised with the strong belief that "the love of money is the root of all evil," but she wants to charge reasonable rates for her massage services, those beliefs can conflict. The result of conflicting beliefs is often odd and contradictory behavior.

The commitment to succeed carries with it the task of monitoring yourself, and noticing if you are doing things that run counter to what you say you want or what you will do. If you say that you want to get 10 new clients, then just sit at home and watch television all day, question what is going on inside yourself as to what it is that is keeping you from your goal. I have known people who accomplished major breakthroughs toward reaching their goals, but then ruined it one way or another. One therapist cut her hand accidentally, another showed up chronically late until he was fired from a job he worked hard to get, and another kept "forgetting" to show up for appointments. While good excuses could be made for all these cases, they resulted in the ending of a job or practice. That is not the purpose of this book.

I suspect there are more than a few good massage therapists who have ruined their practices because of unrecognized fears and conflicting beliefs. I have heard therapists express concern that financial stability would make them lazy or lose their conscience, that clients leaving them would be too painful, or that success would make them greedy and heartless. Knowing yourself and your beliefs can help you tremendously if you start to recognize you are overtly or covertly sabotaging your practice. Part of the commitment to succeed is recognizing and changing self-sabotaging behavior before it hurts you or your practice. Below is a list of classic sabotaging behaviors. If you recognize any of them, take some time to think about how they will eventually affect your practice over the long run. Think about the success you want, then ask yourself if it is possible to build your dream practice while maintaining these behaviors.

Showing up chronically late

Breaking promises

Accidents and forms of physical injury

Misplacing or losing things such as telephone numbers

Procrastination

Perfectionism

Getting sidetracked

Being forgetful about business-related matters

Other forms of chronic avoidance such as computer games, television, naps, or sleeping late

None of these behaviors are "wrong" by themselves. We have all done them at one time or another. Accumulated over time and with repetition, though, these can block your success, so pay attention if your commitment is to the success of your dream practice.

Being a Beginner

Most anything in life that is worth doing has a learning or beginning stage. Some people perpetually look for new things to immerse themselves in while others prefer the security of the familiar. For the growth necessary to run a long-term, full-time practice, there are going to be times when you will face being a beginner. These are the times where you will be learning to take action in the face of being uncomfortable or unconfident. While that may not sound like a lot, millions of people live lives of boredom, repetition, and stagnation because they cannot hack being challenged or feeling out of control. It is safe and secure to sit in front of the television with a bucket of ice cream, and even though it is ultimately dissatisfying and empty, a significant percentage of people will live this way their whole lives. Criticisms from childhood, failures in school, teasing, and other traumas associated with being a beginner can lay dormant until we try something new. Then they rise up in full glory and give us all sorts of reasons to stop whatever we are doing to avoid feeling the pain we felt before.

If you do not like feeling like a beginner, it is understandable, but question your reasons. Some people are embarrassed to say, "I don't know," or flinch at the thought of asking anyone for help. The desire to look good and appear intelligent or competent is very powerful. Unfortunately, a commitment to looking good often runs counter to the commitment to succeed, which sometimes requires that you ask basic questions or expose your lack of knowledge during your stages of growth. In these cases, pride and ego can get in the way of learning what it takes to run a successful practice.

The Natural Talent Syndrome

As a child, I grew up reading various book series about young detectives who, no matter what scrape or problem they got into, always seemed able to find a way out of the dilemma by using some skill or talent at which they were naturally good. If the prima ballerina was kidnapped, our heroine would take a few quick ballet lessons, don her tutu, and wow the audience who never suspected she wasn't the real star at the big fund-raising recital for an orphanage. If a painting was stolen, our boy detectives would recreate an exact replica using a battered old photograph and some oils they picked up on the way home from the high school football game, and put their copy in the museum, thus causing the thieves to be confused and throw away the stolen original, which they then recovered, along with the treasure map on the back of the canvas. Okay, I'm exaggerating a bit, but basically the lesson I got from these stories was this: any skill or talent that you needed could be acquired with little or no training or effort. Imagine my confusion when I found that some things in life took quite a bit of effort or that they took more work than my natural talent could handle. I quit doing many things in my life because I truly believed that certain skills should come easily and naturally. When they didn't, I just stopped.

The natural talent syndrome is a step beyond beginner fears, but it is just as dangerous to success. If you have this syndrome, please understand right here and now that in the real world, mastery of the skills and talents necessary to create your dream practice will take study, practice, and effort. Just showing up and relying on natural talent will get you so far, but probably not as far as you want to go. I wish I had learned this lesson sooner. There are a few hobbies and skills that I would enjoy to this day if I had known that it was okay to struggle and work hard for things that did not come easily at first.

The Desire to Learn

One of the most consistent factors I have found among massage professionals with more than 20 years of experience is that they have an intense desire to learn new things while striving to master the fundamentals of their work. I have yet to meet a successful therapist who was complacent and felt like there was nothing else worth learning. From my research, I can conclude that the ability to succeed is inherently tied to the desire to learn. Seminars, classes, books, magazines, conventions, conferences, peer discussions, association meetings, getting together with local colleagues over pizza, and other forms of advanced learning are part of the investment made in a long-term practice. Whether advanced learning helped the therapist alleviate the boredom of routine work, gave more advanced therapeutic skills that created higher demands and fees, or opened new markets with new skills, it seemed to play a role in career longevity. If your commitment is to success, feed and foster your desire to learn.

Gathering Support

The process of moving through the many stages of practice-building can be greatly enhanced by gathering support from people who will encourage you through your growth and change. One of the most critical times in creating a massage career is the time between when the support and structure of the massage school or training ends, and a financially stable practice is built. Many of my former students dreaded going back into their old environments without the support of their classmates and teachers. In some cases, their old friends were not supportive of their healthier lifestyles or were resentful of their willingness to leave behind the "old gang" for a successful career. Not every parent I encountered at our massage school graduations was thrilled that their child

Figure 1–3   Meet with colleagues on a regular basis for support.

was going into massage. And many spouses, especially husbands, were jealous and felt threatened because their wives were going to be massaging other men. If you are a student, setting up a support system while in school can make this transition less lonely and help you keep your dreams alive. Loneliness is a factor that has killed many massage careers, and dreams can die without encouragement, so if your commitment is to success, get support.

You can seek support from people you admire, or from friends and family who want to see you succeed. I also strongly encourage you to join a massage organization or group (or start your own). While there are many benefits to belonging to associations, one of the best is that you can talk with people who understand what you are going through. There is a wonderful joy and comfort in knowing others who really know what it is that you do all day long. One of the best ways to receive support is to give support. I have noticed that many of my friends that I made from volunteering seem to have made successful careers for themselves over the span of many years. I don't know exactly how volunteering helps lead to success in a practice, but in my experience it does. A note I have taped to my computer simply says, "Whatever you want, give it first." If you want support, perhaps you can start by giving it.

If real people are hard to come by for a support group, I have known many people who have called on the spirit of a grandma who passed on, angels, guides, famous people living or dead that motivate you, or any other source to turn to when you need a boost. I highly recommend the book *Think and Grow Rich* by Napoleon Hill because the author develops the concept about creating a supportive "mastermind group." It may sound nuts, but I gather a great deal of strength from the spirit of my grandma, my Reiki guides, and the members of my imaginary mastermind group that includes Annie Oakley; the inventor, Tesla; Franklin, Theodore, and Eleanor Roosevelt; Abraham Lincoln; Thomas Edison; and Xena, Warrior Princess. All right, I'm kidding about Xena, but sometimes when I need more inventiveness in my ideas, I ask Thomas Edison for creative input, and when I need strength in leadership, I wonder what Abraham Lincoln would do in my position. The personalities and traits these people possessed motivate and encourage me when I need them, and when my own mind reaches its limits, I ask how these people would deal with my situation. If an imaginary mastermind group is too "far out" for you, then at least get real people to support you in making your dreams a reality.

Creating Internal and External Deadlines

In the real world where you will build your practice is a phenomenal concept called "time." Getting and keeping real clients that pay real money has to occur in real time, and the difference between hopes and wishes in fantasy time and real success is the factor of deadlines. Without deadlines (or lifelines as some people call them), people will procrastinate or fuss around with a favorite new obstacle, often until their opportunity has passed them by. This, then, pushes them to return to options that are less gratifying but are more familiar and safer. Therefore, a powerful way to overcome many obstacles or fears is to create deadlines for your personal and professional goals. You can keep your plans to yourself, or if you have a support group, tell them your goals and deadlines so that you are accountable to them to keep your word. If you drag your feet on a project, your accountability to the group will create a worse discomfort because you know that others that you care about will know you never made that call or got your business cards made. In essence, you motivate yourself by playing the potential pain of other's disappointment off the discomfort or inconvenience of doing what you promised. As a result, you end up pushing yourself over your block. It's a nifty trick, especially for those of us prone to procrastination.

One of the biggest benefits of deadlines is that they can push you to action before you feel ready. Of the many lessons I have learned from successful people, one of the most important is that they know if they wait until they feel ready, usually their window of opportunity will have passed. Despite their misgivings, discomfort, or quaking knees, they have trained themselves to jump into things whether they are prepared or not. Certainly, they plan and prepare a great deal, but they do not wait until everything is perfect before they move forward.

Time and again I have heard, read, and experienced that when you make a commitment to something, even if you don't know how you will make it happen, miracles happen, amazing coincidences occur, and you reach your commitment by your deadline in ways you never would have dreamed. Without the focus created by a deadline, creative thoughts and lucky breaks just do not seem to materialize. With deadlines, you can get results, crucial to attaining the success to which you are committed.

Managing Expectations

In addition to managing fear, frustration, anger, growth, and change, I also found that successful therapists had the ability to manage their expectations. They had good methods for handling success as well as setbacks when their expectations did not work out as planned. The ability to manage expectations is a hallmark of maturity, and is often learned only through the proverbial school of hard knocks. On the other end of the maturity scale are those who are delusional about their ability to control others and their environment. At the risk of stereotyping, I found, unfortunately, that many therapists who were young, and from the cities or suburbs, were raised with a sense that they have a great deal of control over their lives. The danger of this deluded belief to a long-term practice is that the more control they thought they had, the more likely they were to quit when the going got tough. Added to what is basically a false sense of control is a feeling I got that these new therapists also felt that everything in life should come easily and quickly to them. Their attitudes weren't the natural talent syndrome; they just plain old felt entitled to the good life that was owed to them. It was as if building a practice would be like pulling up to the drive-up window and putting in an order, then getting impatient when it took more than three minutes to have a successful business handed over and neatly packaged.

As a whole, our culture does not have to face great adversity, rely on perseverance, develop patience, or pick ourselves up from failure. Unfortunately, building a long-term practice will probably require all of these at one point or another, and since my commitment is to your success, I am being honest up front so that you don't give up when the going gets bumpy. Miracles, fortunate coincidences, and other good things are a common part of many successful practices, but they are often the reward for persevering and not giving up on your dream. There is no room for the concept of entitlement in the massage field. No one owes you anything and no one is obliged to be your client. I have seen and heard about therapists' behavior while marketing their practices that leads me to believe some folks think that the world owes them a good living just because they showed up.

On the other hand, don't set your expectations too low, either. Your commitment to succeed should balance you somewhere in the realities of this field, which is that we are still a fairly new and growing profession where demand is inconsistent and not at all guaranteed. Your marketing efforts should demonstrate that you have a healthy sense of the value of your work, combined with the humility that you must prove your value to your prospective and current clients on an ongoing basis.

Managing Setbacks

The commitment to succeed contains the ability and willingness to handle setbacks, mistakes, and "failures." Success requires growth and growth requires mistakes. Therefore, the less fear you have of mistakes, the more quickly you can grow. Handling mistakes and setbacks is not always easy. It is no fun to be embarrassed, or admit that you were unprepared or ignorant. This is when your commitment to succeed and your dreams and desires to help others become vital. You don't tell a baby that she can have only so many chances to learn to walk before she has to give up. She will fall down and get up again until she can walk, and that is the same spirit you must take into building a practice. Things in a practice "fall down" often. Clients move, clients die, equipment breaks, you realize you are out of clean sheets, injuries and illness happen, recessions wipe out half your client base, and local laws change. It is all part of the package, or at least, it was part of my package. You may have better luck. Whatever your fortune, how you handle your personal and professional setbacks will determine whether or not you can make it in massage.

Managing Success

If success is something you can handle with ease and comfort, then you are a fortunate human being. If you are like most people, though, success can be unfamiliar and scary. Success can make you feel as out of control as failure does, sometimes even worse. Managing success may take bravery and courage at first, but if you allow success to happen, you will get more comfortable with it. Being at ease with success and radiating the confidence that comes with it, sends out a charismatic aura that draws people and keeps the cycle of success going. Success is not the destination of your career: it is part of the path. Maintaining success over the years usually takes setting new and higher goals, and broadening your personal mission and contribution. In a paradoxical way, the more "impossible" your mission, the more at ease you can be with your achievements. I, most likely, will not see the end of human suffering in my lifetime, but it is what I strive for every day, and each success I have gets me one step closer to that mission. I no longer fear that success will go to my head, or that I will reach some point of accomplishment and see a Dead End sign. If you want to manage success, put it in the context of your personal mission and life goals. This will keep success in a perspective that is both humbling and motivating. To build a dream practice, success must be welcomed and managed. It may take a little practice, but then, most important skills do.

Creating a Personal Mission

The commitment to succeed can be greatly helped by creating or discovering your own personal mission. We will delve more deeply into guiding principles and what I call a North Star Statement in a later chapter, but when success is being discussed, the concept of a personal mission needs to be touched on.

A personal mission may seem a bit grandiose for some people, but for me, having grown up with two parents who were and are very mission-driven, it seems natural and valuable to have a bigger reason for life and work besides simply filling time until death inevitably arrives. At times of crisis or during moments where significant decisions must be made, having a bigger picture or mission for your life can be grounding and stabilizing. My experience with successful therapists leads me to believe that having a bigger purpose or mission has great benefit in sustaining drive and persistence throughout a career. To make mountains into molehills on your road to success, rise high above the basic details of running your life by seeing yourself in the context of your mission and its impact on the world over time. I have found the sobering smallness of my own being and the mere blink of an eye of time I am given here both a motivator and a relief. I want to accomplish much while I am here, but time is neither an enemy, nor a burden.

While I believe that a larger purpose in life can help sustain one's practice over time, most therapists I know were clueless to any specific personal mission when they began their practices. Do not wait to have a personal mission to start marketing and building your practice. Just aim for getting your first 10 clients. The experience of working with your clients will help you discover your personal mission, and the sooner you start looking for your purpose within your work, the more satisfying and fulfilling it will be. Therapists who are happy and fulfilled have much greater odds of succeeding, and if having a personal mission can help you succeed over the long haul, then keep it in the back of your mind as we continue with what it takes to build your dream practice.

As you may now recognize, the commitment to succeed has many facets and cannot be waved away with a simple "Oh, of course I want to succeed" statement. This is a marketing book but the overall purpose of your marketing is to help you reach your version of success. Without a commitment to success, there is no reason to market to get and keep clients. Please, if you are going to enter the game, whether it is the game of life or of your massage career, enter it to win.

Marketing Attribute #3:
A Strong Emphasis on Professionalism

Some of the most important lessons I have learned about marketing have come from talking, not with massage professionals, but with the general public about their experience with massage. During my crosscountry trip, I took every opportunity to ask people about massage, and did I get an earful. Whether it was the clerk at the Rite-Aid store in Denham Springs, Louisiana, or fellow Californians sharing a barbecue dinner at an RV park in Orlando, Florida, I got to hear what massage clients thought about their therapists. And when it came to the topic of professionalism, the conversation sometimes became downright embarrassing.

Frankly, after what I'd heard, I was beginning to think that if massage therapists could show up at an appointment on time or show up at all, were willing to wear shoes and decent, appropriate clothing, and could give a full hour of average Swedish massage without talking about their latest sexual escapade or lamenting during the entire session about a personal drama or trauma, they would be well on their way to success.

After getting over my initial shock at such widespread stories of unprofessional behavior, my overriding feeling was one of sadness. What a waste and a pity that caring and gifted therapists were losing clients and not getting referrals because they were oblivious to their own lack of basic manners, courtesies, and professionalism. I came to realize that professional common sense isn't all that common! In fact, perhaps professionalism should come under the category of "uncommon" sense.

Perhaps because so many massage therapists have the souls of artists, they have difficulty seeing the world from any perspective other than their own. While this perspective is great for art, it is dangerous for professionalism. The successful therapists I met could see themselves through the eyes of their clients, and they adapted themselves to speak, dress, and behave in a manner appropriate to the realities in which their clients exist. Being appropriate does not mean the loss of self-expression, giving up style, or not being yourself. It means paying attention to clients and trying to see, hear, and feel the massage experience from their perspective. Doing a self-review from a client's point of view is a first step toward professionalism, a key marketing attribute for getting and keeping clients.

Professionalism can take many forms and be expressed in many ways. At its core, though, professionalism is a basic attitude of centering your practice around your clients, and their needs, desires, attitudes, and goals. It is not just centered around yourself. There are many ways to demonstrate that you are a true professional, but perhaps the most important demonstration of a client-centered practice is a set of appropriate boundaries. The heart of boundaries is simple. You and your client are two different people, and what is desirable, important, or appropriate to you may not be the same for your client. Of all the reasons the general public gave me as to why they left their former massage therapists, many of their stories came down to a breach of boundaries. Whether a therapist pushed a personal philosophy or religion; gave too much unrequested advice on nutrition, colon cleansing, or meditation; talked about subjects that were too personal for their client's comfort; or just plain talked too much, these people left therapists with good hands-on skills and poor boundary skills.

The inherent nature of massage makes boundary skills even more important than for other professions. Since most practitioners will be in the position of standing over a client who is lying down, naked under a sheet, and being touched, the normal barriers of clothing, personal space, eye contact, and being on the same physical plane are all removed. Without these common social barriers, the client is vulnerable in countless ways, and what may be tolerable in a normal setting can become frightening or uncomfortable while on the table or floor.

I recall one story in particular where a client had been seeing a massage therapist for quite a while, but at some point, the therapist converted to a particular religion and proceeded to bring it up repeatedly during their sessions. Not sharing this particular faith, this client reluctantly stopped seeing the therapist because she felt uncomfortable and pressured, even though the therapist was simply telling her own experiences of her conversion. Two points are important here. One, the therapist should not have taken the client's massage time to discuss her personal issues, and two, the boundaries of religion and deeply held beliefs are not wise to cross. In a normal setting, these two people could have carried on a dialogue and agreed to disagree, but with the client lying down unclothed, she felt defenseless. Sadly, she did not have the heart to tell her therapist why she never rebooked. I feel sorry for this obviously skilled and good-hearted therapist who had no concept of the increased significance of boundaries in the massage setting.

Even something as seemingly harmless as selling products has the potential to push boundaries and damage a relationship. If you sell products within your practice, you can display them, but do not bring them up unless the client asks about them. Unsolicited selling can be invasive, and if and when you do discuss products for sale, talk about them with your clients before or after the session, not while you are standing over them. Clients, like most human beings, want to be accepted and loved, and some people may feel a pressure to buy something from you for fear that you otherwise might "abandon" them. Combine the fear of losing acceptance with a position of vulnerability, and you may make a sale, but you also can lose a client. Some people in the massage field feel that product sales are also an issue of ethics because the power dynamic between therapist and client is so unequal. Whether selling products is ethical or not, I do not know. This is a marketing book about getting and keeping clients, and all I can do is speak from personal experience: I lost a client because of a health care product I sold. For me, that was the last time I sold products in my practice, and it was a boundary lesson I learned the painful way.

On the other side of this boundary equation are we massage therapists, many of whom think it is perfectly normal to touch naked strangers. It wasn't until a noticeable number of people asked me how I could stand the thought of "touching all those people" and how "icky" doing massage must be, that I came to realize I have a very different set of boundaries than much of the population. Personally, I have no problem with doing massage, and I enjoy my work very much. However, just because massage is fine with us doesn't mean that everyone likes giving touch or even getting touch. Somewhere between the more open boundaries of the typical massage therapist and the more vulnerable boundaries of clients is a flexible line that must be negotiated differently with every client, and sometimes, even from session to session.

Professionalism contains a few basic rules on boundaries, but they really come down to your ability to recognize where you and you clients are different, then respecting their position. The first step of recognizing where you and your client differ is probably the most difficult because most people think others think and feel as they do. Neutrality can be very helpful on touchy subjects, especially with new clients who do not know you very well. Human beings have a very strong sense of "tribe." If you are too different from their tribe on some crucial topics such as politics or religion, you can lose them as clients. Remember, marketing is anything that affects your ability to get and keep clients. Stepping over clients' boundaries is one of the most common ways to lose them.

Some special boundary areas to watch for include:

- religion
- politics
- beliefs about body, nutrition, stress, family, and relationships
- application of bodywork such as level of pressure, method of draping, nonmassage touching, working areas where client has said not to work, techniques, and amount of time spent in areas they want
- conversation such as personal stories, asking personal questions, or telling stories about other clients
- dress codes such as wearing clothing that is revealing, provocative, disrespectful, or that is greatly different from what the client wears or would expect from their stereotypes of massage professionals

Figure 1–4   **How do you see yourself as a massage professional?**

- comfort with nudity, the physical environment such as temperature, and music preferences
- language such as use of massage jargon, unfamiliar terms, foul language, or slang

Your Professional Self-Definition

Professionalism, especially in the realm of boundaries, calls for an understanding and recognition of, and respect for the differences between you and your client. Part of your job is to watch, observe, and listen to your clients so that you will know what they expect of you as a professional. However, a key factor in meeting their expectations of you is your own understanding or perspective of yourself as a massage professional. One of the difficulties our field faces is that we have such different identities as individual practitioners, it is hard to know what "professional behavior" is on any kind of common basis.

One story in particular really drove home the point of our differences for me when I heard about a group of old men who have been working for years at a hot springs resort. They continue to insist on calling themselves "masseurs," and they still get paid about $5 an hour. Their self-perception is that their massage work is of the same value as the kitchen help and hotel maids. They are deferential, cordial, and "at your service" because that is how a professional at their level behaves. On the other side of professional self-perception, I was accosted at a convention by an attendee at my marketing seminar who felt one of my marketing techniques was "unethical." That was quite a surprise to me. As he railed on, I heard him make reference to his "medical ethics." I realized that his self-perception is that his work is equal to that of a doctor's, and his definition of professional behavior was shaped by different standards than the other seminar attendees. Some therapists consider themselves having professional standards similar to hairstylists, estheticians, and other service people of that caliber. Others view themselves as artists, and abide by their own codes and standards. No one way is correct. In each case, the practitioner was directed by his or her own definition of professionalism, and was living by the ethics and behaviors that matched it.

As a marketer, your self-definition will affect your marketing message, the kind of client you try to reach, and the behavior you display around your clients. You need to choose it carefully. Each self-definition opens some doors and closes others. If your work is of medical level and caliber, then your professional presentation will need to match that to draw clients who want and expect that kind of treatment. However, choosing a medical image will likely turn away people looking for more of a relaxing or spa-type experience. Whatever your choice of self-definition, realize that the consumer wants to trust you and feel safe with you, and your level of professionalism needs to portray to them that you are trustworthy.

Rules and regulations about professionalism can fill pages of text, but I would rather focus on the distinction or attitude of professionalism so that you can be a professional under any circumstances. Perceive yourself through your clients' eyes, respect your differences, set boundaries, give your clients' needs and wishes priority, and create a self-definition that calls for maturity, stature, and exemplary behavior.

Marketing Attribute #4:
A Commitment to Excellent Customer Service

If I were to distinguish between professionalism and customer service, I would say that professionalism is about doing what is expected of you, and customer service is about doing what is unexpected. I found this distinction during my interviews with massage clients when I asked them what they liked about their massage experience. Surprisingly, the happy clients mentioned minor things such as electric foot warmers, flannel sheets, and customized aromatherapy oils. They talked about how much their therapist seemed to care, asked about their lives, and sent birthday cards. Given that many schools and therapists place a primary emphasis on bodywork modalities, I was shocked to discover that most clients I interviewed rarely talked about the technique the therapist used or even mentioned the bodywork itself. Unless the therapist was hurting the client with too much pressure or was using a painful technique, when an interviewee went back in his or her memory bank to answer my questions, most of them talked about what I call the ancillaries: temperature, music, oils, pillows, conversation, number of minutes in a session's time, flowers, and other mental bric-a-brac that these clients gathered up to form their impression of their massage experience.

Quite honestly, I think that the majority of the American population still has no idea what constitutes a quality massage, much less has the vocabulary to discuss or describe a good massage. If asked, they take the bodywork they get, focus on the ancillaries, and explain their experiences from them. This is not a license to do low-quality work; good hands-on skills are very important, but customer service is much more than just efficiently and effectively massaging muscles.

The Center of the Universe

At the soul of customer service is a desire to help your client feel cared for, important, and special. In their heart of hearts, clients believe they are the center of the universe, and if during the brief time of a session they feel you have treated them as such, they will come back to you again and again. If you truly aim to help your clients feel cared for and special, it will be natural for you to think of and do the thousands of little things that add up to excellent customer service. Listen to what prospective clients say about what they want and meet those needs, and imagine what you can do above and beyond those needs. Then watch happy clients return and refer their friends. While customer service is primarily for the marketing function of keeping clients you already have, the attitude of genuine caring comes through from you in most every situation you find yourself when you are trying to reach new clients. The word extraordinary should be your motto for customer service; it's all the extras on top of the ordinary, or all the unexpecteds on top of the expecteds.

When I asked people what was important to them about their massage therapist, and what they felt shaped their decision to choose or stay with a therapist, these were just some of the many elements of customer service they focused on:

Personal attention and genuine interest in the client as an individual.

Amount of time spent in a session, especially if the therapist was doing "taxi meter" massage.

Results of bodywork and whether the therapist could help specific problems.

Quality of work and how the therapist's touch felt.

Accessibility to book or change appointments, including rapid response to telephone calls.

Flexibility of scheduling, including occasional forgiveness for last-minute changes.

Preference given for prime-time spots for long-term clients.

Caring, remembering details of personal life or stories told, and wanting to help.

Compassion for their lives, emotional needs, and physical condition.

Friendship and conversation, especially for those who felt lonely or isolated.

Education about their bodies, how to care for themselves, and why things were hurting.

Going the extra mile, and researching or learning new techniques to help specific problems.

Creating an inviting massage environment.

As a professional, you will be expected to do a good quality massage, but if you can add compassion, caring, education, a marvelous place to relax in, and real help for physical problems, you have moved into the realm of customer service. If you continuously ask yourself how you can make your sessions extraordinary, or even how to make them one of the highlights of your clients' week, you are thinking in a place most businesses do not bother to go. Excellent customer service is quite rare, and if you want to spend more time working and less time marketing, provide great customer care and let your clients market for you.

Many great books have been written about customer service, but of all the books I have read, the one that has the most direct application to the personal service of massage is the classic *How to Win Friends and Influence People* by Dale Carnegie. The nature of the client/therapist relationship warrants a deeper understanding of how to relate to and affect others, and if you want to truly serve your clients well, read and reread this book. Human beings have some very core needs that this book can help you understand, and its principles of how to treat other people speak to the heart of customer service.

Skills at the Soul of Success

C H A P T E R

2

CHAPTER
OBJECTIVES

After reading this chapter, you should be able to:

- describe the seven levels of the Perception Continuum of massage.
- educate clients with common misconceptions about massage.
- identify elements necessary for creating and maintaining client trust.
- describe a professional image you want to convey.
- identify six methods of establishing value in your clients' minds.
- identify 10 common human needs that massage can meet.
- identify factors that affect your prices.
- describe three expectations that clients have of their massage experience.
- deliver a professional introduction.

If attributes are the heart of your marketing, then at the soul of your success are a handful of fundamental skills you must practice in order to bring your heart to the people who need it. To build a dream practice requires five skills necessary for what it takes to reach new clients, rebook those clients, and get personal referrals. Building on the foundation of the four core attributes from the last chapter are what I call the five essential skills of success. These skills are:

1. Shaping Client Perception
2. Creating and Maintaining Trust
3. Establishing Value
4. Setting and Meeting Expectations
5. Reaching Out to Clients

Marketing Skill #1: Shaping Client Perception

To build a practice in your community, your marketing strategy needs to take into account what the people in your community think about you and massage. One of the primary goals of marketing is to shape the perception of you and your services in your potential clients' minds. For most businesses, this is a pretty straightforward process. However, massage therapists face some very interesting issues about how the public already sees us, which makes shaping perception a more challenging skill. At this point, massage is going through a period of great transition, and no matter where you work in this country, you must market to a public that fits somewhere along what I call the Perception Continuum.

The Perception Continuum

The Perception Continuum registers possible levels of perception that the public has about massage. It loosely identifies ways you may be perceived by those you encounter so that you will be better prepared to market accurately and effectively to them. On the Perception Continuum, your potential client is at one of the following levels:

Level 1: Not aware of massage

Level 2: Aware of massage, but has misperceptions about it

Level 3: Aware of massage, but doesn't see its value

Level 4: Ready and willing to get massage, but is confused about who is legitimate, what modality to get, or where to find a quality therapist

Level 5: Open to massage and gets them occasionally

Level 6: Regularly getting massage from one practitioner

Level 7: Getting massage from different types of bodyworkers based on need

Depending on where your potential clients are on this continuum will determine what you need to say or do so that they will want to book a massage with you. However, during this time of transition, it is difficult to know what lurks in the minds of those potential clients standing next to you in line at the grocery store. They could think that massage is just for rich people on cruise ships, or they could want a massage and not know how to find a trustworthy therapist. So, how do you create your marketing strategy if you don't know how people see you? In this section on bare bones marketing, we are simply going to make some educated guesses. In later chapters, we will cover how to create an effective marketing message and develop more specific strategies, but for now, we're going to take a deep breath and wade right out into the world of clients. Don't worry: here's an inner tube.

Paddling Along

From my experience on the road and 17 years in the field, the first calculated guess I would make about the Perception Continuum is that most of your potential clients are going to come from people at Levels 4 and 5. These are people who are interested in getting a massage and either have not had one yet or who are not committed to a local practitioner. They do not need convincing to try massage, and you are not actively competing with other therapists for them. Usually, they simply are waiting for the right therapist to come across their path. I say this for two primary reasons. The first is that years of determined efforts by massage professionals, schools, and associations have made a huge impact on creating legitimacy for the field. Alternative health care has repeatedly proved itself as a viable option for Americans, and massage is continuing to gain the credibility and recognition it so richly deserves. More and more people are experiencing the value of massage, getting results they haven't been able to get elsewhere, and increasing their willingness to pay for protecting or improving their health.

The second reason that a whole crop of eager clients are out there looking for you is that massage has enjoyed a marked surge in popularity in the public mind. For some marvelous reason, mass media advertisers have embraced and promoted massage as what I call "The Poster Child of the Good Life." People at Levels 4 and 5 are familiar and comfortable with the images of massage they have seen on television or in magazines, and most likely, massage has made it onto a few million personal wish lists. Now I'm just guessing about the few million wish lists, but I have repeatedly had the experience of talking with people about massage whose wistful follow-up response was "Oh, I've always wanted a massage!" This remark usually is accompanied by the person's hand instinctively reaching for a sore neck, shoulder, or low back, and a sort of pitiful moment of rubbing complete with a sad look in their eyes. If ever there was a marketing moment where you can open a working relationship with them easily, this is it! Their perception is shaped, their desire is apparent, their need is almost universal, and there you are, the answer to their wish list.

For people who do more than just dream about a good back rub, the typical response is "I've been looking for a good therapist! Are you available or can you recommend someone?" I know marketing is supposed to be harder than this, but I really think the field is ready to be harvested in many places, and for people at Levels 4 and 5, the only marketing strategy you need is to show up and start talking.

Now, here's the fun part in all this. Despite all our popularity, if you asked a group of people what massage is good for, you're not likely to get the same answer. This is a smart marketer's dream! We have a public perception that is largely positive, but it is still vague and malleable. This means you have a lot of say in shaping how your potential clients perceive you. We have the option, like no other profession has, of creating an appealing marketing message that reaches into just about any segment of society you desire to serve. Whether your massage is therapeutic or medical, for injury rehabilitation or sports enhancement, or is more for relaxation or stress management, you have the ability to shape how people in those markets perceive you. And because of the malleability of the profession at this time, you can reach and serve more than one market without having to change your marketing tools because people will read into you what they hope or presume that you are.

Sinking Beneath the Surface

People at Levels 4 and 5 do not need to change their minds about massage before they will consider booking an appointment with you. You don't have to "get them to the surface" of accurate perceptions before they will take the risk of trying your services. However, people at Levels 1 to 3 must have their minds and perceptions changed before they will get a massage. Marketing to Levels 1 and 2 people who do not know about massage or have misperceptions about it, can be time-consuming, costly, and without much return. For people who are unaware of massage, any form of marketing either can move them swiftly up the Perception Continuum so that they book with you, or it only may take them part way up, and some other massage therapist later on will benefit from the groundwork you laid.

Level 2 people can have many misconceptions about massage, and they are in what I like to call the "3-H club." They think that massage therapists are in one of three categories: Helgas, Harlots, or Hippies.

Helga is the stereotypical big, beefy Swedish gal in sturdy shoes shown often in advertisements pummeling the socks off some bug-eyed man wrapped in a white towel in the steam room. I don't know about you, but I think it's not a very appealing image. However, it is common enough that some people think this is what massage is, and to get them as clients, you will have to change their perception. Education is the most effective tool in this case. You can explain to a person that pounding on clients has its place, but by comparison, here's what you do in a typical session. Many people think that massage is a painful experience, and since most people don't like pain, you will need to convince them that your touch is wonderful and far from painful.

Harlots refers to the infernal associations that massage therapists are prostitutes, which has been the bane of this profession for way too long. While this continues to be an issue, I think there is good news on this front. When I started my practice in 1984 in California, the common public perception I encountered was that massage was a cover for prostitution. However, over the years, and especially after my crosscountry research trip, I found this public perception quite changed. In fact, I was struck that massage students I spoke with thought that people perceived them as prostitutes, but when I talked with residents in their area, the public had a much higher view of massage than the students did.

In fact, the tables already may be turning on the parlors. I heard a story that may be the wave of the future from people in a town a bit north of San Francisco. A group of women tourists accidentally went into a massage parlor looking for legitimate massage. Much to their surprise, it wasn't quite the day-spa experience they were looking for! The clients pressed a formal complaint with the city, much to the amusement and joy of local therapists. Talk about a switch! Now, this does not mean that therapists still aren't harassed by clients or hounded by vice squads. It simply means that more people in the general public have a more accurate perception of legitimate massage than they used to. Fortunately for us, their demand for legitimate massage is changing the political landscape.

For the remaining folks who still think massage therapy is in the same category as parlors, you will probably run into a few somewhere during your career. In my own case, I have been able to educate some male clients I have encountered with the "harlot" misperception. With a bit of effort, I was able to demonstrate to them the value of massage without sex, and they actually became good, steady clients for many years. Working relationships with other men I have not been able to dissuade from an enduring hope that somehow I would become a harlot terminated rapidly. If your state or city has few if any regulations concerning massage, be prepared for perceptions about sexual massage. In that way, you can take extra caution when reaching out to clients and more clearly define your marketing image so there is no mistaking your legitimacy.

As for the hippies contingent from the 3-H club, there is still a perception that massage is some woo-woo, glow-and-flow kind of experience, complete with burning incense and space music. Actually, quite a few therapists make a good living doing the glow-and-flow routine, but it's not for everyone in the general public. People with this perception can be educated about the benefits and applications of other methods and modalities of bodywork, but it may take some doing. With the hippie perception, or any other stereotype, you are still starting your marketing "below the surface." If a person only perceives you as a stereotype, you first have to undo their image of you, then work up to an accurate perception of you and your work. Only then can you gain trust and create value in the buyer's mind. Undoing stereotypes and educating people is a large part of marketing massage to Level 2 people, and if you have the desire and patience to try to go for members of the 3-H club, please read the second section of this book for more tools and skills.

Swimming Upstream

Gaining clients from the last levels of the Perception Continuum will take more than just showing up and being seen. In Levels 5, 6, and 7, you now face the marketing issues of competition and differentiation. For most people starting out in massage, they are neither likely to be actively competing with established practitioners, nor do they know enough about themselves or their markets to know how to differentiate themselves effectively in the minds of their potential clients. If you face great competition or are ready to differentiate yourself so that potential clients will understand and value what you offer, then you will be helped by the second section of this book which offers many strategies for dealing with competition. Most of the successful therapists I have met, though, know their competition is not with other therapists but with ignorance, misperception, and lack of trust and value in the public mind.

Someday, massage will have what many of us have been working toward for years: full public awareness and value of the profession, widespread accurate and positive public perception, demand for bodywork specialties based on needs, and regulatory laws that are clear, consistent, and massage-friendly. Until that time arrives, the skill of shaping perception is critical to success. It begins with understanding what public perceptions already are, choosing which level of client you are willing and able to work with, and developing a marketing strategy appropriate to that level of perception. That said, for the level of marketing we are dealing with in this first section, study the four core attributes, go after the many people who are looking for their first good massage, apply the next four skills, and you will have done enough to get and keep clients to start your practice.

EXERCISE: Handling Negative Stereotypes

- If you are in a class or group, break up into pairs and choose a Partner A and Partner B. Partner A acts as a potential new client while Partner B is the massage therapist in an imaginary social conversation at a party. The partners have been introduced briefly by the host, along with the information that Partner B does massage. When the host excuses himself to talk to others, Partner A turns to Partner B.
- Scenario 1: Partner A says: I always thought "masseuses" were just prostitutes with fancy covers. What kind of "masseuse" are you? Partner B responds: Let me tell you about the differences between legitimate massage professionals and massage parlors.
- Partner B must find the words to reeducate this potential client so that he or she understands legitimate massage, can value it, and build up enough trust so this person will book an appointment. Partner B needs

to play with words and phrases that educate others without sounding upset, annoyed, condescending, or professorial.

■ Scenario 2: Partner B says: I see those massage ladies on television pounding on people. Is that what you do?

■ Partner A responds: Well, not exactly. Let me tell you the differences between my work and those stereotypes you see on television. Partner A needs to find a way to reshape a preconceived notion so that the listener is more accurately educated.

■ If you are reading this book by yourself, practice saying aloud what you would say in response to these two questions. You may or may not ever get these two common misperceptions dumped in your lap so unceremoniously, but be prepared. These thoughts may be lurking in the minds of others, and you will do yourself a favor by having a solid ready answer to versions of these questions.

Marketing Skill #2: Gaining and Maintaining Trust

As you have seen with the Perception Continuum, there are many different attitudes, opinions, and beliefs that prevail about massage. Recognizing and dealing with those perceptions are important elements to your success because they affect greatly your next marketing skill; the ability to gain trust.

Trust in the massage field is critical for two reasons. One is that potential clients must trust the practitioner enough to let themselves be touched. The other is that practitioners must trust that the client has no intention to harm or harass. During this transition time in this profession, gaining and maintaining trust is a two-way street between client and practitioner and, therefore, takes more skill and effort than in other professions.

Trusting the Practitioner—How to Help Others Trust You

As humans, our ability to trust is based on our accumulated experiences over time that teach us how to judge other people. For ease of processing the millions of bits of data we encounter every time we meet new people or are in new situations, humans have created a shorthand method of dealing with others and our environment. This shorthand has many facets, but the one we have to deal with most in creating trust is called stereotyping. Stereotyping helps us make quick decisions in unfamiliar situations, and it is a skill that has been crucial for survival from time immemorial. While stereotyping may not be politically correct, it is deeply imbedded into our psyches. As a massage therapist, it will be helpful to learn what kinds of stereotypes people have so you attract instead of repel them.

Handling Stereotypes to Gain Trust

Before you are able to gain trust, you will be evaluated and judged on many stereotyping factors by your potential clients. What you will be dealing with is essentially a form of prejudice, or a prejudgment made about you before you will be allowed to massage them. While it may not seem fair that people make instantaneous decisions about your massage work based on how you are dressed, how you talk, or how you stand, that's just the way it is. People have to gather data about whether or not you will be safe and trustworthy, and their strongest preliminary impressions of you initially will be based on your personal presentation. To let their psyches know you are someone they can trust, they will use as many of their senses as they can to determine their feelings about you.

What Clients See in Your Personal Presentation

The first sense your potential clients most likely will use to evaluate you is sight. People will look at your clothes, your posture, how you move, what your body language says, how you style your hair, and any other visual clues they can gain about you. You don't have to be a beauty queen, dashingly handsome, or dress like a model; you simply have to look like someone who is safe enough to touch them.

If your potential client is a friend or an acquaintance, your personal presentation and appearance may not be as crucial, but it is still important. You need to understand that no matter how well you know people, touching them with massage is a different level of connection and may be scary for them. Regardless of whom you are massaging, friends or strangers need to trust you first, so look and act the part of a trustworthy professional no matter what.

Common sense would suggest that everyone knows to look professional. However, one of the biggest complaints I have heard from massage employers is that therapists arrive for work with clothing, hair, and makeup entirely inappropriate for creating trust, safety, and mutual respect between client and practitioner. I wish I didn't have to go over this, but personal appearance is such an issue in gaining trust that it must be dealt with honestly and spelled out clearly.

Personal Appearance Do's

The rules for a massage professional's personal appearance are pretty basic. Wear clean, comfortable clothes that can let you move easily, be washed frequently, and are acceptable to your clients. Wear hairstyles that keep your hair off your clients and represent the image you want to create. If you wear makeup, keep it professional looking. Wear shoes that are comfortable and that can support your feet for hours of standing.

Carry your body with pride. Stand tall, radiate confidence, smile, make good eye contact, hold your head up straight, and look like you are someone who has a good, safe, wonderful touch. Whenever you deal with clients, it is helpful for you to come across as relaxed, competent, capable, friendly, and ready and willing to be of service. These are attributes I would certainly want before I turned over my time, my money, and my body to someone else. Overall, imagine seeing yourself from your clients' eyes. Ask whether your personal presentation sends the message that your client can trust that they will be well taken care of.

If you do not feel confident or capable, or are a bit shy, practice carrying your body as if you were confident, capable, and outgoing. Your mind will believe what your face and body are portraying, so when in doubt, smile big, straighten your shoulders, and move with purpose. As one of my very successful colleagues used to love to say, "Fake it till you make it!"

Most of my best students lacked initial confidence in the quality of their work, but despite their fears, they went out, presented themselves as if they had benefits to offer their clients, and ended up helping people. Their real confidence came later when they realized that they actually did good work. While that process took a while, they worked at presenting themselves well on the outside despite how they felt on the inside.

Perhaps the best way to decide how you will present yourself can be based on the concept of congruency. Basically, congruency means that everything you say, do, wear, and so on, has a feel or an aura to it that is consistent. Congruency is part of what your clients will look for in determining their trust in you, so if you want to be perceived as a professional who offers quality service, you have to look and act the part or they won't believe you. The congruency of your self-presentation is both for you as an individual and you as a stereotype of your clients' perception of a massage therapist. Where they are on the Perception Continuum can make this a little tricky to figure out, but if you follow the basic appearance "do's," you should be fine no matter what other people's preconceived notions are.

Personal Appearance Don'ts

Perhaps more important in creating trust than the more general personal appearance do's are the much more specific personal appearance don'ts. I shudder at some of the outfits I have seen on so-called professionals, and have listened in horror to employers and clients telling stories about what massage therapists have worn to work. Being taken seriously as a professional is greatly undermined by a poor personal presentation. If you want to command high fees and/or gain new clients, don't do the following.

For women especially, do not wear tight, revealing clothing including leotards, unitards, catsuits, tube tops, halter tops, tank tops, low-cut blouses, or shirts that reveal the midriff. Short skirts, short shorts, cut-offs, bicycle shorts, or anything equally revealing or provocative need to be kept out of the professional wardrobe. There are no clothes police out there enforcing these suggestions, but if you want to avoid sexual harassment by clients and be treated as a professional, dress appropriately. I don't want to sound like a prude, but frankly, the less skin you show, the better.

Personally, I don't like to be given a bunch of rules to follow, so let me explain my concerns about this topic, then you can choose whether or not you'll consider my suggestions. I had the great fortune of growing up in the Philippines where touch was commonly practiced between friends. The casual contact of holding hands, leaning on each other, or sitting close was normal and acceptable. On moving to America, I soon discovered that the only people you are "allowed" to touch are family members or partners of the opposite sex. This unfortunate situation basically means that for most American adults, and especially men, touch means sex. I have had the privilege of having a few male clients who were honest enough to talk with me about their experiences of getting massage. Of the many things I learned, the one that surprised me most was that many of these men wanted to try massage, but originally hesitated getting it because they were afraid they would become aroused because touch meant sex. This fear of arousal and subsequent embarrassment is not talked about very much, but I am going to guess that it probably keeps many men from getting massage. While this topic is not one I would address directly with prospective clients, you can address it indirectly with professional attire and a no-nonsense attitude and energy. If a man is concerned about arousal and sees that the therapist dresses provocatively, he

Figure 2–1   What does your personal presentation tell your client about you?

may opt to just say "no" rather than risk the overwhelming training of his psyche. From what I have learned from some male clients and students, it is difficult at first to be touched and not get aroused. However, men can be trained that touch can be pleasurable, nurturing, caring, and therapeutic. Arousal is not harassment, and it is not the practitioner's fault if the client gets aroused. That said, your comportment and dress make a huge difference between whether arousal becomes harassment or does not occur at all.

For male practitioners, your personal presentation needs to be professional as well. In particular, it needs to tell your clients that you will not be coming on to them or that you are open to them coming on to you. With the small but growing number of stories I heard during my travels of male practitioners inappropriately touching female clients, gaining trust soon may become more of an issue than it used to be. The topic of repressing or transmuting sexual energy so that it doesn't affect, frighten, or annoy clients is beyond my ability to address here. However, as more males at a younger age go into massage, I hear more instances of women concerned by the sexual energy they feel from male practitioners. As stories like these spread, male practitioners will have to work with extra caution to demonstrate that they are safe and trustworthy. It is unfortunate that the misbehavior of the few can do so much damage to the many, but it is a reality our field faces and must honestly address to maintain our positive public perception. I personally do not know how to tell therapists, male or female, how to repress or redirect sexual arousal toward clients, but it is a skill that must be learned. Otherwise, a long-term career will be very difficult to build.

Given the concerns mentioned here, presenting a professional image becomes an even more important step toward demonstrating trustworthiness. The rules for men are basically the same as for women. The less skin you show, the better. Tank tops, sleeveless shirts, bicycle shorts, tight pants, unbuttoned shirts, or trying to look sexually attractive are all potential signals to female clients that they may need to be on their guard, and keeps them from establishing trust and getting the most benefit from their session. And guys, please keep your shirts on. One poor woman I spoke with had her therapist strip off his shirt in the middle of the massage and drop beads of sweat onto her. This woke her most unpleasantly to the sensation of cold drippings on her back, followed by the startling realization that he looked naked when she looked up to see what was falling on her. While sweating onto clients is an equal-opportunity no-no, taking clothes off in a session is highly unprofessional.

As a general recommendation, stay away from stained, faded, or torn clothes; T-shirts with controversial slogans, images, or pictures of heavy metal bands; gangsta wear; overalls; and ill-fitting clothing. If you do choose to wear white clothes, make sure they are nice and white, not dingy and gray. Again, no fashion police will arrest you if you wear such clothes to your sessions, but that type of dress basically marks the wearer as an amateur. Sloppy attire also can be interpreted by your current or potential client as disrespectful, and it is definitely unprofessional. Your goal is to gain trust and instill value, but neither of those is easily attainable when you are wearing inappropriate attire.

Shoes are a whole different topic, and the issue for some people is whether to wear shoes or not. If your practice is going to be barefoot Shiatsu, then this is not an issue, but many therapists face the question of wearing shoes while working. I don't have strong recommendations either way, except for the time you meet new or potential clients, or when your current clients are arriving and leaving. Even with your current clients, I still recommend that you wear shoes when you greet them and say good-bye. With first-time clients, shoes are part of shaping their perception and gaining trust, and basically should be worn on introduction. I feel strongly about this, especially based on a sad but true story one of my clients told me.

My client was going to see an acupuncturist, and because I was out of town for an extended period, decided to try a massage from the massage therapist who worked in the acupuncturist's office. When it was time for my client's appointment, the massage therapist opened her office door, walked into the lobby in bare feet, and introduced herself. Although a bit taken aback, my client chalked up the bare feet to her old hippie perception of massage therapists and let it go, or so she thought. In and of itself, greeting a new client in bare feet may not seem like a big deal, but it cast an initial doubt in my client's mind as to this person's professional level.

As my client told me later, this first doubt then caused her to notice other trivial things that she might otherwise have overlooked. Once the door of doubt was open, things went downhill. By the time the session was over, she had taken her first misgivings, added them to some minor but bothersome observations and feelings, and had come up with the final decision that she would never book another appointment with that therapist.

What intrigued me most about my client's story was that one moment of lost trust virtually undid the rest of the massage therapist's marketing. Amazingly, this therapist had numerous and sophisticated marketing tools including a great business card, a fancy brochure, a secretary to book her appointments, and was included in the office website. She even had the great marketing advantage of offering insurance coverage through prescriptions from the acupuncturist, and to top it all off, her hourly rates were lower than mine. One would think by having all these wonderful elements of marketing in place that success would be guaranteed, but it wasn't. This massage therapist made the mistake of losing trust by poor self-presentation, and it ultimately cost her a client.

The skill of creating trust has other elements of self-presentation to consider. Personal adornments such as jewelry, makeup, tattoos, and body piercings are also part of how people judge you. Forms of personal self-expression are touchy subjects, and many people will have many opinions about them. Therefore, the only way I can rise above opinion is to state what I have experienced. Basically, the older, wealthier, or more conservative your clientele, the more judiciously you will need to present yourself. Of course, there are exceptions to every rule, but for most therapists, multiple body and facial piercings, tattoos, and other counter-culture adornments will make it harder to gain trust with clients in mainstream America. Not everyone is bothered by piercings and tattoos, but many folks are, and some will worry that if you are willing to hurt or scar your own body, how well are you going to treat theirs?

It is not fair, but in marketing, perception is reality, and much of America still has negative perceptions about piercings and tattoos. I have known a number of successful therapists who are highly decorated, but their bodywork is extraordinary and their marketing is almost all word-of-mouth referrals. Their new clients have a high level of trust based on the referrals, which will likely supersede their prior prejudices. However, even though their current clients may be fine with their adornments, I have wondered if they hesitate to buy their mothers or fathers massage gift certificates from these therapists for their birthdays.

Jewelry that can scratch clients, long fingernails that can gouge skin or prevent effective hand use, or makeup that looks like it belongs in a night club are among many other topics of personal presentation that come down to the basic question: is your need for external self-expression worth risking the loss of a client? Personal presentation isn't about what is right or wrong, or even about what everyone else is doing or wearing. Your choices come down to whether or not it matters to you that your potential clients trust you, even before you touch them. If they do trust you, they are more likely to book, then rebook and refer. This is how you build your dream practice in the real world. If they don't trust you, you will have to keep working to get more new clients; and if no one trusts you, eventually, you will have to get out of massage altogether. No trust, no practice. It's that simple. For some people, this is a difficult choice, but at least you are getting to make an educated choice knowing that your personal appearance is a crucial part of building a strong practice.

Running the Gauntlet

On a similar theme, there is a game I have observed among some massage therapists that I want to address here. The game is sort of a challenge to prospects and clients, and the challenge goes something like this. If you can get beyond my exterior presentation, you have passed the test and will be allowed to be my client. The exterior presentation can be sloppy or inappropriate dress, excessive tattoos, body piercings, wild hairstyles, and all sorts of external defense mechanisms that force people to pass through a gauntlet before they are allowed into the castle.

Having done this myself, and having talked to my students who used their external presentation to feel safe by screening out "shallow" people, I can attest to the fact that these defense mechanisms work. They keep people away, or at least put them on their guard and make them uneasy. The prevailing feeling was, "If people can't hack how I look, they don't deserve to be my client."

My experience of massage therapists as a whole is that we are a different breed of cat, and we enjoy being mavericks, pushing the envelope, being nonconformists, and being impossible to pigeonhole. We like being different and making people question the thousands of assumptions they make about their health, their bodies, and their prejudices about people who are different than themselves. Attributes such as these are what make massage therapists fascinating people who have the capacity to change others' lives.

The downside of using external expressions to represent these great attributes is that they can prevent prospects and clients from being able to trust fully that the person behind this exterior will be loving, caring, tender, and capable of relating to who they are. This lack of trust, then, makes it very difficult to get clients. As I discovered at the beginning of my career, the world that I wanted to change had very high gates and very tight locks that were designed to keep "alternative" people like me out. After banging on those gates with how I used to look and dress, and not having anyone let me in, I reassessed my strategy and made changes. I found that if I dressed and talked pretty much the way that my target market of potential clients did, they undid their locks, opened the gates, and let me in. My goal as a massage therapist was to help people, and because I really wanted to serve others with my touch, I chose to take down my external barriers.

If you like to look exotic, funky, or basically counter-culture, I recommend that you enjoy this form of self-expression during your nonworking hours, but please do not use it as a screening mechanism for clients. That is not fair to them, and it is not fair to you. Remember, this is a marketing book, and my purpose is to help you get and keep clients. Issues of individuality and self-expression are not my favorites to discuss because they are often loaded with emotion and personal beliefs. However, I would rather deal with the discomfort of someone disagreeing with me than have them face the difficulty of trying to build a practice with an exterior presentation that creates mistrust and keeps people away.

In summary, the essential skill of creating and maintaining trust in your potential and current clients is crucial to building your practice in the real world. At this time in our profession's history, we face a number of challenges to creating trust, but they are not insurmountable; they simply take more attention and conscientiousness. If you have the fundamental attribute of desiring to serve others, put the time and effort into doing whatever it takes to gain trust. Trust is what gives you the opportunity to serve.

EXERCISE: Designing Your Personal Presentation

■ Write down five words that you would like your clients to use to describe you. These words can be the image you want to portray, the aura you want to convey, or how you want people to feel around you.

Example: I want my clients to see me as safe, loving, effective, considerate, and interesting.

■ For each of your five words, write down five things you can do in your personal presentation to demonstrate those characteristics. Think from your clients' perspective of what would help them feel the way you want them to.

Example: For my clients to experience me as being safe, I will wear polo shirts and khaki pants; arrive on time for our session; speak with conviction and confidence, but not too loudly; do a familiar premassage routine; and stand back from the peephole of the front door so they can see that it is me ringing their doorbell.

I know a few of these are odd, but as you can see from the example, all sorts of things can affect how your clients perceive you. Think of every step of your time together and what you can do to present yourself so that your clients trust you.

Reverse Trust

The second element of trust in building a practice revolves around whether or not you, the therapist, can trust your clients. Especially because of the issue of misperception about massage and prostitution, and because of unpredictable sexual arousal by clients, this is a topic to be taken seriously. Two primary factors of trusting your clients will greatly affect your ability and willingness to market your services. The first is whether you can trust that your client won't harass or harm you. The second is whether or not you trust you can reach your clients without harassment by various law enforcement agencies. This isn't much fun to talk about when all you want to do is help others with your massage, but this angle of trust—or rather, mistrust—has shut down the practices of too many quality therapists for me to not address it with blunt honesty.

Trusting the Client

At this time, the large majority of massage therapists are women, and for those of us working out of our homes or doing outcall, being able to trust potential clients is critical for your safety as well as your success. To obtain safety and success calls for marketing options that screen out potentially dangerous clients while still making you visible enough to attract legitimate ones. Unfortunately, much of the traditional marketing strategies of advertising, public relations, and media exposure can attract the heavy breathers. I have spoken with colleagues who have Yellow Pages ads that are clear as a bell with words like "nonsexual" or "therapeutic only," and give a license number or an association logo to add legitimacy, all to no avail. People still call looking for sex. The heavy breathers are pretty easy to spot. They ask questions such as "Do you do full body massage?" or "Do you work on all the muscles?" or "Do you do extras?" These and other transparent code words are a dead giveaway to what they are really looking for. At the risk of possibly offending a legitimate client, my colleagues who use mass media marketing have carefully crafted answers and a whole set of questions that don't accuse the caller of anything but do screen out potential trouble.

For anyone who wants to avoid this type of harassment, about the only safe way of marketing is by word-of-mouth referrals, which we will cover in great depth in the following chapters. Whatever type of marketing you use, you always will need to screen your clients (which we will cover later also). For now, just realize that once again we face marketing issues that are unique to our field and require different marketing strategies than anyone else has to use.

Trusting the "Authorities"

The second factor of reverse trust is whether or not you know you can go about your business of getting and keeping clients without being harassed by state or local authorities. I have found that this issue is not often talked about, but many of us work in areas where authorities still conduct what are akin to witch hunts on legitimate therapists, and it greatly affects our ability to market. In fact, as one of my colleagues who has been fighting for fair licensure in San Francisco recently quipped, just about the only massage people working legally in San Francisco are the prostitutes. Obviously there are legitimate therapists working legally in San Francisco, but it amazes me that even in one of the most liberal cities in the country, massage therapists have a hard time getting a license to practice. How sad that the parlor owners have the money, connections, and know-how to gather up phony school certificates and pay the right people for licenses for call girls, when qualified therapists have to fight for the right to get a license to practice.

From my research, I have found that San Francisco is not the only place that makes it difficult to practice legally. A significant number of practitioners I interviewed across the country were working without a business license, either because they could not get one, or the process was too prohibitive or demeaning. After hearing stories about therapists being forced to put drains in the middle of their office floor so they could hose down the room after each session, or being set up by vice squads with undercover agents harassing therapists for sexual favors so they could bust them, I can see why so many people opt to work without all of their appropriate licenses.

My mother (also a massage therapist), who is a minister's wife and the picture of a quintessential grandma, had to go through the vice squad ringer. She had to get a doctor's clearance certificate for sexually transmitted diseases, endure a police background check, have mug shots taken, and go through months of foot-dragging before she got a city license to do on-site massage in an office building. Another colleague of mine was told that the city where she lived only gave out four massage permits because "we don't need more than four masseuses in town." Being the fifth or fiftieth massage therapist in town means practicing illegally.

I look forward to the day that our field is regulated fairly and without the specter of prostitution hanging over it, but that day is not yet here in many parts of the country. Many people have fought for years to be treated fairly by regulating authorities and their work has paved the way for the profession to grow, but there is still much work to be done. It is only through our ongoing efforts that massage will get its due, so it is important that you do what you can to work legally.

If you are fortunate enough to work in an area that treats massage therapy like any other service business, you can have fewer concerns about who you can trust and you can use more forms of marketing safely. If not, then you will have less room to trust others and your practice will need to be built almost exclusively from personal referrals. Informal marketing and talking with people you meet can get things started, and the material in a later chapter on Mutual Marketing also can be of great assistance.

Overall, the issue of reverse trust is one of the biggest our profession faces. My hope is that as our field continues to grow and gain legitimacy, these concerns will fade off into the distance and just be old war stories horrified newcomers hear at conventions or read about in old marketing books. Until that day arrives, though, many practitioners who are basically forced to keep a low profile will need to market "under the radar" and trust their intuition about whom they can trust in the process of building a practice.

Gaining and maintaining trust takes forethought, practice, and an ability to respond appropriately to the real world. Knowing what it takes to gain trust requires stepping outside of yourself and your reality, and seeing what it will take to invite others to join you in your growing practice. Whatever form of marketing you choose, make one of your goals to show that you are trustworthy to touch another human being. Trust is the foundation of your success. Do everything you can to build on it.

Marketing Skill #3: Establishing Value

If you have done what it takes to gain the trust of people who can potentially become your clients, you can take the next step in building your practice. The third essential marketing skill you need to get people under your hands is the ability to establish the belief in their minds that your work is valuable to them. Fortunately for us, massage is so valuable to so many people for so many different reasons that this skill can be mastered with some good thought and effort.

If gaining trust is the emotional part of a person's decision to get a massage, then believing in its value is the intellectual justification most people need to commit the time and money for your services. Depending on where people are on the Perception Continuum will affect how much they value massage and how much they are willing to pay for it. If your primary market is the group of people who are already looking for a good massage therapist, creating value will not be too difficult and will not require a huge marketing campaign. If your primary market needs to be convinced of the value of massage or have their misperceptions changed, then you will have to work harder on this skill.

However, no matter where your potential clients are on the Perception Continuum, they all have basic needs that are core to being human. You can establish your practice in many ways, but one way is to decide what basic human needs you are able to meet with massage, then market your desire and expertise to meet that need. The ability to establish value in other's minds will be based on which needs of theirs you can meet and how much they want those needs met. To explore this further, let's look at a series of questions we will work through together so that you will be prepared to provide the valuable service of massage to those who need it.

There are six questions for establishing value.

1. What universal needs do human beings have?

2. How do massage and bodywork meet those needs?

3. What is your ability and desire to meet those needs?

4. Who is your competition that already meets those needs?

5. What are those needs worth to your potential clients?

6. How do you set a price on your ability to meet their needs?

Question 1—What Universal Needs do Human Beings Have?

Human beings have a vast number of wants. However, we have a much smaller number of true needs that are core to us as a species. Depending on whose material you study, there are some very interesting interpretations about which of those needs are most important or more universal than others. In the hundreds of books I have read and hundreds upon hundreds of hours of seminars I have attended that deal with human behavior and motivation, my favorite summary of human needs comes from Tony Robbins, a human behavior specialist. Simply stated, the two core human needs are to avoid pain and gain pleasure. Basically, we do what we do to feel good or stop hurting. If this is the case, and I think it is, massage therapists are in luck! Of all the other service professions in existence, very few of them have the ability that we do to offer both pleasure and pain relief simultaneously. In addition, compared to virtually every other medical service, our clients are happy to keep their appointments. I mean, really, how many people truly look forward to seeing their dentist, or say "I've been looking forward to this all week!" when they get their annual checkup. Oh, the advantages we have!

Figure 2—2   The value of a massage is flexible, and depends on the wants and needs of the client.

Avoiding pain is a multitrillion dollar investment human beings make. We have vast armies to protect us from the pain and fear of insecurity, we take drugs and alcohol to numb our minds and bodies, and we do everything imaginable to escape the pain of boredom. To gain pleasure, we take extraordinary measures to feel loved, look good, attract a mate, and grow and learn.

If I were to mix and match the needs I have studied, I would put them into the two primary categories of avoiding pain and gaining pleasure with some specific divisions added relevant to us as bodyworkers. In both categories, I see there are divisions between mental, emotional, physical, and spiritual/energetic needs. I'm going to list some of the many needs that humans have in each category. As you read them, ask yourself if these are needs with which you are willing and able to help people. Each of these needs is important to large numbers of people. The more you understand these needs, the more valuable you will discover massage is in meeting so many of them at once.

Pains that People Want to Avoid that Massage Can Help

Mental Pain

  stress

  being overwhelmed

  boredom

Emotional Pain

  loss

  insecurity

  loneliness

  insignificance

  isolation

Physical Pain

   lack of touch

  Musculoskeletal

    stress-related tension

    postural

    movement repetition or overuse

    soreness

  Conditional

    tired or fatigued

  Injury

    sports related

    job related

    accident or trauma

  Illness

**Pleasures that People Want to Gain that Massage
Can Provide**

Mental Pleasure

  self-awareness

  self-understanding

  exploration and learning

  performance enhancement

  variety

  conversation

  clarity

  epiphinal

  zoning out

Emotional Pleasure

  feel loved

  feel safe

get attention

acceptance

me too, popular

feel important

feel successful, arrived

feel better

feel attractive

feel pampered

treat myself and taking care of myself

deserve it

smug and superior

happiness

feel special

relationship with you

sense of belonging

sense of significance

sense of security

feel connected

feel needed by you

make a contribution to you

gain approval

Physical Pleasure

touch is healing

feels good

letting go

performance enhancement—sports, activities

look good—younger, vibrant, posture

ensure wellness

better able to care for self and others, including children

remain mobile

be pain free

be healthy

feel better

live longer

feel attractive

I think you get the idea that massage can be valuable to a lot of people for many different reasons. These are just some of the few needs that we can meet, and I'm sure you can think of more.

Exercise: Meeting Your Clients' Needs

Take a look at this list again and ask yourself these questions.

■ Which of these needs can I help people with right now? Put an X by those needs.

■ Which of these needs would I enjoy helping people meet? Underline those needs.

■ Which of these needs would I want to help people with, but I need more training? Put an O by those.

■ Which of these needs do I have no real interest in? Draw a line through those.
Now, take out a sheet of paper and write down how and why massage is valuable. At the top of the paper write Massage is Valuable Because I Can Help People . . .

■ Below that, take the needs you have underlined and marked with an X and make a new list that is tailored to you. Play off of the basic needs and make additions to the ones that are meaningful to you. If you can think of needs that you want to meet that are not on these pages, by all means, write them in. Your page can look something like this.

Example:
Massage is Valuable Because I Can Help People . . .
Feel less lonely
Figure out why they are hurting and help them make changes
Run faster
Let go of their stress
Be able to move better, such as when picking up grandchildren, getting into the bathtub, working in the garden
Feel successful, like they've "arrived"
Feel special
Be touched because no one else touches them
Understand what is happening to their bodies
Have a safe place to cry
Just let go and relax
Feel okay about their own bodies

■ Write a full page, or more if you like. Once you are done, look at your list in amazement. We have so much to give that so many people want and need! And this is just the tip of the iceberg!

Now that we have some idea of what needs massage meets, we can look at the next six questions for establishing value.

Question 2—How Do Massage and Bodywork Meet Those Needs?

Massage has the marvelous advantage of helping people because it has direct and indirect benefits. The direct benefits often are what we talk about in traditional marketing. Increased circulation, better range of motion, decreased blood pressure and blah blah blah are all great sounding, but they aren't usually what people really want to buy. These are results of massage, and they are what we are comfortable talking about. But they aren't always the bottom line of what motivates people to spend the time and money on your services. At some core level, human beings need the touch and closeness of other human beings, and massage has the ability to meet those primordial needs.

This duplicity creates a bit of a dilemma in marketing. First, it's not polite to run ads that say "Are you lonely? Does nobody touch you? Are you embarrassed by your body? Do you want something to brag about to your neighbors? Then come get a massage and I can help!" I don't actually know if ads like that would work, but I don't have the guts to try it. The second dilemma is that most people want marketing messages proven to them. How does pressing on muscles help people feel less lonely or learn to accept themselves at a deeper level? I don't know how; it just does. I have lots of anecdotal evidence that it does, but how and why I do not know. While we are gathering evidence in research studies proving the value of our work, what people really want to buy is often what we cannot prove.

Not being able to talk about the indirect benefits of massage, and not being able to prove a lot of those indirect benefits, leaves us with a few options. We can talk about the direct effects, the relaxed muscles, lower stress, and whatnot that appeals to the justification side of the brain. I would add to that a second option that may sound a little hokey but which is based on intention, one of the most powerful tools we use during bodywork. I figure if intention can work on the table, it can work in marketing. If you hold in your mind the knowledge of the value of massage, and communicate with silent intention the ways that you can really help people, I believe they can hear those silent messages. We all have to bear pretenses imposed on us by society, but we communicate on all sorts of levels beneath those pretenses and I think we can market from there. The mere act of touching another human has woven into it cure-alls for many problems, and skilled touch brings an even deeper level of ability to help.

Frankly, if we humans were smart enough to sit around and groom each other like our distant ape and monkey cousins, we'd be a lot more peaceful, happier, and satisfied with life. However, since we're all too suave and sophisticated for that now, we don't get the amount of touch we need, and there is gathering evidence that it makes us unwell and unhappy.

If you have a select group of potential clients that would not be offended by your honesty about the indirect effects of massage, such as the ability to brag to the neighbors, you can experiment with that as a marketing message. If you have a lot of competition with other massage therapists and want to stand out in the crowd, then take the risk and emphasize the indirect benefits you can offer them. Whether you have a formal marketing program or talk to people you encounter in your everyday life, keep in mind the many needs you can meet and approach people with the confidence of knowing how much you are able to do.

I am a big advocate for skilled touch, and I always encourage practitioners to keep growing and learning professionally. However, because of all the indirect benefits we offer through our time, attention, and mere touch, you already provide a valuable service, even if it isn't the latest and greatest bodywork modality to come down the pike. Your power to help most of the needs on the list for relieving pain and gaining pleasure can come from good basic massage skills applied well, along with compassion, caring, and what most everyone wants: a little attention.

Question 3—What Is Your Ability and Desire to Meet Those Needs?

One of the joys I experienced as a teacher was seeing the marvelous differences among my students. They were all in class to learn the same skills but I knew each of them would end up with very different types of practices. The beauty of massage is that we can apply our basic skills with very different outcomes depending on the needs of the clients we are drawn to serving. When you are trying to understand and establish your value in the marketplace, there are a number of things to consider, along with your desire and ability to meet those needs. To create the highest value for yourself and your clients, consider the following:

Your inherent personality.

Your background, which includes your training and life experience.

Your upbringing.

Your personal beliefs and values.

Your desire to serve.

Your ability to serve.

Let me give you an example from my own life to make this clearer, and then I'll have you try it. From my inherent personality, I have a soft spot in my heart for little old ladies, I am curious and fascinated by people, I love being relaxed, and easygoing. My background includes a long history of childhood illness, numerous sports injuries, worldwide travel, and growing up as a missionary child. My upbringing taught me to respect everybody, be kind and generous, and to help wherever I was able. My beliefs and values tell me that service is the highest calling, and that one person can make a big difference. My desire to serve with massage comes from my enjoyment and affinity for touch, and from the satisfaction I get working with the elements of body, mind, emotions, and spirit. My ability to serve is grounded in my love of anatomy, my study of athletic performance, my initial massage training and numerous seminars, and teaching thousands of students.

Looking over this shoot-from-the-hip synopsis, I can see how massage would be a natural career for me, and why I have been drawn to the needs of the kind of clients I serve.

EXERCISE: Getting to Know Yourself

- This is a stream-of-consciousness exercise. In it, your only job is to think about yourself, who you are, and what you like to do. The clearer you are about what you like and what is important to you, the more you will consciously gravitate your practice toward meeting other's needs in a way that is mutually beneficial and enjoyable.

Take out six pieces of paper (yes, six!) and on each one, write the following subjects at the top, one subject per sheet.

1. My inherent personality.

2. My background, which includes my training and life experience.

3. My upbringing.

4. My personal beliefs and values.

5. My desire to serve.

6. My ability to serve.

■ For each topic, write—as fast as you can—all the words and thoughts you can think of in three minutes. Don't edit your work or worry that it doesn't make sense. Just free-associate with the words and see what comes up. When you are finished writing, take a look at your words. Then go back to the prior exercise, Massage is Valuable Because I Can Help People, and read over that list. If you discovered new needs you can serve that are a great fit for your personality and skills, add those to your "Massage is valuable" list.

Keep these two lists where you can find them easily. As you work through the rest of this book, keep thinking about who you are and what needs you can meet for other people. This is the secret of creating value.

Question 4—Who or What Is Your Competition that Already Meets Those Needs?

Competition is probably one of the most misunderstood facets of marketing massage that I have encountered. I have heard students and practitioners complain about crowded markets, and blame local schools for "pumping out" graduates, all with the firmly held belief that this somehow will take away their access to a minuscule pool of clients from which to draw. Since the pool of clients is comprised of the millions of people who have never even had a massage, I believe that we have a huge reservoir of clients to draw from, and we would be better served exploring what our competition really is so that we can market effectively instead of blaming and complaining.

If competition is whatever affects people's hearts, minds, and wallets so that they don't book a massage with you, then I would have to say that your biggest competition is with ignorance. Combine ignorance with mistrust and lack of value for your services, and you've just identified your main opponent to success. This means that marketing is primarily educational, and the purpose of marketing is to tell people about the benefits and values of massage.

Another area is the competition we face from many other products and services that have nothing to do with massage, but that are able to meet the different needs that massage can serve. If you recognize this, you can compete with their draw by addressing your comparative benefits. If you market to stress-management clients, your competition can be psychotherapists, biofeedback experts, or hypnotists. The benefit of massage over these services is that you can help clients learn stress-management skills while helping undo the physical manifestations of stress in their bodies. None of the other services can use touch as part of their stress-management assistance, leaving us with an incredible and enviable advantage.

Because massage has the great flexibility and malleability to serve many markets and needs, we have amazing marketing angles. But sometimes, that flexibility can become a two-edged sword. Since our service and fees can be judged and compared with values in other competing industries, you will have to know more about those industries as you try to establish your value in your buyer's mind.

For example, let's say your market is the group of people in search of relaxation and pampering. Their mental budget for massage can be weighed against other pampering category expenditures such as a nice dinner out, a weekend getaway trip, or a facial. Essentially, you are competing for their pampering dollars, and your value as a pampering experience needs to be the same or better as other experiences outside of massage in order to get their business.

Similarly, let's say you are aiming for the market that has a goal of spending money on what makes them look or feel good. Here, you are competing with hairstylists, aestheticians, personal trainers, a new pair of shoes, a sack full of makeup, or a visit to the plastic surgeon. Discretionary income can be fickle in this market, and if your clients are on a semitight budget, it may come down to a massage from you or a new handbag. Your job is to generate enough value in your clients' minds so that if they want that new handbag, they will cut something else from their budget before they cut massage.

If your goal is to build a practice in the medical massage market, you face competition from other medical services. I would like to sound a few warning bells about this market. Until there comes a time in our industry that a widespread designated training for medical massage comes along, some therapists are tiptoeing dangerously along the boundary of the limits of our scope of practice. Some states have high education standards, clear-cut licensing requirements, and real preparation for the world of medical massage, but most states don't. On that note, be careful that you do not diagnose, treat, or prescribe.

On the marketing front, you will be in competition for medical dollars—which the massage profession has already done quite well—but we could close doors on all sorts of other markets if we get too wrapped up pushing massage into the medical model. Massage has proven itself efficacious and viable for centuries without getting caught in the medical model trap, and we could be shooting ourselves in the foot if we try to force it in that direction. People are fleeing Western medicine in droves and running to alternative therapies for many reasons, so why model ourselves after a sinking ship? I think that many people go to doctors because they want a professional's time and attention focused on them, and their aches and pains, but since insurance companies only allow doctors a few minutes per patient, clients get a pill but no attention. We have the ability to give the time, listening ear, and caring attention, and it is part of why our popularity has soared. Compete in the medical market if you so choose, but realize that the reasons people see doctors are often deeper than the symptoms they claim, and massage can be much more helpful for those silent needs beneath the symptoms.

If you have advanced training and a therapeutic bodywork specialty that gets you good results with injuries and soft tissue problems, you can do well in the medical massage field. You may choose to work in a doctor's office or work on your own with referred patients. In this case, your competition can become your ally. And, as you consider other competitors from other professions, I encourage you to consider the possibility that they also could become allies and great sources of referrals. Those aestheticians, hairstylists, and makeup salespeople all know lots of people who might want massage, so be a smart marketer and befriend your competition.

If you are fortunate enough to live in an area where you have competition with other massage therapists, consider yourself lucky! This means that other therapists already have been training the general public and moving them further along the Perception Continuum toward accepting and valuing massage. Your job is a lot easier because of those around you simultaneously working to educate the public. Your fellow massage therapists are your allies, not your enemies. Your primary battle is with ignorance. Many therapists have sacrificed much of their time, money, and energy to change the hearts and minds of the general public, knowing full well that someone else will reap the rewards of their efforts. Massage therapists have no need for a scarcity mindset. Scarcity makes us miss the opportunities right in front of us, and frankly, any person who has a body is a potential client. As far as I know, most of your clients will have bodies, and until every body is being massaged, there is room for us all.

One of the primary ways that I, and a few other successful therapists I interviewed, got started was because of referrals from other massage therapists. I started my practice with three referrals from a therapist who was leaving the area. In another case, the original therapist didn't like the long drive to a particular client, and referred her to a new therapist in town. The client became the start of a whole new practice. Get to know other massage therapists around you, and learn and grow with them, working together instead of against each other. You may build a whole practice from a departing therapist. As you will see later in the book, there are dozens of ways to reach untapped markets, so keep your mind open and let go of any notions of scarcity. It's a very big world out there!

Question 5—What Are Those Needs Worth to Your Potential Clients?

Part of marketing is evaluating what a product or service is worth to a customer or client, and what factors affect that worth. Why, for example, would people pay $30 for a bottle of wine at a restaurant when they know they can buy it at the grocery store for $15? Has the wine's inherent value suddenly jumped? Of course not. However, the restaurant setting and the experience of being out on the town makes the desire stronger at that moment, and the worth becomes negotiable. If a person purchased stock in a new Internet company for $10 and it jumped up to $100 in value, where has the increased value come from? In reality, that stock is just a piece of paper, but its value has changed because the people involved in buying and selling it agree on its new value. As you may notice if you follow the stock market, agreements about a stock's worth change frequently, and often because of factors that are unpredictable or out of the control of the principals involved.

In trying to establish the worth of massage, many factors affect it, but here's the rub: you will find it almost impossible to figure out those factors, and they change constantly. Value and worth are what we agree they are. Is a massage more valuable because it is given at a beachfront resort in Maui instead of in a spare bedroom that is now a massage office? Is a massage more valuable to the recipient if it costs $125 instead of $40? Is a massage to help restore range of motion to an injured knee more valuable than a shamanic-style session with burning sage and a crystal layout on the chakras? Is it worth more to a client to be able to brag to neighbors about getting massage, or to have less lower back pain? Is a massage worth more because the practitioner thinks it is? To all of those questions, the best answer I can think of is "It depends." Worth depends on what the practitioner and the client agree it is. Whatever needs you meet will vary in value from client to client, and over time. So, why bring worth up at all? Because worth is flexible, and you have the power to shape it.

The first and most important place where worth is shaped is in your own mind. If you truly understand how many needs and wants you fulfill for others, you will have more confidence and belief in the value of your work. With that confidence comes an increased ability to explain the many needs you meet and to persuade others to accept the value that you place on massage. If you set the value, others will agree or disagree, but it is set.

I remember seeing this principle in action with a student who had been in his massage training program for about seven weeks. He knew a basic sequence, had, um, shall we say, unrefined skills, and no prior massage experience. Once he learned his initial sequence, though, he was off and running getting clients, led by his unshakable belief that he was some great gift to the world. I marveled that he was convincing people that he was skilled, that he was charging $75 an hour, and getting it back in 1991. I don't know how many of his initial clients returned or referred others (which are the crucial factors for success), but he sure started off with a bang.

Even more interesting to me were this man's classmates, many of whom had much better innate talent. Despite their better hands-on skills, they lacked confidence to the point that some were even hesitant to work on family and friends for the after-school practice we encouraged them to do. From a teacher's point of view, I was dismayed and confused. The student with the worst skills and arrogant attitude was getting clients who were paying more than my clients, and the students who were truly gifted were having a hard time thinking their talents were worth anything. This experience, and many more like it over my years of teaching, brought me to the realization that the practitioner's confidence was a significant factor in establishing worth at the beginning of a practice.

I wish I could say that building a dream practice in the real world was fair, but I can't. If you don't understand your own value and how to communicate its worth, success can be elusive, no matter what your skill level.

From observing my students, I have seen three primary elements involved in the process of establishing worth, especially in the beginning stages of building a practice.

1. Belief in ability and confidence level

2. Ability to communicate

3. Level of skill

I saw all sorts of combinations of these elements: gifted students with no confidence, arrogant braggarts with no sense of touch, caring hearts who were afraid to talk to people, blowhards with real talent who were secretly fearful, and average hands with save-the-world hearts and missionary mouths. In the short run, the advantage seemed to go to those with confidence and the ability to communicate it, regardless of their skills. Over the long run, where repeats and referrals became a factor, the level of skill became the predominating factor, even for those who had some lack of confidence. In fact, on the whole, I noticed that those with lower confidence were often more competent because they were willing to learn, grow, and get better, while those who were supremely confident rarely had any notion to improve what were often poor to mediocre skills. Over time, those who honed their craft developed confidence borne by experience, and their ability to establish worth in their clients' minds grew as they did.

My recommendation in all this is pretty simple. If you have low self-confidence, work on mastering your hands-on skills, and look at and value the many needs you meet that do not require a high level of skill. Most of my original clients, who were elderly widows, came to me because they were lonely, wanted someone to listen to them, and needed a loving touch. Basic Swedish was good enough for them, and it was the level of work I was able to do. Over time, I continued to learn and studied my anatomy when I was faced with a client problem I didn't understand. With deeper experience and better results, my confidence and understanding of my worth grew. If your confidence isn't the greatest, start somewhere, anywhere, and let your confidence build over time as you practice your skills.

On the other hand, if you think you are the greatest massage student or practitioner to hit the planet, then you have a great advantage in getting your initial clients. If you have the skills to back up your beliefs, then you have what it takes to establish worth over time. That said, I must confess I always dreaded getting students who thought they were really great right at the start of training. If they were genuinely talented, they could be a real joy; but if they weren't, it was bad news for the whole class. In many ways, the more confident the unskilled students were, the less they seemed able to really evaluate their own work and the less coachable they were in improving their skills. Their attitude was, "If I'm this great, why do I have to pay attention to this teacher or listen to feedback from my classmates? I know what I'm doing!" They were pushy and careless with their classmates, often rough with their work, and were too above-it-all to participate in exercises unless they were in the mood.

Unfortunately, when students like this want to build a practice, they take their no-room-for-improvement attitude and apply it to their clients. Even if clients tell them that the pressure is too hard or say that they do not like anyone to touch their feet, these types of practitioners arrogantly ignore them because they maintain the attitude that they know best. The core attribute of the desire to serve becomes sublimated by the desire to be right, and the results are disastrous for the client, the practitioner, and the field. This type of practitioner manhandles and injures clients all too often, but because of the ability to draw in new clients with their confidence, they may not notice that return and referral clients are few and far between. Clients who have been mauled by therapists with distorted views of their own worth and expertise are rarely likely to try massage again, and certainly do not spread the good word about massage to their friends. By comparison, if a person gets a bad haircut from a new stylist, he or she will go look for a new one; but if that same person gets a bad massage, that may be it.

If you fit the profile I have just described, please open your mind to the possibility that your skills are not as good as you imagine. If you are in school, look outside of yourself for feedback about your work, ask for help in improving your skills, practice saying "I don't know," and become accustomed to the notion that other's views are as viable as your own. If you think you already know everything and your favorite phrase is "I already know that," you are in serious trouble for maintaining a long-term practice. There is a line I like to use that basically says "The more you know, the more you know you don't know." If you believe you already know it all, then you are clueless about the vast amount of knowledge in a wide range of disciplines that would be helpful for your practice. I am not being so blunt to be mean. My goal for this book is to have every therapist become successful, and I have watched too many know-it-alls burn brightly and then flame out by not addressing the issue.

If you are already practicing, give value to your clients' preferences and be there to serve them, not dominate them into taking whatever you dish out. Worth is established because of agreement between you and your client, and if your view is that your clients' wants, needs and opinions aren't that important, it makes for a skewed and often short-lived relationship.

The successful practitioners I have interviewed have an interesting blend of confidence, humility, pride in their work, attentiveness to their clients' needs, and an unquenchable desire to continue learning and growing. They recognize the value of their work, give credence to their clients' feedback, and work together with their clients to set up a trusting and value-driven working relationship with mutually agreed on worth that improves over time.

Question 6—How Do You Set a Price on Your Ability to Meet Their Needs?

The value of your massage varies from client to client and from day to day, depending on how their needs change or how well you have met their needs. For example, if a carpenter comes to you because of low back pain and after a few sessions that pain is gone, his need for massage for pain relief will drop. He either will stop getting massage or will find other reasons to continue with you for maintenance or less therapy-oriented purposes. What he valued about massage has changed. Do you change your prices because his needs change? In most cases, no; your prices will remain the same. That is because value is only one of many factors that is considered when you set the prices for your sessions.

Setting prices is one of the major issues in marketing no matter what field you are in, but it becomes even more of an issue with massage. With so many different needs and markets that we serve, there is no common standard for pricing in the industry. This leaves you with the need to consider other factors for setting your prices besides just what other massage therapists are charging.

Your prices may be affected by some or all of the following.

What markets you have the desire to serve.

What needs and expectations you have the ability to meet.

How big the market is for those needs.

What your market is willing and able to pay.

What your "competition" costs.

Your personal and business expenses.

Your financial goals.

Your work location—home, office, outcall, or other settings.

Length of session.

How you present yourself to your market.

What you perceive your work is worth.

Your attitude about money.

What stage your practice is in—new, established, and so forth.

For a new practitioner starting out, your prices will be more affected by these factors. Later on, if you develop an incredible reputation, can help people with their bodies very quickly, and have established yourself, the rules can definitely change. I've taken seminars from massage experts who charged $100 for a 15-minute session because that's all the time they needed to get the results for which the client came to them. They were world-renowned practitioners and teachers, and believed their method of treatment was superior to what Western medicine and other bodywork modalities had to offer. If you get to that level of expertise, then you have more leeway with prices and how you choose to set them. Until that happens, though, your prices will need to be more in line with what the market will bear.

In the world of price-setting, two primary groups should be considered. One group comprises what is known as the "value" market. These are people who base most of their buying decisions on price; the lower the price, the more likely they are to buy. The second group is more of the "quality" market. Buyers in this group are willing to pay for the level of quality they want in a product or a service, even if the price is higher.

At this point in our profession's history, most of our clients are in the "quality" market. These people are more experimental, willing to be the first to try the hot new rage of massage, and will pay for a good experience. The quality market wants a good value, but they are willing to pay well to get what they want. The interesting thing about this market is that low prices can turn them off. If you do not put a valid price on your services, this market will perceive your value as beneath their standards. Their belief is that if the price is too low, something is fishy. This more sophisticated market probably has some dollar amount associated with massage based on what they have seen during their travels to resorts, spas, and hotels. People will usually pay more for most products and services when they travel than they will at home, but they will have a frame of reference, nonetheless, when they start looking for a massage therapist back home.

As for the value market, they will become more of a factor as a higher percentage of the population tries massage. However, these "me-too buyers" who follow the trends set by the quality buyers will want a piece of the action, but they are not as willing or able to pay the price. This group is willing to settle for less, but they want a low price as part of the bargain. There are many more people in the value market, and if you want to appeal to them, do massage package specials, low-cost half-hour sessions, and make your prices accessible and appealing. As the value market starts getting interested in massage, pricing will become more competitive, but there will be a larger customer base discovering the joys and benefits of massage. We may never get to the day when Massage Hut franchises dot every corner or shopping mall in America, and compete with Massage Shack for clients in search of low-cost rubdowns, but then you never know.

If you want to appeal to both markets, I recommend that you have a "massage menu" that can fit almost any budget. Don't have one set price to which people either say yes or no. Have multiple options from which to choose. Package deals, couples' discounts, holiday specials, premium add-ons such as aromatherapy, or short sessions all give potential customers the ability to say yes to becoming your client. As for the ubiquitous sliding scale, I don't recommend it. People at the bottom may like the discount but can end up resenting feeling poor, while people at the top of the scale will resent paying for the same service for higher cost just because they have more money. Quite honestly, my experience with the very wealthy is that they can be the most guarded with their money.

To get around trying to set one price for the same service for different markets, have slightly varying services so that prices cannot be directly compared. A massage menu lets people purchase the service level and price they are comfortable with and can afford. Also, since your competition comes from so many angles, having a menu makes it more difficult to compare multiple prices and options. The goal of the menu is to move the decision-making process from "yes or no" answers to "which option to choose." Your best marketing is direct demonstration of your hands-on skills, so make it as easy as possible for potential clients to say "yes." Once they are under your hands, you can establish your value so that they choose to return for the same service, or upgrade to a higher service level and price point.

There aren't a lot of hard and fast rules about setting the prices on your menu, but I prefer to have prices with odd numbers because they are harder for people to mentally divide and assign value. For example, if I charged $60/hour, that is easily divisible to a dollar a minute. This may cause some people to pause and wonder if they want to spend a dollar a minute. If I charge $65 for an hour and ten minutes, most people can't do the math on the spot and take the price as a lump sum which often feels more acceptable.

If you choose to have a massage menu and want a good, high-end option list for the quality market, think for a moment about when people will pay high amounts of money for a product or service. Think about what

---

Massage Menu
1-hour Swedish Massage
90-minute Swedish Massage
1-hour Deep Tissue Massage
30-minute Hand and Foot Massage
Aromatherapy Massage
Salt Scrub
Hot Rock Treatment
Herbal Wrap
Chakra Balancing
Posture and Gait Assessment
Pamper Package
Chair Massage at your party or event $X/person—minimum 5 people
$X/person—6 or more people

Figure 2–3   Offer a variety of services at various prices to appeal to different markets.

changes the cost of a particular item so that it becomes more or less expensive. In our quirky human nature, there are a number of fairly classic factors that people will spend more money for, and interestingly, massage touches on quite a few of those factors. Read the following list and ask yourself which of these possibly may affect the prices of your upper-end services.

Factors that Increase Price

People will pay more for things that are:

rare

exotic

unusual

status symbols

convenient

unique

highly prized

sought after by others

hard to come by

uncommon

extraordinary

entertaining

a break from the routine

exclusive

new and exciting

People also will pay more for:

what gains other's approval

what shows superiority or affluence

what others agree is valuable

times of celebration

fast results

good reputation

Whether you are in the world of fine art, fine wine, precious gems, or massage, many of these factors in combination add up to higher demand and, therefore, higher prices. For some of these elements, such as being too unusual or too hard to find, I don't recommend them if you are just starting your practice, and haven't established your value and reputation. However, once your value is established and agreed on with clients, everything becomes flexible.

For example, I know a number of practitioners who live and travel between two states every month. Their practices are booming and their prices high. For one thing, they are so hard to book with that people sign up months in advance. These practitioners have a small, exclusive "club" of clients who jealously guard their standing appointments and who like to brag about it. Since these massage professionals provide excellent customer service, and have good skills and solid reputations, they have strong appeal and command high prices.

In a combination of a few of these factors, one client I spoke with who goes to a high-priced jet-setting massage therapist thought it was cool that "my masseuse lives in L.A." half the time. Of course, the clients in Los Angeles think it's cool that she spends half her month in San Francisco, and round it goes. Unless your practice is strictly medical, do not discount the value of bragging rights. I honestly think that more than half of my original clients in the 1980s came to me for the primary, but unspoken, purpose of being able to one-up their friends. The utter joy they had of taking a telephone call in the middle of their in-home massage and being able to say "I can't talk now. I'm getting a massage" was just amazing. You know you have truly arrived, and so does everyone else, if you get to say, "Not now, dahling, my massage therapist is here."

On a little tangent here, I want to address the ongoing debate about what touch professionals are called, especially with the term "masseuse." Most people in this country do not have the savvy to know the difference between our myriad titles in the far-flung realm of massage and bodywork. While I advocate gently training people to call you by your proper title, it is poor marketing to take offense where none was intended if you are called a masseuse or masseur. Even at the school where I work, we get regular calls from people who want to go to "masseuse school." In almost every area of the country, when I told people about my research project for this book, they invariably asked, "Oh, are you a masseuse?" Their question was asked with no connection to prostitution or intention of being degrading, which shows that our years of work have changed public opinion, but we're still such a new field that many people don't yet know what to call us. If I can educate people about the differences in titles, I do, but getting upset or angry at simple ignorance, which I have seen numerous therapists do, doesn't help establish trust and value which is the purpose of your marketing.

Now back to pricing. I've met practitioners who use exotic methods such as working with hot rocks, rain therapy, or soul retrieval, and many people come to them who are willing to pay the accompanying exotic prices. The market may be smaller for such specialties, but when the "been there, done that" crowd wants something new and different, the exotic methods are just what they are looking for.

In later chapters, we will cover many different additions you can make to your basic massage so that you can appeal to different markets and price points. For now, though, open your mind to the possibility of offering more than one service for one set price.

The Other Side of Pricing

While the prior material focuses mostly on the market and factors that affect what your potential clients will pay for massage, the other side of pricing covers your financial needs and goals. A dream practice in the real world means earning real money. This brings up two issues that have hobbled countless practices. The first issue is how you feel about money; the second is your financial planning. Since this is a marketing book, I will not go into financial planning, but I have included some great books in the Resources section on how to handle the money you earn.

Throughout this book, I have frequently reiterated that the purpose of marketing is to get and keep clients. In actuality, the real bottom-line purpose of marketing is to earn money, and, more specifically, to make a profit. Now that you have taken a look at the many needs people have, the value you provide for all these needs that you meet, and taken into consideration how clients feel about money, it is time to examine how you feel about money.

My experience tells me that practitioners in this field have, at best, mixed feelings about money. Many students I dealt with felt guilty or shameful about charging money for the "gift" they had been given with massage skills or even an innate healing ability. When I taught classes on marketing and business skills, students would sulk, skip class, or rage against the evil capitalist machine that was devouring the pure sanctity of massage. Money was bad, desire only led to heartache, charging the market rate was discrimination against poor people, selling healing was immoral, having more than enough to pay the rent and put food on the tables was corrupt, and so on, ad nauseum.

Then those same people who said it wasn't fair to charge for massage would gladly go pay $80 for a psychic to tell them what lay ahead in their future. I'll save you the $80 right now. I foresee a very bumpy road and a job pouring coffee if you don't get over negative associations with money. Money is an exchange of energy, and if you are putting out good, helpful energy in the form of massage, it is right that you get paid back in a form of energy of equal value. That energy can return in the form of trading for a service, a product, money, or anything else that balances out what you have given. This is not a subject I take lightly, and if receiving money for the value you offer with your massage is difficult for you, treat the issue with serious respect.

Where these negative feelings show up most is in pricing. While it is important to be competitive in your pricing, I have seen much damage done to long-term success by consistently undervaluing and underpricing services. Nothing will kill a practice faster than being substantially underpriced. It's pretty simple, actually. Without adequate income from massage, you can't make a living and pay bills. If that goes on too long, you eventually will have to change professions.

If you are uncomfortable talking about money or telling people your prices, you are actually pretty normal. However, to be successful, you will have to work through that discomfort until you can look potential clients square in the eye, and tell them your prices and services without squirming. Remember, the value your client perceives starts from you, so you have to exude that value before they will accept your prices. I highly recommend that you stand in front of a mirror and say what your prices are. Say them until nothing on you flitters or flutters or flinches, and keep going until your face and body are fully behind that price.

For further help on this very important topic, there are a number of books included in the Resources section that I read that helped me over this hurdle about money. They gave me clearer and healthy distinctions about money, and helped me enjoy my work, my clients, and the money, compliments, and gifts they give me in ways I never could have before. One of the hallmarks of being human is that we have the desire and privilege to contribute to other people's lives. If you give a massage and then deny the recipient the ability to contribute back to you in kind, you are, in essence, denying them their humanity. If you give value, be willing and able to receive value. It is a crucial step toward success.

EXERCISE: Practicing Pricing

The purpose of this exercise is to get you to a level of comfort with pricing so that you can talk to potential clients about money with confidence and ease.

- If you are in a class or group, get a partner. If you are reading this by yourself, work with a mirror. If possible, the partners should sit facing each other, almost knee to knee.

  Partner A asks Partner B; "I hear you do massage. What do you charge?"

  Partner B answers, "I charge $20."

  Partner A asks Partner B the same question four more times. Each time the answer is $20.

  Then Partner A asks the same question, but the new answer is "I charge $50."

  Repeat that question and answer four more times. Then change the price to $80 and repeat that price four more times.

  Then switch and work the other way.

  When finished, if you are in a group, take the time to discuss the different feelings that came up at each price point. If it is just you and the mirror, tell yourself what you noticed.

- For the second half of the exercise, Partner A asks the same question, only this time Partner B answers with the dollar amount he or she plans to charge initially or wants to raise rates to. As Partner B answers, Partner A observes all body language including eye movement, head position, hand movements, breathing changes, color changes, facial expressions, tone of voice, and anything else that can indicate whether or not Partner B is comfortable and confident with that price. Partner A keeps asking the question until Partner B can name the price with no signs of discomfort. If there is any form of incongruity such as dropping the chin, bouncing a knee, or blinking too much, Partner A will tell Partner B what is noticed and keep going with the question and answer stage until all symptoms of incongruity stop.

  For those working with a mirror, repeat your price to yourself until you come across as sure, confident, and believing that your services are worth the price you are quoting.

When Worth and Price Collide

In a subject about as huggable as a cactus, let's now mix the two domains of worth and setting price. The value of your services is an agreement between you and your clients, and your price becomes a factor of agreement as well. Regardless of which market you are targeting, phrases such as "I deserve . . ." and "I am worth . . ." have to be calculated realistically in the real world of competing for your client's dollar. If you are dragging around your affirmation cards and chanting to yourself that you deserve $100 an hour but no one else agrees with you, that dream practice may remain a dream. There is a vast difference between what you are worth and what your services cost. Everyone on this planet is a priceless individual and has inherent worth, but that is different than setting a price for a service you offer.

Deserving and earning are two different distinctions, so please, don't mix up the critical issue of price in the morass of "deservingness" and personal worth. It is a self-defeating head game that I bet has cost untold numbers of therapists their dream of a successful practice.

If you want to create a dream practice in the real world, accept your inherent worth as a human being, work on your skills so that you can have genuine confidence in your ability to serve others, and set prices that work for both you and your clients.

Marketing Skill #4: Setting and Meeting Client Expectations

To be able to create a dream practice in the real world requires the ability to set and meet clients' expectations. However, once again, massage faces some unique issues on the subject of expectations. If you were a doctor and a patient came in with a broken leg, the expectations are pretty clear for everyone involved that the leg will be set. Massage, however, has so many modalities and methods of application that it is impossible to know what a client expects without asking. Add to this the variables of the Perception Continuum and you've got too much potential for misunderstandings and client dissatisfaction. Clients can have an accurate perception about massage, but think that you have a skill level or use a massage method that you haven't learned. They can have a misperception and think that all massage has to hurt to be effective: if your work doesn't hurt, they're upset. Whatever clients think, you need to find it out, otherwise they might leave disappointed. I wouldn't include the skill of setting expectations as a Bare Bones essential if it wasn't for my observation that its presence was a common denominator for successful practitioners and its absence wasn't noticeable with unsuccessful practitioners. When our field becomes more established, this skill will be less critical, but for now, the general public needs to be helped in setting appropriate expectations.

Setting and meeting expectations is crucial for building your practice because without this ability, it is virtually impossible to build trust, establish value, or serve the needs of others. Customer service of any caliber would be difficult to provide if you didn't actually know why someone came to see you. I know this seems really basic, but understanding what clients want allows you to fulfill their hopes and expectations of their time with you. If you are able to ethically and legally give clients what they want and expect, the marketing function of rebooking clients and getting referrals becomes your path to success.

Setting expectations requires two major communication skills: the ability to listen and the ability to educate. The skill of listening has two parts. There is "listening to" which means you hear and understand the actual words and explicit requests that the client makes, and you respond to them as a professional. Then there is "listening for" which is reading between the lines or listening to the subtext of the implicit or unspoken requests, often part of customer service. As we covered in the section on what needs clients have, most people won't just come out and say they are lonely, want someone to like them, or want someone to listen to them. The basic human needs such as being accepted, valued, respected, and loved are part of the unspoken subtext that is always there, even if it is covered up with official sounding expectations such as relieving that nagging low back pain. Successful therapists know how to listen to and for client expectations that are both explicit and implicit, and then meet those expectations.

Each of your clients will have a unique set of expectations, but there are some common ones that most clients have for which you can anticipate and prepare. Listen for these expectations as you do your telephone screening, intake interview, or other premassage conversations, and you will be better able to meet your clients' expectations or educate them to change their expectations. Some key expectations to listen for are the:

- anticipated results of the session.
- quality or method of application of massage.
- modality or technique used.
- attitude and approach of the therapist.
- anticipated feelings during and after the session.
- ambiance of setting.

We will cover these expectations thoroughly in the chapter on rebooking because met expectations are what bring clients back and lead them to refer. However, I want to touch briefly on three of these broad expectations so that you can better predict what is wanted from you. Understanding these key expectations can help keep clients happy by preventing broken expectations, disappointment, frustration, and misunderstandings.

Client Expectation #1: Anticipated Results of the Session

Clients can expect some interesting results from massage. Depending on their preconceived notions, clients may expect that massage will be a nice rub-down, or they may think they are going to be "fixed" from an old high school football injury in just one session. Your task is to ask them questions until both you and the client are clear about what they expect. Sometimes, clients do not know what they expect, at least consciously, so get them to talk about their expectations until they can articulate them. This saves having them sub-consciously become disappointed later when the massage wasn't quite right, but they can't quite say why. In their minds, it wasn't that it was a good or bad massage; it just wasn't right, and they're not coming back. Questions to get people clarifying their expectations can be very simple. My favorites are:

"What can I do for you today?"

"What are your goals for your session today?"

When they answer, say "Great! Anything else?" Keep asking them

"Anything else?" until they run out of expectations.

If the answers from these more generic questions do not reveal expectations, get more specific and ask about results they are hoping for. Or you can be right up front and say, "I want this to be an outstanding massage for you. If you can tell me what your expectations are, I will do my best to get the results you are looking for." Don't be surprised if you see a few jaws drop with a statement like this. Few clients ever experience customer service at this level, but once they have recovered from their shock, they will know they have come to the right place.

If your skill or experience level is not very high yet, I would actually stay with the more generic questions. That way, people don't suddenly set expectations too high, then become disappointed later. I saw this principle in action at the car dealership where I get my oil changed. An oil change used to be a straightforward process. You booked an appointment, brought in your car, sat in the lobby, drank bad coffee with floating globs of nondairy creamer, watched the news channel, and got your car back in about an hour. I was happy. Then the dealership (I somehow blame the corporate marketing department) got the idea of drop-in service with a 30-minute guaranteed turnaround time. They wouldn't take appointments; it wasn't necessary in this new, improved customer service campaign. Unfortunately, reality and marketing departments are often bad com-binations. The last two times I "dropped in" for my oil change, the service de-partment was backed up, the wait was longer than 30 minutes, and I left upset because they threw off the schedule I had planned. In reality, I was still sitting in the waiting room drinking bad coffee for about the same amount of time as I used to, but because my expectations were elevated and then not met, I was no longer happy. That is bad marketing. I'll give them another chance, but the moral of this story is, don't set expectations you can't meet.

If you believe that you are able to meet your clients' expectations about the results they are seeking, I recommend that throughout the session, you tell your clients what you are doing and how your work is meeting their needs. This form of education is invaluable in creating trust, establishing value, and shaping positive perception. I call this "on-the-table marketing" and it is probably the most important form of marketing that you can do.

If your clients have expectations of results that you don't believe you can fulfill, you have a number of options.

1. You can bluff your way through the session and hope they can't figure out that what you are doing won't really help them. Not only is this unethical but also really bad marketing. People who are upset talk a lot more than people who are happy and satisfied, and bad word-of-mouth is a powerful thing to overcome.

2. You can explain to your clients what you think you can do for them, but be clear that their expectations are too high for your level of skill. This is not uncommon, and I have had many new clients who expect that I had the skill level and diagnostic abilities of orthopedic doctors. There is no shame in saying what I can and can't do. Sometimes, I have gotten better results with clients than their doctors did, and sometimes I haven't, but I am very up front about my scope of practice and ability level, and then let the client decide if he or she wants to stay. In these cases, I am resetting the expectations to be more realistic, and I have yet to have a client walk out because I wouldn't promise the moon. In cases where expectations are unrealistic, I go to great lengths to educate the client about my strategy, and discuss my approach or methodology so they know I am making a good-faith effort to meet their needs. Even if I realize that one strategy such as trigger point work is not working, I tell them so; then I choose a different strategy such as resisted stretching, explain it, and get back to work.

3. You can refer your clients to other massage therapists or medical practitioners who can meet the level of expectation they have set. Again, there is no shame in this. I have referred a number of clients to a colleague with a whole set of skills I don't come close to having when I think she can meet their needs. Sometimes, good customer service is simply referring the client elsewhere. Be careful with referrals, though. If the client is not satisfied, it can backfire. Only refer to someone you know and trust.

Client Expectation #2:
Application of Massage and Modality or Technique Used

Preconceived expectations are not limited to what results the client hopes to get from massage. Sometimes, clients think they know how those results are going to occur. For example, if a client says "Just shove your elbow into that sore point on my shoulder and work it real deep for an hour," the therapist must listen for the real need (the client wants his shoulder to stop hurting) and then educate the client as to how to reach the same goal in a different way. In this kind of scenario, the expectations surround the application of massage and the method used. The client, with his limited knowledge, thinks that direct pressure is the best method, deep work is the best application, and a long period of time on one spot is going to be most effective for releasing pain.

How this exchange is handled makes all the difference in the world for having a satisfied client. If you respond by saying, "Well, that's a really bad idea. Pressing in one spot for an hour is pretty stupid," you've just lost a client. I know that most people don't actually use phrases quite as blatant as these, but sometimes this attitude is conveyed by therapists despite the words used. One of the major reasons that patients are leaving traditional doctors behind is because they feel unheard, and they object to having their fears and concerns dismissed. Patients are rarely given credit for their own intelligence and experience of their bodies, and they resent it deeply. Massage therapists need to avoid the mistakes made from other medical or service professions and be respectful, even if the client has some expectations that are a bit erroneous or unrealistic.

A better way to handle this client who believes he knows how you are supposed to work is to reeducate him. I would probably say something like, "Well, you're the expert on your body and it sounds like your shoulder is hurting. Tell me more about your shoulder." Once he was done talking, I would say something like, "I hear what you're saying about your shoulder. Now, again, you're the expert on your body, and I'm the expert on massage. I need to tell you that if I just worked on your sore shoulder with deep pressure for an hour, I would probably hurt you more, which I don't think you'd like. Let me give you some options for how we can help your shoulder without hurting it further, and then you can decide."

In this exchange, the client feels heard, learns more about you and your work, retains his power of decision, and has his unspoken needs to be valued and respected met. The odds are high that you will have a grateful client on your hands who now has higher trust and value for you and your work because of how you handled his expectations.

If your massage modality is fairly different from the standard stereotype of Swedish, you will need to become good at reeducating clients on how and why your methods work. For example, I use both Polarity and Reiki, which I find to be incredibly powerful tools. Since most people think that they need to feel a lot of pressure to get results, I have to compensate for that expectation. I either mix in heavier work with my lighter energy work, or I take the time before the session to educate my clients about what I am doing and why, and tell them what they can expect to feel. During the work, I ask specific questions that help them focus their attention at a higher level of awareness so that they do feel the work. I frequently retest the area with pressure or range of motion, and ask if it feels better. This focuses their attention further while helping them assign value to the work. They may not feel the work happening, but they feel the changes in their bodies. This lets them maintain their expectation that they feel something, and, therefore, it is working.

The Importance of Anatomical Knowledge

If you look at the prior examples of how to reeducate a client's expectations about results or application, you probably will notice the common denomina-

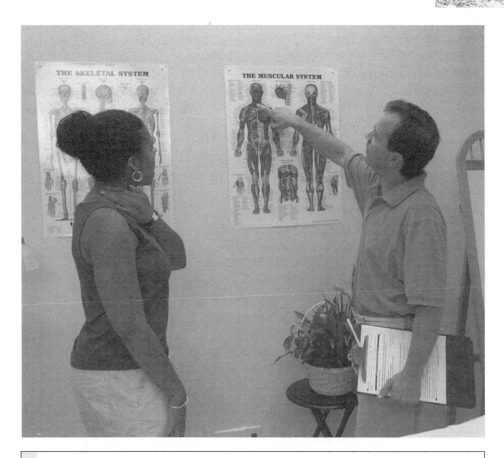

Figure 2–4   Educating clients about their bodies is some of the best marketing you can do.

tor of good communication. In these cases, good client communication is grounded in your understanding of your work and of the human body. Basically, the more you understand about what you are doing, the better you can set expectations. In my opinion, underneath this ability to communicate about client expectations is one of the most important marketing skills of all: a thorough and conversant knowledge of anatomy. Understanding anatomy enables you to explain to clients what is being done during a session; describe why one technique will work when another won't; demonstrate how the muscles work in relation to each other; and justify strategies, techniques, and amounts of time spent in a given area. Speaking the language of anatomy lets you give words to your clients' vague sensations, and show them pain patterns, compensation patterns, and other mysteries that you now seem magical in understanding. In short, clear, anatomy-based communications that validate and illuminate your decisions creates three things unpurchasable in advertising or traditional marketing: a sense of trust, an accurate and positive perception of the therapist, and an understanding of the true value of massage.

Nothing is more fascinating to people than themselves. Educating others about their bodies, how they work, and how they are going to be treated is the ultimate in customer service and marketing. Educating a client before, during, and after a session creates the right expectations; delivers what is promised; and reminds them what they purchased was valuable, and worth the time and money spent. When client expectations are met, and they are happy and satisfied, they will market and promote you better than any formal marketing program could ever do.

Client Expectation #3: The Attitude and Approach of the Therapist

Deep within the hearts of humans and animals alike is a constant craving for attention. This craving is possibly one of the most important of the silent expectations and human needs that clients have when they come for their massage. It is very different from expectations about results or methodologies because it is not based on skills, but on the attitude and personal approach of the therapist. As stated earlier, many people firmly believe they are the center of the universe and want to be given treatment befitting their status. People aren't just muscles and movable joints. They have hopes and dreams and fears and needs, and your "tableside manner" lets them feel human and happy, or like slabs of meat to be greased up and pushed around until their time slot is over.

To be blunt, if you have an excellent attitude, genuinely want to serve people, and treat each client like gold, you probably can have mediocre skills and do quite well for yourself. You also can have excellent skills and a less appealing attitude and get away with it. I've known a few therapists who are about as approachable as a pincushion but they do great work, and their clients accept their no-nonsense demeanor and take-care-of-business attitude. If you are dour, bristly, standoffish, pushy, arrogant, or abrasive, you can make it in a practice, but you'd better be an outstanding clinician. If you will not treat people like they are the center of the universe, be prepared at least to give them the results they came for. Since the desire for attention can be met in many ways with the simple mechanical application of touch, you can still meet this need, but the experience will be much better for you and the client if a caring heart is behind the work. Millions of people ache just to have someone look at them and welcome their presence. If you have the bigness of heart to do this, you have already served your client well. The best of all worlds for success is to have a positive demeanor, make people feel important and special, and provide excellent massage. It is an irresistible combination.

I feel compelled to tell a story here. It's a bit odd, but bear with me because it speaks to what we need to understand about human nature, and our role in healing physical hurts and hurting hearts. I went to a fast food restaurant for my favorite meal, the children's hamburger meal, complete with an elaborate toy that I wanted for my nephew. The toys are the main reason I eat at these fine establishments, and while I was watching some children to see which toys they got, I saw an interesting drama unfold. A little boy about two-years old was playing with his toy when a man entered the restaurant and loudly greeted a little girl who was seated at the table beside the little boy. The girl called back in greeting and immediately raised her toy triumphantly for his approval, which he promptly gave. The little boy was sitting with his father who was obviously tired, distracted, and disinterested in his son's plastic toy. The boy turned to this stranger and raised his toy in hopes that the man would give him the same kind of acknowledgment he gave the little girl. The man did not see this boy raise his toy for his approval, but the boy went through a repeated cycle of holding up the toy, not getting acknowledged, and then looking down at his toy with increasing despair. It was as if the value of his toy was diminishing in his eyes because it didn't get another person's attention and approval. After numerous attempts, the boy dejectedly put his toy down and gave out a most tremendous shriek, whereupon he got all the attention he wanted, even though it was negative. I was fascinated. How core is our desire for attention, for approval, even for a little eye contact? And what damage have so many suffered from a lifetime of small but painful moments such as I had just witnessed? These wounds are just as painful as torn ligaments or pulled hamstrings, and they are part of what clients bring to us in their silent expectations. There is no job description that says your attitude and approach needs to bear these silent hopes in mind, but now you know they are there, and you can do wonders for yourself and others by meeting them.

Marketing Skill #5: Reaching Out to Clients

One of the funny things about creating a dream practice is that you need clients to make your dream a reality. So how do you get clients? According to most every successful massage therapist I interviewed, they got clients one primary way: they talked to everybody about massage. Yup. That's it. I know it doesn't sound very sophisticated or difficult, and actually, it's not. For people who started out with a private practice, talking to family, friends, acquaintances, hairstylists, grocery clerks, neighbors, waitresses, people in the park, co-workers, folks at the gym, in line at the store, or waiting in a restaurant all resulted in a casual conversation where massage was discussed and a client discovered.

The 10 X 10 Rule

I have met very few therapists who began with any formal marketing strategy, or who had delineated a target market at which to aim. If someone would come in, lie down, get a massage and pay, that was high standard enough. One strategy, from one of the most successful therapists I know, was to "just get 10 clients." Following her short massage training in a converted back bedroom of her teacher's home, her big marketing strategy was to talk to everyone she could about massage. With no brochures, flyers, public speeches, or website, she talked and talked until somehow, she rounded up 10 clients. Now, some 25 years later, her practice has grown and evolved tremendously, but she still feels that the simple goal of "just 10 clients" was a great way to start. If I were to add another rule of 10, I would use what one of my colleagues called the 10-foot rule. His policy was this: anyone within 10 feet of him was fair game for a friendly conversation where he got to mention that he was a massage therapist. He didn't ask for business; he just talked about himself and what he did for a living, which is pretty standard conversation faire for most Americans. The people who were looking for a therapist were thrilled to meet him, and his informal marketing was more than adequate to get new clients who then rebooked and referred him into a full practice.

How do you start a practice? I'd start with the 10 X 10 Rule. Set a goal for 10 new clients; talk to everyone within 10 feet of you, somehow including the word massage; and keep talking until you get those 10 clients. It's that easy and that hard. If you have an easy time talking to people, your work will entail how to introduce the topic of massage. I recommend that you ask other people what they do for a living. When they are done and ask you what you do, the door is open for you to step in. One therapist I interviewed gained a significant percentage of her practice by regularly wearing a T-shirt or polo shirt that had the word "massage" on it. People who read the script on her shirt got into conversations about massage, and gave her an easy opening to tell about herself and her services.

I wish I had something fancier to tell you, but virtually every massage therapist I have met started with some version of this tactic. If you have a hard time talking with people, then part of your marketing strategy will be to do whatever is necessary to either get more comfortable talking with others or get others to talk for you.

I am not being facetious about this oh-so-basic strategy. It has worked for thousands of therapists and it can work for you. However, if you want fancier marketing methods, much of the rest of this book has specific skills and tools for reaching people through as many ways and means as possible. So keep reading! Your practice awaits you!

The Only Marketing Tools You Really Need

CHAPTER

3

CHAPTER OBJECTIVES

After reading this chapter, you should be able to:
- design a basic business card.
- select and use an appointment book.
- create a professional address and telephone list.
- use the telephone effectively when dealing with clients.
- deliver a professional introduction.

Your core attributes, marketing skills, and massage abilities will be the primary determining factors in your ability to build your dream practice over the long term. However, in your process of getting and keeping clients, there is one more key factor to consider: how to choose and use your marketing tools.

In this Bare Bones section of the book, we are going to review the only marketing tools you really need. I have chosen them because they are the only tools the vast majority of successful therapists use. In the next section, we will cover marketing tools as elaborate as you desire, so if you work in a highly competitive massage market or want to build a practice very quickly, the advanced tools in the later chapters can help. Advanced marketing tools, however, take more money, time, and skill, and often are more effective when you have a clearer idea about who you are, what kind of work and clients you enjoy most, and what level of skill you can promote. If you are a massage professional just starting out, these basics are what I recommend for getting your first 10 clients. And they may be all the tools you ever need to succeed!

There are only five marketing tools you must have to enable people to gain access to you and to book their appointments.

1. Business cards

2. An appointment book

3. An address book with telephone list

4. A telephone and answering machine

5. A professional introduction

Basic Marketing Tool #1: Business Cards

Business cards are one of the most important marketing tools you can use in building a massage practice. On the surface, the purpose of business cards is simple. It gives people a way to get in touch with you to book an appointment. However, cards can serve multiple functions such as the ability to act as tiny advocates, spreading the word about you while you are busy elsewhere. The more cards you have out in the world and in other people's hands, the more voices you have speaking on your behalf, multiplying your opportunities to book appointments or reach referrals. Basically, a business card is leverage, and the more leverage you have, the more you can spend your time doing massage instead of marketing.

At its most basic, a business card needs only three things on it: your name, your title, and your phone number. Beyond these three elements, everything else is secondary. You can have a very simple, plain business card that will serve its purpose by letting people remember who you are, what you do, and how to contact you easily.

If most of your clients come to you from personal referral, how your card looks is not that critical. Most of my clients come to me by word of mouth, and the first time my new clients see my card is after they have arrived for their first appointment. My card is helpful in showing that I am a professional, but it is a referral, not a card, that brought clients in the door.

If you will be using your card in more professional types of networking where other professionals give out your card on your behalf, you may need more than a basic card. The recipients of your card will place more importance on how your card looks since it is one of their only ways of judging you. In those cases, your card must speak for you. If you are going to post your card in a public place with no other form of personal representation, it must say the volumes and give the impressions that people need to make a decision to call. To start with, though, you will probably be doing most of your own marketing and speaking on your own behalf, so your card mostly will serve as a basic reminder tool.

Let's look at the three elements of a basic card: your name, title, and telephone number.

Basic Business Card Element #1: Your Name

For most people, your name is a pretty straightforward line on your card. I recommend that you use your full name, unless you are Madonna or Cher. So far, no massage therapists I know of have reached star status, but there's always a first for everything! On a more serious note, if you work in an area where you face good odds of being sexually harassed by clients, you may choose to put just your first name on your card. You can do that as a form of protection, or keep your home telephone unlisted so that you cannot be traced easily. Another possibility is to choose another name or a pseudonym. Maybe it's a California thing, but a lot of my students seemed bound and determined to change their names while they were in massage school. If you decide on a new name or insist on using a nickname, at least make sure that it represents you well. In marketing, brand names are highly valued, and if you want to "brand" yourself with an unusual name for people to remember, you may choose to do so. Remember, though, that if your family and friends are referring you under your old name and your card has a nickname that is different, people may get confused. If you change your name somewhere down the road because of nicknames, marriage, or other reasons, I recommend you have transition cards with both names on it and have your answering machine give both names. That way, people with personal referrals or old cards who get your answering machine won't be alarmed thinking they reached a wrong number and hang up.

Basic Business Card Element #2: Your Title

Your title is the next element on your business card, and how you choose to describe yourself with your title can make a big difference in how you are perceived. The general public does not have much knowledge about the different titles that massage therapists earn in their schools or specialty seminars, and frankly, our field is so confused about titles that it has been difficult to come up with a common standard. Since there are no nationally agreed on titles, I recommend that you consider creating a title that is fitting and appropriate to describe yourself. For example, the title that I earned in school is Holistic Health Practitioner and Educator, but no one knew what that title meant and it did not carry much value in the marketplace. What was a more appealing title to most people at that time and in the area that I lived was the word "massage," so I called myself a Professional Massage Therapist. When I introduced myself, I started with the word "professional," which created a particular expectation. Then I sandwiched in the word "massage," which in 1984 had some negative undertones, before the word "therapist" so I had two words with positive, strong perceptions propping up the weaker word.

Marketing is about creating an impression and answering the needs the public has for your services, and your title can be very powerful in telling people that you offer what they want. Ethically and legally, you cannot say you are licensed or certified if you are not, but beyond that, think carefully about how you want to describe yourself. Unless you are required by some local or state regulation to use certain titles, I recommend you use words that the general public will be attracted to.

For example, your school certificate may say Certified Massage Therapist, but if you serve a market of executives, your card can read Stress Management Expert or Stress Management Massage. If you are into sports massage, consider having a title such as Sports Massage Specialist. If you serve multiple markets, you can have two or three different cards with different specialties listed. If you are networking with business executives, take your cards that list you as a Stress Management Expert; and if you are at an adult league softball game, take your sports cards. In a future chapter, we will look more closely at developing specialty markets. If you decide to market to a specialty group, then I recommend you have cards for that group.

Basic Business Card Element #3: Your Telephone Number

Besides your name and title, your card needs to give some way for people to contact you. The most common contact method is a telephone, though some people use the Internet more than a telephone. Due to the nature of massage and possibility of harassment, some massage professionals choose to have a separate telephone line for their businesses. If you work out of your home, or go to your clients' homes or offices, I recommend you get a second line that is unlisted so that your address remains safe.

Depending on your practice, you can have numerous ways to be reached. You can have a cellular phone that lets clients access you quickly and easily, and I highly recommend it if you do outcalls. It's great if you get lost or hit traffic. When I got my first car phone in 1986 for $1,500, it gave me access to booking spur-of-the-moment clients that more than paid for the phone. You can have voice mail, an answering machine, or an answering service. If you have clients that travel a lot, you may consider getting a remote voice mail that operates 24 hours a day so that they can call you from other parts of the country or the world without waking you up. If you move a lot or know that you will be changing residences in the near future, a voice mail can be a stable telephone number that lets people find you no matter where you live. If you really want to go all out, you can get an 800 number. The benefit of an 800 number is that your area code never changes and you don't have to reprint your cards every time a new area code change happens.

Your name, title, and telephone number are all you need for a Bare Bones business card. In a later chapter, we will cover graphics, e-mails, addresses, types of paper, type styles, colors, photos, logos, two-sided cards, folding cards, and layouts. For a basic business card though, you can walk into any printer or major office supply store and choose a basic design from their predesigned layouts, give them your information, and let them do the rest. It really is that easy.

Whatever you do, *do not wait* to get your first cards. Do not wait until you design the perfect logo or choose an official business name. Do not wait until you have filed a fictitious business name, or have saved $200 for a formal photo shoot or graphic artist. I talked with a therapist who asked me what more she could do to build her practice. When I asked to see her business card, she didn't have one because she hadn't designed it yet. And she had been in business for three years! It is better to wait for inspiration than to wait for clients to show up. Just get your first 100 cards with your name, title, and telephone number, and get them into people's hands. Do not make any excuses: just make cards. Later, when your practice is underway, you can put more time, money, and understanding into creating a graphic representation of you and your work. Whatever you do, don't leave home without your business cards. Potential clients are everywhere!

Basic Marketing Tool #2: The Appointment Book

Owning your own business or being a massage employee requires some tools and disciplines you may have never had to use before. For a massage therapist, an appointment book is a crucial tool for managing a practice or building a new one because you basically sell two things: your reputation and your time. Most of marketing is about creating your reputation, but how you manage your time, and how you book and keep your appointments is equally important to your ultimate success. If you have never used an appointment book or time management system, it may take some getting used to, but I cannot emphasize the importance of these tools enough. Even if you have used a calendar or appointment book before, scheduling your life and practice together takes forethought and planning. In addition, your appointment book is a marketing tool. How you use it while booking appointments can continue to create trust, instill value, and shape perception.

The Bare Bones appointment book can be used for many purposes such as holding your business cards and giving you a place to put all those checks that clients give you. For building your practice, there are four primary uses for an appointment book.

1. Scheduling your time.
2. Setting boundaries.
3. Setting goals.
4. Booking appointments.

Scheduling Your Time

Massage therapy is a service that typically is sold by time. Clients can book an hour session or a 15-minute session, and they pay for your time, often by the minute. Therefore, how you handle your time greatly affects your ability to make a living with massage. The first principle to consider is that time, like money, is a commodity, and there are ways to perceive and handle time that can lead to success or business failure. Money and time are inexorably linked in our field, and while there are many ways to work with these two elements, there are a few lessons and viewpoints that can be helpful to us in the touch and service professions.

One of my favorite principles about time is that it is fluid and malleable. Time often seems to stand still when I am doing massage, though at other times it seems to fly. Your clients also experience odd distortions of time during their sessions, usually concluding that a good session is too short and a bad session feels interminable. Even though your clients are paying for a set amount of time, their personal experience of that time is malleable, and that can alter how they perceive the value of their session and affect their decision to rebook.

What I have discovered is that there is often a difference between when the clock says a client is done and when the client "feels" done. I know this sounds a bit esoteric, but I often have found that the client "feels" done a few minutes after their clock time runs out. It is as if they are subconsciously testing to see if I really view them as special and important, and will work to a point of completion instead of turning into a pumpkin the second the clock strikes twelve. After testing this discovery numerous times, I have come to the conclusion that my attitude about time greatly affects my clients' perceptions about how much they trust me and value my work. I have found that if I feel rushed, they feel that the session seemed short, but if I'm relaxed and at ease, they don't mention the time. I also have found that if I give a few extra minutes of free work past their expectation points, their experience of time expands, and their trust and gratitude rise exponentially. Somehow, just as with money, if you have a spirit of generosity with time and give from a place of abundance, you are blessed back tenfold.

Generosity of time and a spirit of abundance are not the same as being codependent and having weak boundaries. Treating your clients as if they are the center of the universe does not mean giving away lots of free time. Where the practicality of time crosses the marketing need to maintain trust and value is a middle ground of scheduling, which brings us back to the appointment book. As you schedule your work time, I believe it is valuable for you to pad your session time with a few extra minutes. If you have a very busy practice and have sold all of the minutes you have available, you don't have to do this. You can schedule clients for tight time frames and have rapid turnover with moments to spare in between. Some people prefer to practice that way, and that is fine. However, if you have a few minutes to spare to work longer, let a client lie on the table and snore, or not feel rushed getting changed, I believe you have just done some excellent marketing. For clients with the fear of abandonment, loneliness, or low self-esteem, those extra minutes are like gold, and your gift of that time creates incredible loyalty.

Those extra minutes scheduled also can be good for you. Massage is a physically and often emotionally demanding profession, and the risks of burnout and injury are increased with overbooking your schedule. The stress of rushing, working too fast, or becoming anxious because a client is slow getting up and is cutting into the next appointment is very detrimental to your health and your practice. Padding your schedule with a little extra time can compensate for all those amazing delays that happen that throw off tight schedules.

If you have an office, anticipate people being late, taking a long time changing, fumbling for their checkbooks, talking while they get out their appointment books, and so on. If you do outcalls, give yourself time for traffic, getting lost, and stopping for gas. It will do your blood pressure a lot of good to be prepared for unanticipated delays and to plan accordingly.

People are not widgets you can shove down the conveyor belt. Many of them want a personal connection with you, and that takes time before and after the session. My suggestion is to plan on that time and enjoy it. I genuinely like my clients, and the times of talking during my set-up and take-down are some of my favorites. If you book clients too close together, it can become easy to get irritated at the tiny delays to your perfectly planned schedule. Being antsy, preoccupied, and rushing in and out the door aren't quite the marketing message you're looking for. If you have a few minutes in between clients, you can always do stretching or meditation, so either way, padding your schedule works out well for you.

Setting Boundaries

In the start-up stage of a practice, it is common to take clients from anywhere you can and book wherever possible. If you can, be flexible in the beginning and do what you can to get new clients, but once you are more established, it is appropriate for you to set more boundaries on how you schedule your clients.

One of the goals of this book is to have you enjoy a long-term career, and therapists who book clients indiscriminately and set no boundaries around their schedules are likely candidates for burnout. Your job is to create a balance between serving your customers when they are available and taking care of your own physical and emotional well-being. Since massage therapists are inherently caring and want to serve their clients, it is easy to become unbalanced in our scheduling, and to work too hard, too late, or to book too many clients on the same day or too close together. If you have weak boundary skills or struggle with codependency, acknowledge it and plan accordingly by setting up your schedule and only booking clients in preset time blocks. If you are a people-pleaser, overeager, or only think about how much money you can make, then you need to be very careful about how you schedule yourself.

Oftentimes, we don't know we have overstepped our boundaries until we are on the other side of them. If you find yourself rushing between clients, driving home too late at night, or missing dinner with your family, you need to reconsider how you schedule your clients.

Calendars

One way to handle overbooking or underbooking is to make good use of your calendar or appointment book. I recommend an appointment book that has a month-at-a-glance section where you can schedule the times of your appointments, and a section where you can write out your daily to-do lists, telephone numbers, addresses of and directions to clients, reminders of things to do for your personal and professional goals, and anything else you want to record about your business. You can get more advanced appointment books and electronic systems if you like, but for now, we will cover what is absolutely bare bones essential: a fill-in calendar.

Any office supply or stationery store carries calendars. I recommend that instead of getting a calendar you pin up by the telephone, you get a portable time management system. That way, you only have one calendar, and you can take it with you to your office, your clients, or anywhere you will need to know your schedule and when you are available for appointments. Please do not try to crossreference two calendars, and don't try to keep appointments in your head or on scraps of paper. As a professional, you need to book clients confidently without worrying about overlapping with some vaguely remembered dentist appointment written on your home calendar. Organizing a practice is very different from going to a job or school. You will be booking your life, sometimes to the minute, and you need the right tool to keep you relaxed and confident that you will be in the right place at the right time.

Setting Goals

When you are starting out building your practice, I recommend you have a set goal of how many clients you want a week, then use your calendar to visually remind you of those goals. Book in working hours for yourself, and if you don't yet have a client for set time slots, work on getting a client for those specific times. Empty spots alert you to your need for clients for those particular time slots. By knowing when to make a more concerted marketing effort to fill those time slots, you can more effectively meet your goals. The more specific you are with your goals, the more likely you are to meet them. For many reasons, it is more powerful to have a goal of getting a client for a 4:00 P.M. time slot on Thursday than it is to tell yourself "I need to get new clients."

A Balanced Life

If you are starting to get busy in your practice, a calendar helps you book your time for balancing your practice with the other elements in your life. To help reach your goals while maintaining some balance, I recommend you create a time frame for the hours you work so that when clients call to book an appointment, you can put them into one of your pre-designated time slots. This helps you sound more confident and busier, which helps build trust between you and your new clients. It sounds better to say "I have appointments available on Monday at 2:00 P.M. or at 3:30 P.M." than to say "My schedule is totally open and I can book you any time." People want to go with a winner, and you don't want to sound like you're sitting around waiting for your first client to call because very few people want to be that first client.

There are other advantages to booking in your personal time. A client was looking over my shoulder, requesting a booking for a time that I knew I was unavailable due to personal reasons but I had not written anything down in that spot. After that, I learned to preplan and write in my personal appointments on my calendar page so that clients wouldn't ask for time slots that were unavailable. This practice also helped me not be tempted to cancel things in my personal life just because a client happened to want that time slot. The more inclined you are to overbook, the more important it is that you schedule your personal life into your calendar so that you maintain balance and avoid burnout.

Booking appointments

Booking appointments is where the marketing rubber meets the road of sales. There are two distinct types of booking moments, and they each require two distinct skills. One moment is the time you book a new client for a first appointment; the other moment is when you rebook a current client. In both cases, your appointment book is part of the marketing process, and how you physically handle your book sends volumes of information to your client. First of all, just having an appointment book in your hand indicates you are serious about doing business. Second, how you hold your book or gesture with it while you talk gives indications that you are ready to move the conversation to a moment of decision.

First-Time Appointments

First-time appointments may be made on the telephone or in person, but opening your appointment book tells you and your client that it is time to get serious. Somehow, when a piece of paper becomes part of the process, it means an expectation is now present that a commitment is requested. If you can see your potential client while you open your calendar to book an appointment, you can watch for signs about levels of readiness to get a massage. An appointment book out with a pen poised over it is a signal to decide, and if you see hesitation or resistance, your marketing is not yet done. More information may need to be given, more reassurance offered, or more listening done before that pen writes something down. If your potential client is ready to book, look for one of those empty spots you highlighted and fill it in. Then write down that date and time on a card, and give it to your new client. You are on your way!

Rebooking Appointments

In rebooking clients, your calendar also can be a useful tool to move the postmassage conversation forward. With clients who book on a session-by-session basis, the time after the massage is when some clients get clingy and want a few more moments of special attention. There is a delicate balance between cutting to the chase of setting up your next appointment and having your time frittered away. For some of my elderly clients who are not in a rush, this is when I especially have noticed that I am judged for being genuine in my caring. What I learned is that if I talk a few minutes and then start opening my appointment book, they subconsciously know that their time is up and I will be leaving soon. Perhaps I am overly protective of my clients in their hazy, happy moments after the massage, but I have scheduled in time for those moments, and I use my appointment book as the signal for them to conclude this session and plan for the next one.

If you are rebooking a new client after the first massage and are a bit nervous, your appointment book can help. We will cover rebooking extensively in a later chapter, but for a basic rebooking, you need your appointment book, a few carefully chosen sentences, and occasionally nerves of steel. If you work at a resort or hotel where rebooking is not part of your job, your income won't depend on rebookings, but if you have a private practice, they are crucial to your success and you need to handle them well.

After your session is over and your client is dressed, sit down with her for a debriefing and talk about how you worked toward the goals and results she wanted. If she agrees that she received the massage she expected, simply ask for a rebooking. Even if you are nervous or feel you could have done a better session, don't make excuses for your work. If you are constantly trying to improve and learn to be a better practitioner, then you can be confident that you did your best at the time, and you can exude that confidence in your rebooking. Touch your appointment book, indicating that you are ready to talk business, and say something like "I enjoyed working with you today, and I'm glad I could help with your (whatever her goal was). Would you like to book another massage?" Then be still and listen. If your client says yes, then open your appointment book, pick up your pen, set a time, fill in an appointment card, hand it over, and close your book. If your client does not want to rebook, then read the chapter coming up on rebooking. Clients who rebook are going to be your best source of referrals, so take the time and have the right tools to make the rebooking process simple, smooth, and professional.

Keeping Your Appointments

Using an appointment book is a discipline, and it may take practice to get used to looking at it regularly and not making promises without it. When you write down an appointment, you basically have given your word, and you need to do everything in your power to keep your word. The marketing function of gaining trust is dependent on you keeping your word and your appointments. If you want to be head and shoulders above your massage competition, make sure you show up for your appointments, and make sure you are on time.

I met a woman in the Hollywood area who makes upward of $200 a session doing outcall massage to ritzy hotels. She has limited training and basic skills, but when I asked her why she gets so many plum assignments from the hotels, she had a simple answer: she shows up when she promises to, and she is on time. It seems that responsible and punctual therapists are a hard commodity to come by in the massage field, which is too bad. Having an appointment book can help you with the details of keeping your word, scheduling your time realistically, and managing your responsibilities. However, it is up to you only to make promises you can keep, and then keep them. The hardest part of keeping promises is not to make them if you don't plan to keep them. If you don't want to book a person as a client or work on a Saturday, say no. The word "no" is one of the best words you can learn to say, because then when you say "yes," you can trust that you mean it.

If you often find yourself running late, needing to cancel at the last minute, or forgetting things that are important to your work, you will need to make some adjustments beyond using an appointment book. Your reasons can be as deep as old rebellion issues, a subconscious fear of success, or just plain inexperience in the discipline of managing your time and commitments. Remember, you either get good excuses or good results, but if you want to succeed, your reputation needs to be based on results. Since you are selling your reputation, the better it is, the more money you can command. A strong reputation requires a strong trust in your word, and if your word is weak, then work on making it strong. If you are just plain old forgetful, make your appointment book your constant companion. Write down everything you need to do and refer to your book often. Your appointment book can be a huge factor in your success, so get one and use it.

Use It, But Don't Lose it

The last factor of using an appointment book is being able to find it when you need it. After experimenting with portable calendars of every size and type, I finally found what was most important was having one that I could find easily when a client called to book an appointment. There are few things more embarrassing than racing around the house shouting "Hold on, hold on!" into the phone while a client waits for me to unearth my appointment book. After experiencing that unpleasant scenario a few times, I decided I needed to do something different. It's called changing a bad habit into a good habit. Because I need to take my appointment book with me most everywhere I go, I have had to develop a discipline of habitually putting my book in the same places when I am at home at my writing office or in the car when going out for various appointments. This new habit has made my life so much easier.

If you are prone to misplacing things, or seem always to be looking for your missing keys or wallet, you will need to develop a set of habits for yourself. One of my mentors, a successful entrepreneur named Ted, gave me one of the best tools to change a bad habit into a good one. Since I have learned this tool, I have never again misplaced my keys, wallet or appointment book. The tool is comprised of two simple phrases, but the words can shape your self-perception, personal beliefs about yourself, and ultimately, your behavior. The phrases are: "That's like me," and "That's not like me."

To make sure that you don't misplace your appointment book, pick a designated place to put it when you are at home, at work, or wherever you use it. Make a commitment to yourself always to put your book in that one spot. Then, when you go into your home or office, head right to that spot and put your book there. When you put it down, acknowledge yourself with a simple "That's like me." This trains your mind to keep repeating your new habit. If you race into the house and start to put your book down somewhere else, simply say, "That's not like me." Habits often are based on self-perception, and when your self-perception expects you to do one thing and you do another, it jars your awareness. This momentary jarring is your signal to pick up your appointment book and move it to its designated spot. When you put it down in the right place say, "That's like me," and get on with whatever you were doing. There are many ways to change a habit, but this method can be easy and very effective.

I realize that simple things such as being able to immediately find your appointment book when a client calls may seem trivial, but they aren't. Mundane as some of these points may seem, they are all little pieces of shaping your clients' perceptions, and added together, they determine your overall image as a professional.

Basic Marketing Tool #3: An Address Book with Telephone List

In a service business such as massage, your primary asset is your client list. Keeping track of your clients in an organized manner gives you the ability to access them for scheduling, marketing, sending birthday and holiday cards, or any other reason you want to get in touch with them. Your client list also can be used to demonstrate the value of your practice. If you want to get a business loan, enroll investors, sell your practice, rent an office or otherwise prove your creditworthiness and earning potential, your client list may be required as one of the tools you use to back your claims. Your client list also is part of your tax records, and may be needed to prove to an auditor that you are a legitimate business and have rights to the tax deductions you claimed. While every precaution needs to be taken to ensure the privacy of your clients, this list is one of the only pieces of evidence you may have that your practice exists, so keep it maintained and guard it well.

Dozens of ways to document your client list are available, ranging from customizable software programs with business card scanners to basic address books. Even if there is a picture of a puppy on the front cover, an address book is vital to running your practice. If at all possible, get a calendar or appointment book with a section for listing clients. That way, when a client calls and leaves a message on your machine to change an appointment but doesn't leave a telephone number, you can find the number and schedule in one book. I recommend that you have one section for clients and that you do not list your clients separately by last name throughout the alphabetical pages. It is painful to admit, but every so often the last names of my more infrequent clients slip my mind. If I had listed them in the alphabetical pages instead of in my client section, I would have lost track of them among all the other contact names I have.

Even if you have files and forms with all of your clients' information in them, a centralized and portable list makes it easier to get hold of your clients, especially if you do outcalls. You can write down addresses and telephone numbers only, but for each of my clients, I like my appointment book's address section to include their:

■ name
■ address
■ home telephone

- work telephone
- cell phone
- e-mail
- birthday
- date of first massage

For clients I don't see that often, I write in directions to their homes and what I charge them, since both can slip my mind if months have passed between appointments.

For Bare Bones basics, this simple system is enough to get your practice off the ground without too much expense, hassle, and procrastination. Just like with your business cards, go to a business supply store, get a basic address book or appointment book with an address section, and start using it. Later, when you want a fancy leather-bound time management system, an electronic organizer, or computer program to hold all your information in one place, you will know better what you want and what you need to keep track of your clients and business.

Whatever system you use, I recommend that you do an occasional backup of your information. Whether on your computer or by photocopying your pages, keep your client list in a few places so that if, heaven forbid, you lose one source, you will not lose this most important information.

Basic Marketing Tool #4: A Telephone and Answering Machine

Marketing requires multiple forms of communication, but one of the primary ways of handling your reaching, rebooking, and referral of clients is over the telephone. How you handle the telephone can tell a lot to your callers about your level of professionalism, and your manner can greatly affect their level of trust in you.

I remember one instance of this principle in action when I was returning a call to a massage therapist who worked out of her home. I really did not have any prior impressions of her until I called, and her teenage son picked up the telephone and greeted me with a surly, "Yeah?" Not knowing if I had called the wrong number, I asked for the massage therapist, whereupon the boy dropped the phone on the counter and yelled, "Mom! Phone!" Somehow, no matter what this woman had to say after that, I already had created my first impression of her, and it wasn't good. Again, it can seem unfair that we are judged as professionals by our nonmassage skills or by others around us, but if I were an apprehensive new client alert to every detail to see if I was going to feel safe in someone's environment, such a telephone reception would have sent me running.

Marketing on the telephone works two ways: incoming calls, when a prospect or client calls you; and outgoing calls, when you call a prospect or client. Each of these requires different communication skills, but they both require professionalism. Let's take a closer look at what it takes to market on the telephone.

Incoming Calls—Option One

Incoming calls have two possible outcomes: your callers either reach you in person, or they don't. Both scenarios create a lasting impression on your caller. For that reason, the telephone etiquette used by you, a family member, colleague or receptionist, or your outgoing message on your answering machine is important. It may make the difference in the success of your practice. There are a few elements in your telephone manner that indicates to your caller whether you are a trustworthy professional or an amateur. They are very basic rules, and may seem simplistic, but in calling massage professionals across the country, I have so often experienced these rules ignored that I am including them here.

To represent yourself as a professional, when your telephone rings:

- assume every call is a business call.
- smile before you pick up the telephone; it brightens your voice.
- always say who you are; immediately answer with your name and/or your business name.
- remember to be of service and sound happy to hear from the caller.
- greet the caller by name, and ask "What can I do for you today?"
- be quiet and listen.
- have a pen and paper handy, and know where your appointment book is.

If a prospect (someone who is considering becoming a client) calls, he or she is in one of two possible states. One is a state of readiness and a desire to book with minimal information and conversation. In my experience, when prospects called me because one of my clients referred them to me for massage, they already had made up their minds. All they wanted to do was go over a few details and book the appointment.

The first time this happened, I started to trot out my marketing spiel because I assumed the man calling me would need to know all sorts of things about me and my work before he would book with me. I was wrong. This person was a high-powered executive who had very little time, knew what he wanted, had made up his mind and, quite frankly, wasn't interested in what I had to say. He had heard from a friend of his that I was a good massage therapist and that was all he needed to know.

The second state of readiness of a caller is when the prospect has heard about you from a referral or some other source, but wants to know more before making a decision to book an appointment. How you handle this call makes or breaks your future working relationship. In the beginning of the conversation, I ask as many questions as I can to find out what the caller wants or needs.

Ask:

"How can I help you?"

"How did you hear about me?" (create common ground if from a personal referral.)

"Have you had massage before?"

"What were you looking for from a massage?" (This is a good screening question.)

Then:

Listen as long as you can before you answer their questions.

In everything you say, remember you are opening a potential, long-term relationship.

Always strive to establish trust and value.

Take notes as they talk, especially noticing how they phrase their words.

Reword questions if you are not clear about what they mean.

Ask for some form of decision and move the caller to take some step.

Finally, trust your gut reaction. Early on, I learned to trust my gut instinct, and I turned down new clients a number of times because my intuition told me to. In a number of cases, I never really knew why my internal warnings went off, but in a few instances, I later learned that the person had a severe medical condition that I could have aggravated. When I worked for a large company while I was a new massage student, one of my coworkers was angry because I wouldn't massage her. However, something felt very wrong to me. Then, about a week later, she left work in an ambulance with a bleeding ulcer. My guess is, based on her personality, that she would have blamed me for aggravating her medical condition and probably would have sued me. If you are not used to using your intuition, pay attention to hunches, inclinations, uneasy feelings, or hesitations. Whatever you decide, pay attention to what happens as a result so that you can learn to trust the information you receive about your new clients on more subtle levels.

Common Questions

While I cannot predict every question a prospect will have, there are three questions I've heard over years of receiving calls that you need to anticipate and be ready for. These questions will be about your work, your fees, and unfortunately, the occasional question that tests your legitimacy. I have experimented with various answers to these questions and I am including what I have found that works. My answers may not work for you, but be prepared so that you can smoothly and professionally respond to these questions. When in doubt, respond to a question with your own question and get clarification before answering questions you aren't sure about. The more your prospects talk, the more you will know, and the better you will understand what needs they have so that you can let them know how you can meet their needs.

Following are three versions of these common questions, including the answers I typically give and the rationale for those answers. Every question you are asked is an opportunity to market yourself, so formulate your own answers with the intention of shaping your caller's perception, establishing value, and creating trust.

Q: What kind of work do you do?

A: That depends. I have a wide range of skills and depending on what my client needs from me, I pick and choose what will help them most. What can I help you with?

Rationale: Massage therapists are like most other professionals; they become so used to their own industry jargon, they no longer notice when they are using it. If a woman calls and asks you what you do and you say a very specific modality type she is unfamiliar with, you may have just shut the door on her. The immediate perception of you is that what you offer is untrusted because it is unfamiliar, and is not what she wants. It does not matter that the jargon term you used is actually what she wants; she may have already made up her mind that you can't give her what she wants. To avoid that mistake, ask her what she wants first, then tell her how you can help her using the words she gave you.

Q:	How much do you charge?
A:	That depends. I offer a wide variety of services in my practice. What kind of work are you looking for?
Rationale:	In any form of negotiation, do your utmost to avoid giving out a price until you have a good idea of what the client wants. I recommend that you have a "massage menu" and that you have services that hit a variety of price points. People are funny about money and pricing, and if you have only one service and one fee, their only choices in response to you are "yes" or "no," or to negotiate. If you have a range of services and prices, your options greatly increase the odds of a "yes." Just like a menu at a good restaurant, your offerings can tantalize more buyers than by having only one item on the menu. Short, affordable services like on-site massage or foot reflexology can be offered alongside package deals of 10 massages for a discounted price. Don't sell yourself short by offering just one massage. As you listen to your clients talk, think about how you can best be of service and make offers that will get them under your hands. Also, listen for elements that will affect your prices such as how long a session they want or need, what time of day they want a session, and how far you have to drive if you do outcall.

I prefer to not charge extra for driving long distances. Instead, I wait until I learn where the caller lives, then give a flat rate for a single session that will absorb the cost of driving time and expenses. Everyone wants to think they got a good deal, and tacking on an extra fee because you live far away can rankle some people.

Q:	Do you do full-body massage/give extras/do release massage? (These are some common euphemism or code phrases that really ask if sexual favors are part of the session. Other phrases may be used, so if a question of this nature sounds odd, you may be dealing with someone you need to screen out.)
A:	Let me clarify what you mean. I work holistically and feel it is important to massage the body as a whole, but unfortunately for my profession, sometimes the term "full body" means that the customer is expecting a sexual massage, which is not what I do. If that is not what you meant, my apologies, and please understand that this, unfortunately, is an issue with which my profession still has to deal.
Rationale:	Massage as a cover for prostitution has not been eliminated yet. Therefore, there is a possibility that the caller may be a threat. Questions of this nature need to be dealt with firmly and directly. If the client is looking for sexual massage, this is your safest opportunity to protect yourself. It may be uncomfortable in the moment to accuse someone essentially of soliciting you, but once you hang up, it's over. Not dealing with it directly, then booking an appointment endangers you greatly, so you must have the courage to confront the caller on the telephone if you suspect anything. If you still are not sure about the caller after your initial answer, you can simply ask "So what is it that you are looking for?" Then be quiet and

listen until you feel confident in the response. It is better to risk putting off a real client than to get stuck in a dangerous situation. If you feel something is off, push the caller until you are sure what kind of person you are dealing with.

Finally, regardless of what questions are asked, remember that ignorance is your biggest competition. Take time to answer questions, assume that the caller knows very little about massage, and listen well so that you can best educate your caller. Education is still one of our field's best forms of marketing, and incoming calls are your golden opportunity to educate clients.

Incoming Calls—Option Two

The prior material was based on the premise that you actually answered your telephone. If you are busy with your life and practice, however, you will have fewer opportunities to answer your telephone and give your caller the impressions you desire. If you do not answer your telephone, then someone or something else should. In this day and age, most people, especially those interested in massage, will probably not bother calling back if your telephone just rings and rings. That leaves you with having your impressions created for you by another person and/or a machine.

When Other People Answer Your Phone

If you have a home-based or outcall practice, the odds are high that your home is your office. If you live alone, one telephone is fine, but if you have family, children, roommates, or anyone else living with you, get a separate business line. You need tight control over the impressions created for your callers, and unless those living with you are well-trained, do not let them speak on your behalf.

Figure 3–1   Professional telephone manners are crucial to building a successful practice.

My father is a minister, so our home telephone always was ringing with calls from members of his congregation. At a very early age, my three sisters and I were trained to answer the telephone respectfully, giving our names first, and politely taking messages or finding our parents to tell them who was calling. We were taught not to yell for our parents, but to go find them, and not to bang the phone down since that hurt the caller's ear. We were taught to ask to spell out names we couldn't spell and to repeat back numbers for callbacks. I thought this kind of message-taking was normal behavior, but I have had enough conversations with children or teens who have horrible telephone manners to conclude that if children have access to your clients, you may be doing a disservice to your practice if you don't train them.

If you can train others to represent you well, great, but otherwise get a separate line and a machine. That way, you control your message, you don't lose any calls, information is written down accurately, and you have sole access to creating your business image. Plus, it's easier to deduct your business telephone and calls as a clearly definable expense.

If you have an office, you can answer the telephone yourself, or have a machine or receptionist. Since we are in the Bare Bones section of the book, a receptionist is not usually part of a beginner's scenario, but if one is, be very choosy in your hiring. I was boggled when I worked for a large company that spent tens of thousands of dollars on marketing, but paid minimum wage for the receptionist. While the executives were racing around in Jaguars, this poor receptionist was barely making a living, and her resentment was evident in her telephone manner. To get a minimum-wage employee, the company settled for a woman barely out of high school who was not well-spoken, and while she didn't cost much, the problem was that she was the first impression callers had of this multimillion dollar company. Receptionists can make or break a business, but few businesses treat them well or give their role the credit deserved for establishing and maintaining the corporate image. A few lost messages here and there, a customer who has been accidentally cut off one too many times, a bad attitude as a greeting, and voila, business is mysteriously dropping. If you are hiring a receptionist, screen well, do good training, practice with scripts, pay well, give acknowledgment, and treat this person as a full-fledged marketing representative.

Answering Machines and Voice Mail

For about the price of one or two massages, you can buy an answering machine. If you don't have one, get one. Even if you don't like machines much, an answering machine in this day and age is a necessity for starting and running a massage practice.

Marketing to create trust and shape perception needs to be consistent in all facets of your business. For a prospect or client to call you and not reach you, a machine, or voice mail is confusing and possibly distressing. If the caller has some trepidation about getting massage or has concerns about your professionalism, a ringing telephone with no answer can be interpreted as being suspiciously unprofessional. After all, what other business or service profession does not have some immediate response to a caller? Plumbers, hairstylists, dentists, carpet cleaners, and other businesses answer their calls, and so should massage therapists. Clients who want to set or change appointments need to be able to call once and leave a message, not call back until they happen to get lucky to reach you in person. If having an answering system sounds like common sense, it is, but I have called enough massage therapists over the years who simply let the telephone ring to consider this topic as one worth discussing.

Choosing Your Message Machine

If you don't already have a message machine, or have an ancient one that has an outgoing message that sounds like you're talking underwater, here's what to look for in a new machine. First and foremost, get one with a capacity for long incoming messages. Clients leaving messages to book or change appointments, or telling you about a friend they are referring, leave directions, or other information-rich messages that will need more than 30 seconds to give you the details you need. In addition, machines that cut off the caller after 30 seconds create an abrupt jarring feeling. If you are trying to help people feel special and important, but your machine or "telephone representative" cuts them off without warning, an incongruity becomes established. This may sound minor, but because of trust issues, massage therapists are judged more intensely about little things, and little things are what make up your marketing package and professional image.

Opinions will vary on my next machine recommendation, but I suggest that you have a machine with electronic chips instead of cassette tapes for incoming and outgoing messages. Cassette tapes are harder and slower to rewind to hear a message again, or to retrieve remotely, and they can sound worn after a while. Wobbly sounding tapes were funny in old high school film projectors but not on your professional business machine. Saving and deleting messages can be done more easily and accurately by chips, though if you need to save messages for long-term purposes such as court cases where you are working with Worker's Compensation or injury cases, you may prefer tapes.

Message machines come with a wide variety of bells and whistles, and I recommend that you get a high-end model for your business. Cheap machines are never a bargain. One lost message can mean one lost client or appointment which could more than make up the difference between a great machine you can rely on for years, or a junky one that will most likely end up aggravating you and your clients.

Machine vs. Voice Mail

Depending on your mobility and need to access your messages, you may choose to get a voice mail system instead of a machine. Voice mail services give you easy access to your messages no matter where you are. A voice mail can be added to your home or office line, and can pick up callers if you are busy on the telephone or Internet, or if you are out. A voice mail also can be a separate number that goes to a remote telephone center that keeps your location private and acts as a buffer of safety from any form of harassment. If you do get a separate line, have a regular schedule of checking it so that you don't miss a last minute appointment opportunity or a cancellation.

How to Leave a Professional Outgoing Message

As a marketing tool, your answering system has the important task of representing you when you can't answer the telephone. In particular, your outgoing message has the task of greeting your callers, informing them that they have reached you, and otherwise enhancing or maintaining your professional image. In setting the tone of your message, imagine who may be calling you and what they will want from you. A professional message should include the following elements:

- a greeting
- your name and/or business name
- request for further information from the caller
- information on other ways to reach you, if appropriate
- information about when you will return the call

You may choose to add more elements, but these are the bare minimum components to include. Their primary purpose is to help your callers trust that they have left a message with you, not with a wrong number, and that they know what to expect as a next step. I recommend you write down your outgoing message and practice it until it comes out smoothly and easily. Make your sentences short so that you can breathe naturally, and do a few takes on the machine if you have to.

Your Telephone Voice

When you create your message, your voice is just as important in shaping your professional image as the words you choose. Use a friendly voice, speak clearly, and sound as if you are genuinely happy to hear from the caller. Imagine your favorite client or the kind of person you want as a client getting your message, and speak as if you were talking directly to that person. You don't have to fake being perky or sound chirpy; just smile, be confident, and talk.

Sample Messages

Examples are easier to understand, so I have included a few sample messages to put all of these elements together under a variety of circumstances. You don't have to use my words, but these messages cover the bases and can help you write your own message for your own situations.

"Hello! You have reached the voice mail of Monica Roseberry. I'm sorry I missed your call, but if you leave your name and number, I'll be happy to call you back as soon as possible. Thank you for calling, and remember to wait for the beep."

"Hello! You have reached the massage therapy office of Monica Roseberry. I am either out of the office or with a client at the moment, but your call is important to me. If you leave your name and number at the tone, I will be happy to call you back as soon as possible."

"Thank you for calling the office of Monica Roseberry, massage therapist. My office hours are 11 A.M. to 7 P.M., Monday through Friday, or by special appointment. If you would like to schedule an appointment or book with me for a free consultation, please leave your name and number, and the best times available for you, and I will call you back today."

"Hello! You have reached the message center for Monica Roseberry of Outstanding Room Only Speaking and Education Services. I will be out of town on a speaking engagement until October 6, but I will be checking my messages every evening and will call you back as soon as possible."

"Hello! You have reached the message machine for Monica Roseberry. I am out of the office today, but I will call you back when I return on Friday the 12th. If you need to speak with me before then, please call my cell phone at. . . ."

You can add other words to these few elements, but don't make the message too long or use it as a mini advertisement. I would rather create my first impressions myself, and I want to know more about my caller before I start crafting those impressions. I speak more rapidly and get to the point with my executive-type callers, but I'm slower and more personable with my elderly clients. I'm more familiar in tone with long-term clients and more formal with new ones, and I want to choose my tone in person, not let my machine do it. Therefore, I keep my message short and simple enough to get my information across, and leave a professional but malleable image.

Anything beyond a simple message risks alienating a client who is very different from you. Cutesy sayings can be annoying to no-nonsense business-people, and background music of any type can put off callers who don't like your musical selections. I have gotten massage therapists' messages ranging from seemingly endless New Age music, followed by dreamy-voiced "Leave a message!" to heavy metal riffs with "You know what to do!" shouted as the only message. Then the therapists wonder why no one leaves a message and why they don't have enough clients. Please, use professional wording and keep the music off your outgoing message.

Establishing your preference in music as the first impression a prospect gets about you sets a number of precedents. First, it subconsciously suggests that your practice is about you, not about your clients. This distinction is really subtle, but it is important to understand. It may sound harsh, but in essence you are forcing other people to listen to your music whether they like it or not. This one factor has the potential of warning the caller that other elements of your practice may be just about you as well. Clients who have been forced to endure a prior therapist's conversation topics, music selections, pressure preferences, and temperature settings are wary of getting another self-centered therapist, so don't set off their alarm systems with your choice of music. You may like wooden flutes or Led Zeppelin, but leave it off your outgoing message. If your caller doesn't like your music, your first impression will not be a good one.

The second precedent that music sets is the possibility that the caller may leap to a narrow and incorrect stereotype that may be difficult to overcome. If the caller was hoping for a therapeutic, no-nonsense practitioner and is treated to a minute of what I have heard called "ding dong" music, she logically may leap to the conclusion that you are one of those hippie types and not what she was looking for. The odds of her leaving a message have decreased, and even if she does, the therapist will have to start below zero in undoing the caller's negative stereotype. I don't want to belabor the point, but in marketing, details matter, so maintain control of your image by leaving your message as simple as possible so that no one can read into it something you did not intend. Be professional, personable, and brief on your message, and learn more about your caller before you reveal too much about yourself. In that way, you don't accidentally talk yourself out of a client and instead, build a trusting and beneficial relationship.

EXERCISE: Creating Your Outgoing Message

- On a separate sheet of paper, write down three outgoing messages that will represent you and your business well.

- If you are part of a group, practice your outgoing messages with five other people and get their feedback. If suggestions are made that can improve your messages, rework them until you find one that works well for you.

Taking Messages

Your telephone and answering system most likely will be your primary link to your current and potential clients. The information coming in through your telephone line will have an impact on your business, and how you handle that information can greatly affect your success. Information such as telephone numbers, addresses, directions to drive, appointment times, referral names, and the like, should be stored in a manner where details can be retrieved at will. Taking messages on scraps of paper, backs of envelopes, or on sticky notes may seem convenient at the moment, but this can end up leading to lost or misplaced information just when you need it most.

For a basic Bare Bones message system, I highly recommend going to an office supply store and getting a telephone message book with carbonless copy pages and tear-out message sheets. These books have many advantages. For those of us with home-based businesses, the big message books are hard to lose in a pile, and no one is likely to walk off with your book to make a grocery list. This means that when the telephone rings, you can always find a piece of paper to write on, which doesn't seem like a big deal until you have a client on hold while you rummage around for a piece of paper. The tear-out sheets let you take a message with you, but the carbonless copy page stays as a permanent record you can refer to months later, which can be invaluable. If you need to prove that your telephone is for business use for tax purposes, these message books also can serve as a record of your business use. Using a message book may take a little discipline at first if you aren't used to it, but in the long run, it will save you time, frustration, and valuable information. The process of getting and keeping clients usually requires calling people back sometime during your marketing process, so get good at and be consistent with how you store the information that lets you reach your callers.

Outgoing Calls

Marketing on the telephone also occurs during your outgoing calls. Since cold-calling is still not a recommended venue for the personal service of massage, you don't have to work up a sales pitch, but you still need to be prepared for calling potential clients. Outgoing calls can be first-contact calls such as when a client or networking partner hands you a telephone number and says they have a referral who is interested in massage. Other outgoing marketing calls occur when you return calls from current or potential clients, confirm appointments, or make follow-up calls after a massage session. These topics will be covered thoroughly in later chapters, but a few basic rules need to be put in place about what to do with messages left on your answering system.

The basic marketing tool of your answering machine is very powerful, but only if you call the people back who left you messages in the first place. When a client or prospect calls you and asks you to call back, how you handle the return call can mean the difference between a paying client and a lost lead. Returning calls may be easy or difficult for you, but there are some basic, professional rules to follow. If at all possible, return calls within 24 hours, and sooner if you can. If incoming calls are about scheduling appointments, it is a professional courtesy and smart business sense to return the call promptly so that your clients can solidify their schedules. If any percentage of your clientele books massage as an impulse buy, your turnaround time for callbacks is even more important; otherwise, you may miss opportunities in the short and long term.

When you call a client or prospect back, a few simple courtesies can help create trust and demonstrate your professionalism. Your call can result in one of three ways: you can reach your caller in person at home, at work, or elsewhere; you can get someone else on the telephone; or you can get an answering system.

The Unfamiliar Caller

When you return a call to someone who is unfamiliar to you, start the conversation by giving your name and asking for the caller by name. I simply say, "Yes, hello, this is Monica Roseberry. I am returning a call from Tim Smith." If you have reached the person directly, remind him of who you are. "I'm the massage therapist you called this morning. How can I help you?" Then be quiet and listen closely. Ask as many questions as you can to figure out his needs before you talk so that you can craft your responses well. Notice, by the way, that I start the conversation with the word "yes." "Yes" is a powerful word, and opening your introduction with it starts you off with a positive feel and leads the person answering toward a more open position. Experiment with saying "yes" early and often, and notice if people lighten up a bit.

If you do not reach your unfamiliar caller directly and someone else answers the telephone, be careful. If you have reached your caller's place of work, use the same opening as above, but do not reveal the nature of your call. This opening makes it easier to forward your call to him, and you will get through the answering system with less delay or prying questions since it is a returned call. Since this is not a current client whose staff may be familiar with you, do not tell anyone else about the purpose of your call, or say "I'm calling Tim Smith about getting a massage." This can cause a serious breach of privacy and can be embarrassing to a potential client who might work with others who are near the low end of the Perception Continuum. Even if you have reached a home telephone, be judicious. Tim's visiting mother may answer the phone and have concerns about Tim getting a massage. If you cannot get through to your caller, leave a message, but keep it vague. "Yes, this is Monica Roseberry. Please let Tim know that I returned his call from this morning. He can reach me at this number until 5:00 P.M. today, or after 10:00 A.M. tomorrow morning. Thank you!"

Reaching a machine or voice mail is a good possibility, so be prepared with a brief but also vague message. "Yes, hello, this is Monica Roseberry. I got your message this morning and I'm sorry I missed you. I will try back in a while, or if you get this message before I get a chance to call back, you can reach me at this number between 3 and 5 P.M. today." This gives you the opening to call back in case you don't hear from the caller again, which can happen.

The Familiar Caller

When current clients or people you know leave a message, you can be a little less formal in the return call, but still keep it professional. When calling familiar people, you can reach them in person, another person can answer, or you can get an answering system. If you reach your client, still start with your name, and I recommend using your full name. Few things annoy me more than having someone call and say, "Hey, it's me!" That gives me three words to sift through the voice files I have on hundreds of people, and I am put on the spot trying to figure out who this caller is before feelings get hurt. After you give your name, get to the point, especially if your client is at work. "Hi, Karen. It's Monica Roseberry. I got your call this morning. What can I do for you?" The ubiquitous "How are you?" leaves you in the position of possibly interrupting her work, or yours. I've had a few lonely clients who taught me the dangers of a simple "How are you today?" and what that can do to my time.

Current clients are usually more specific with their needs such as changing times or booking appointments, but if they are not, train them to tell you exactly what they want if they leave you a message. That way, when you call back, you have a ready answer, whether you reach them directly or must leave a message. Oftentimes, you can do a great deal of work and never talk to anyone in person, as long as you are clear. "Hi, Karen. It's Monica Roseberry. I got your call about needing to cancel on Wednesday at 3:00. I can either rebook you on Thursday at 3:00 or 5:00, or on Friday at 5:00, so let me know which works best for you and I'll book you in. If none of those times work, let me know and we'll try something else. Bye!"

Professional telephone skills may be something at which you are already quite accomplished, but if you have never run your own business before, develop new telephone habits that will mark you as a successful therapist and businessperson.

Basic Marketing Tool #5: A Professional Introduction

Almost every successful massage therapist I have interviewed about marketing said the same thing when I asked how they got their original clients. They simply "talked to everyone" until people started booking appointments. Most of the conversations they had were impromptu and informal, but they had certain marketing elements in them that led to a new client/therapist relationship.

Whenever you are around people, whether in formal or informal settings, you have an opportunity to market your practice. Every public situation you are in, from jury duty to standing in line, has potential clients all around you. You will need to be sensitive to the moment and know what is appropriate to talk about depending on your situation, but any conversation is an opportunity to talk about your work, no matter how briefly. If you find yourself in a conversation that turns to what you do for a living, you are now engaged in a marketing conversation, and you need to be prepared for it.

First and foremost of any marketing conversation is your personal introduction. How you describe yourself and your work can pique a person's interest toward an immediate booking, or toward further conversation or a referral. Many people are interested in massage and are just looking for a trustworthy therapist, so you only may have to say that you do massage and the deal is sealed. More than a few times, I have gotten new clients during informal conversations in line at the store, sitting in a restaurant, or lurking near the buffet table of a party. Not every moment is appropriate to market directly, but saying what you do for a living is acceptable conversation in most every setting, and the almost unconscious handing out of business cards is a fairly standard ritual during introductions. Therefore, this makes your personal introduction one of your most important and versatile marketing tools, usable in any situation and capable of building a practice from the ground up.

Many different ways exist of introducing yourself, but somewhere in most getting-to-know-you conversations we talk about our work. If at all possible, get others to talk about themselves and their work before you talk about yours. In this way, you have a better chance to figure out where they are on the Perception Continuum and how open they might be to massage. When others are done talking, they may ask you what you do. This opens the door for you to talk about massage. If they don't ask what you do for a living, pick up a piece of one their stories and tie it in to your work. Making a segue from their stories to yours can be a bit of a trick, but it is an art worth practicing. A simple, "You know, I was talking with one of my massage clients the other day who brought up this very subject . . ." and ta da, you've just introduced your work.

Fortunately, massage is intriguing enough to most people that you often will be asked further questions, and can talk freely about yourself and your work without having to sound like a salesperson. No one likes to feel hustled or put upon in social settings, so keep your tone conversational but still hand out your cards. A final, "Well, if you ever feel like trying a professional massage, give me a call," can be a sufficient opening without sounding pushy. I sometimes even add, "And I give a 100 percent money-back guarantee, so you've got nothing to lose but a few aches and pains." It's a bit smarmy, but it tells people I'm very confident in my work, and I know most people have a few aches or pains from which they wouldn't mind a little relief.

If your personality is a bit more bombastic, aggressive, or direct, you will need to find ways to express yourself more in step with your own character. No one introduction method is right for everyone, and you may need to experiment with different introductions before you settle on a set of phrases that are effective yet comfortable. Results are what matter, and if you can get clients while being flamboyant, cocky, or shy, go with what works for you.

Opportunities for self-introductions can come at unexpected moments and you need to be ready to take advantage of them. For Bare Bones marketing, we will work with your most common introduction which is most likely a 30-second description that can be delivered in many settings. Sometimes dubbed as "The Elevator Introduction," this short, riding-in-the-elevator spiel needs to convey information quickly while creating trust and shaping perception. Establishing value usually takes knowing your listener better to know what needs are important, but that can be done later if the conversation has been extended due to interest created in the first moments.

When someone asks you what you do for a living, or you are given an opening to talk about massage, what will you say? How will you introduce yourself? Hundreds of factors will impact and alter your formal and informal introduction of yourself. We can't cover every possible scenario, but a personal introduction, like your outgoing message, can pack a lot into a few words, and every word needs to carry its weight. Depending on your personality, your introduction can be humorous, serious, or hit points in between. An introduction can include:

- your name, if it has not already been given.
- your title, which you can create.
- a simple description of your type of work.
- an example of your typical client.
- an opening for the next step in the conversation.

I have a few practiced components that I can add in if the listener seems interested, or that I can leave out if eyes start to glaze over. My personality is a bit more comedic, but I pay attention to my listeners and shape my personality to be more fitting for the setting, the mood, and the moment. For example, if the setting is a casual party and the mood is jovial, when asked what kind of work I do, I often reply, "Well, I push people around for a living." When the listener's eyes bug out in surprise and then relief that this isn't going to be some boring story, I know I have their full attention. Then I add, "Oh, I'm just kidding," and touch them quickly, as if I'm teasing an old friend. "I'm a professional massage therapist. I work with everyone from professional basketball players to little old ladies. I love doing massage and helping people feel better. And what do you do?"

Humor can disarm people, and frankly, if your listener has spent the evening listening to others whine about their boring jobs and talk endlessly about themselves, you will be a breath of fresh air. You love your work, you're funny, your work is different and interesting, you help people, and best of all, you're interested in their story. Amazingly, the less you talk, the more fascinating you become! In fact, the more questions you ask of your new acquaintance, the more intelligent and perceptive you appear. It's like magic! This doesn't mean you have to be a doormat to some boorish, overbearing conversation hog. It just means that you are courteous and considerate, and when the questions inevitably come back around to you, you will have a much better idea of what basic human needs this person has and you can talk about your work fulfilling similar needs.

If we go back to the earlier concept of listening to and listening for, you can listen *to* the person tell about family and job, skiing accidents and stress, and too much airplane travel. Underneath that information, you can listen *for* the needs that they wish someone could help them with. When the ball goes back in your court, you can pick up their story line and use it to tell more about yourself and your work. "Oh man, I've got so many clients who fly all the time for work. I'm like the first person they see when they get in from a long flight (which is true). I don't know why sitting so long makes them hurt so much, but it's like I have to unfold them and straighten them out or something to get them back to normal."

Yes, I do sometimes talk this way, especially if the setting is casual; no one likes a boring stiff or someone trying to be pompously impressive. I'm still getting across the message that my services are very valuable to flyers, and implied in the example is the fact that my clients are often wealthy and successful, they make me a priority with their time and finances, and that my methods work. I don't have to beat anyone over the head with the details or toot my own horn; those who are listening for whether my work is valuable and that others like them have trust in me will hear those messages buried deep within the casual lines.

As for touching people as part of a gesture or as a natural part of the conversation, I highly recommend it. Many studies have shown that a simple touch from tollbooth attendants, cashiers, or librarians handing back library cards strongly impacts the touchee's positive perception of their interaction. I remember one study a classmate of mine did in one of my college communications courses. He stood outside the college library and surveyed students about the library. Then he asked the librarians to casually touch randomly chosen student's hands as they got their books or library card. Then he interviewed them as they walked outside the library door. To make a long study short, he found that the students who were touched perceived the library as having better books, more magazines, more helpful staff, and better resources than the students who had not been touched. This wasn't some double-blind study with thousands of subjects, but I learned a lesson from it early on which is that a simple touch can totally change a person's perception of you.

If you find, after you have given your introduction, that your listener is genuinely interested in getting a massage from you, you have a number of options depending on your setting. If the interaction is brief such as in a line or waiting for a restaurant table, give the person your card, but more important, get a card or number you can call yourself. Promise to call, then follow up immediately. Longer interactions can give you the time to be more specific about your work, but be sensitive to your environment. Parties and other social gatherings have unwritten rules about mingling, doing business, and otherwise not cornering someone to talk all night or demonstrate your neck massage technique while curious bystanders gawk. Unfortunately, I've seen this scenario with the poor recipient trying to get out from under the well-meaning clutches of a massage therapist who had no clue how uncomfortable the momentary client was feeling. If you have your appointment book and someone wants to schedule a massage then and there, do so. However, the most likely option is that you will need to call later and set up an appointment when you both have your schedules available. Again, feel free to give out cards, but always get names and numbers, even if you have to write on one of your own cards.

A little tip for such gatherings: write down the date and function where you met the person and what you should do next to follow up. After looking at cards in my desk drawer with no shred of recognition of where they came from, I learned to make notes right at the moment, even if I had to borrow someone's pen. Remember, people like to feel important, and if you make the effort to write down information about them instead of hastily stuffing their card away, you've just gone up a notch in their book because you recognize an important person when you see one. Shaping perception is part of marketing, and even small things such as this can be more valuable than you imagine.

EXERCISE: Crafting Your Professional Introduction

- *Scenario 1:* Imagine you are at a party where you know very few people. You are standing in a circle with a small group of strangers who are talking. The rest of the group has introduced themselves and talked about

their work. The conversation stops for a moment and all eyes turn to you expectantly, waiting for you to take your turn.
Write down what you would say in that moment.

■ *Scenario 2:* Imagine you are standing in line at the grocery store. You are wearing a polo shirt that says something like "Every body loves massage." The woman in line behind you reads your shirt and says, "Oh, I've been looking for a massage therapist! Do you do massage? What kind of work do you do?"
Write down what you would say in that moment.

■ *Scenario 3:* Imagine that you are at a formal networking meeting, and that you face a room of 15 other professionals from other fields who are willing to refer you to their clients and customers. You stand up to address the group to give your one-minute marketing talk.
Write down what you would say in that moment.

If you are in a group setting, practice giving variations of your personal introduction to three people, and hone it until you can deliver it easily and naturally. If you are part of a small group, I recommend that you stand in front of your group and introduce yourself as a professional, and practice what will become one of your most valuable marketing tools, your personal introduction.

Conclusion

This first section of the book has covered the Bare Bones attributes, skills, and tools that virtually all successful massage professionals have used to launch and sustain their careers in massage. These are simple and basic concepts and principles about how to gain trust, establish value, and shape perception in people's minds so that they book a first massage, rebook, and refer others. At this unprecedented time of growth and change in our profession, these are the primary factors for your success in massage. Mastering these simple fundamentals can help you tremendously in your quest to build your dream practice.

Muscle Marketing
Reaching, Rebooking,
and Referrals

CHAPTER 4

Reaching Skills

CHAPTER OBJECTIVES

After reading this chapter, you should be able to:

- identify factors of your ideal life and work.
- identify elements of an ideal practice.
- explain how to choose a niche market.
- explain how to select the best places to market to find your clients.
- describe the elements of prequalifying clients.
- explain the five Levels of Mutual Marketing.

Muscle Marketing

In the first section of this book, we focused on the Bare Bones marketing attributes, skills, and tools that successful therapists have used for decades to build a practice. These basics are the foundation of success for countless therapists and are necessary for sustaining a long-term practice.

Most massage professionals have not needed to do a lot of advanced marketing because they have followed the fundamental principles covered in the first section, and have built their practices on direct marketing and word-of-mouth referral. However, as the massage field grows and moves through this time of transition into broader acceptance by the general public, more and more avenues of marketing are becoming available to us. This second section of the book aims to take advantage of marketing skills and tools that can propel your practice from dreams to reality. These skills and tools will take more thought, more time, more money, more skill, and more maturity, but if you are ready to take your practice to the next level and are willing to commit yourself to do what it takes to succeed, then buckle up for what I like to call Muscle Marketing.

Muscle marketing gives you two things that are hard to come by with Bare Bones marketing: speed and control. If you want to build your practice quickly, and if you want to reach a bigger market that you directly aim for, keep reading. We will cover many ways to market your practice, and while not every option suggested here may be right for your current circumstances or your personality, consider them for use later in your career.

Muscle marketing covers the Three Rs of marketing. We will take a look at intermediate and advanced skills and tools that can help you quickly and effectively:

Reach your prospective clients

Rebook your current clients

Get personal **R**eferrals from multiple and ongoing sources

Reaching Skills

In the Bare Bones section, your primary skills for reaching prospective clients were talking to people yourself, including using what we called the 10 X 10 rule. The goal of getting 10 new clients by talking to anyone within 10 feet of you can be very fast and effective, but it also can be random, leading to a practice that may not be totally satisfying. As you build your practice, you will discover your preferences for types of people you enjoy working with more, massage modalities that you find more effective, or other facets of a practice you will want to adapt or adopt toward making your dream practice a reality. The more you know what you want, the more quickly and effectively you can build your practice. Therefore, the next level of reaching clients requires these three skills:

1. Knowing yourself.

2. Choosing your ideal clients/niche market.

3. Selecting the best places to market to find your clients.

Two primary philosophies of marketing exist for massage. One says you should see what needs there are in the marketplace, then prepare and shape yourself to meet those specific needs. It's the "find a need and fill it" approach. An example might be that you notice the growing percentage of an elderly population as the Baby Boomers age, and you decide you would be smart to train yourself to be better skilled at working with them. The other way is to take the time to think about who you are and what you enjoy, then attract clients who want what you offer. You may love dance, art, or music, and you decide you want to build your practice serving professionals in those fields. Neither way of choosing is right or wrong, but they are very different approaches.

I saw the first principle in action with a friend of mine. Her father, wanting his daughter to succeed, urged her to get a degree in computer science because he knew she could always find a well-paying job with that degree. She followed his advice and sure enough, she got a good job and is secure in the knowledge that she can always find work. Unfortunately, lurking under the surface of this widely accepted thinking is the fact that she's bored out of her mind, and is doing daily work that doesn't inspire or move her. She is going through the motions of life, but she is not living it. Security is virtually guaranteed for her because she chose to shape herself to meet the needs of the marketplace, but in many ways, she has traded her soul in the process. She has no idea what is important to her or where her real passions lie. But she is now trapped in her bills and lifestyle, and I doubt she will ever get out of the rat race that her well-meaning father steered her into.

When you are developing your practice or shifting it in some way, I would advise the second principle, which is to know who you are and what you want first, then use your marketing to find the clients that are right for you. With more daily satisfaction, happiness, and passion, your odds of succeeding soar.

So, to continue to build your dream practice, we are going to revisit your own unique and individual definitions of what true success and satisfaction are. We started the process of defining success, but now we are going to take it a step further.

Reaching Skill #1: Knowing Yourself

Getting to know and accept yourself is not always an easy or obvious path. However, I find it interesting that the second commandment of the *Bible* is pretty emphatic about this point: "You shall love your neighbor as you love yourself." Whether you read the *Bible* or not, American culture has placed much emphasis on the loving-your-neighbor part, and what I find quite intriguing is the command to love yourself. After all, if you don't love yourself much, you can't love your neighbor much either. If you want to serve and care for, or love others, your first step is to care for and love yourself. Part of loving yourself is getting to know who you are and what is most important to you. Once you know that, it will be easier to figure out how to serve your clients.

Exercise: Creating Your Ideal Life

- There are many avenues to discovering your beliefs, values, passions, goals, dreams, and lifestyle desires, and although this discovery is a life-long process, we'll start here with a mental stretch to open your mind to new or additional levels of awareness of what's really important to you. Now is the time to let your imagination fly. We're going to do an exercise to create a no-holds-barred ideal day, week, month, and year, by writing down how you want to spend your most valuable asset, your time. Since no one else will see what you write unless you want them to, you don't have to sound like a Miss America contestant with everything being about saving the world. For most of us, making the world a better place is an underlying foundation of our goals, but it helps to be more specific. Oh, and have some fun with this. After all, it's your life you're planning. I recommend that you do the following Ideal Life exercises at the rate of three to five minutes per exercise. Our brains create miracles when we are on a deadline, and if you're anything like I am, given too much time, my mental editor kicks in and tells me to write down elements of my ideal life that look good, sound good, will impress other people, make my parents happy, or otherwise have nothing to do with what I really want my life to be like. Be prepared! Your answers may surprise you.

   Here's what to do. First, take a minute to look at the list of possible elements below to consider in your Ideal Day, Week, Month, and Year. Nod when a particular element registers more deeply with you than other ones; say hmmm a lot; and let images, thoughts, or feelings flash by. Then take out a blank piece of paper, label it at the top with My Ideal Day, set yourself a time limit, and write as quickly and unconsciously as you can. When you hit your time limit, stop. Then look at the elements again. Take out another piece of paper, label it My Ideal Week, set your time limit, and write as fast as you can about what would happen during your ideal week. Then do the same for your month and year.

   Ideal Life Elements

   Relationships

   Friends

Family

Growth

Learning

Challenges

Money

Health

Well-Being

Awareness

Hobbies

Work

Leisure

Travel

Health

Food and Drink

Sleep

Entertainment

Music

Sports

Play

Sights, Sounds, Feelings, Tastes, Smells

Interests

If this is the first time you have ever been given the opportunity, or perhaps even the permission, to think so freely, so boldly about how to live your life, notice how you feel. The first time I did this kind of thinking and writing, I was exhilarated, frightened, hopeful, doubtful, surprised, and suspicious. I experienced a hodgepodge of mixed and contradictory feelings rattling my self-perception and shaking my previously unquestioned sense of "reality."

If your Ideal Life exercises came up with a surprise for you like "I want to draw greeting cards" instead of "I want to do sports massage for the U.S. Olympic Team" like you thought it should, don't worry. What bubbles up from your unfettered subconscious is a set of thoughts to consider, evaluate, accept, or let go of. They are not commandments written in stone. However, if a revelation comes to you in the process that needs serious thought, even if it has nothing to do with massage, go ahead and pursue it.

Knowing Your Ideal Practice

If your ideal life didn't include any work or clients, then we may be in a bit of trouble here since this is supposed to be a marketing book for how to get and keep clients. However, if you see that much of your passion is, say, surfing, then maybe you should consider a practice that caters to surfers. Having just spent a week where I got to watch surfers wipe out repeatedly, I can bet that they need massage, and that enough of them can afford it to start or build a practice. You may not be into surfing, but whatever passions and interests came up in the prior exercise, keep them in mind as we now turn to focus more specifically on your practice.

The skill of knowing yourself enough to reach new clients includes knowing:

- what kind of hands-on work you want to do.
- what benefits you want to offer your clients.
- what services you can offer in addition to massage.
- what setting you would work best in.
- what work time frame is most suitable for you.
- what kinds of clients you want to have.

Choose Your Work

Given your ideal life, and your passions and interests, what kind of hands-on work do you want to do? What convictions do you have about the body and about health? What kind of touch do you want to give? What is the intention of your work? What are you trained and qualified to do? Where do you have depth and experience, both in massage and outside of the field? What are your interests? Where do you foresee areas of growth for your work? Do you want to do massage more for stress reduction or as an indulgent, marvelous luxury? Do you want to work with tricky injuries and holding patterns, and use in-depth anatomy knowledge and complex strategies? Do you have a gift for releasing chronic tension or compensation patterns? Do you prefer the emotional aspect of massage and know that touch can help in ways that words could never reach? Do you like digging deep into tissue, or do you prefer laying-on-of-hands styles like Reiki or Polarity? Would you like to be a broad-based practitioner offering a wide variety of modalities to a wide variety of people, or would you prefer having a specialty and targeting a narrow market?

Choosing your work is part of the process of creating a niche for yourself which is a big step toward developing your marketing plan. In essence, you are choosing your own persona, identifying yourself in the marketplace based on the work you choose. Since public perception about massage is still vague, you can create your own titles and massage categories to fit your work, becoming the expert and having a marketing angle for defining yourself in your prospective clients' minds.

Having clearly defined work lets you differentiate yourself in your marketing, especially if you face competition on the general market. You can develop a unique specialty and become the first in your community to offer services in new categories such as massage for entrepreneurs, carpenters, hip replacements, or anything else that can distinguish you from your competition.

In this time of transition in our profession, we have ample room to explore and invent ourselves, and to create niches that never previously existed. Start with what you know and like, and don't worry about others with advanced certificates, more experience, or better brochures. There is always room if you know how to make it. Please don't wait until you are "good enough" to choose a niche. Start with a niche doing work you think you will enjoy, and make a conscious effort over the years to continuously improve. That is how you become good enough.

In the section on Establishing Value, we looked at what needs humans have that massage can help. Addressing those many needs to relieve or avoid pain, and to gain pleasure, can be one of the factors of choosing your work. Wherever you can crossmatch your passions and interests with other people's needs can become the point where you develop your work. If you have

Figure 4–1   Massage can go just about anywhere!

a passion for ballet, market your practice to a ballet troupe. If you love archaeology, dig up a group you can accompany to an excavation site. Do they need massage after days of lifting stones and carefully brushing dust off ancient pottery shards? Of course they do! Do you love river rafting, snow skiing, mountain climbing, or racecar driving? Can you imagine your table set up where the rafts come ashore, in the ski lodge, or at the bottom of the mountain where all those aching bodies are desperate for you? Since massage is portable and is useful in endless settings, let your mind open to the possibilities of where and how you can work. Given this vast variety of markets, if one segment of the market seems overcrowded with other massage therapists, you can adapt your work, create a new marketing message, and appeal to a whole new segment that other therapists haven't reached yet. With the broad appeal and flexibility of massage, this wouldn't be hard to do, and it's how you can love your work for many years.

Know What Benefits You Want to Offer

One way to further identify the kind of work you want to do is to consider what kind of benefits you want to offer your clients. We are fortunate in our profession because massage offers a vast array of benefits to countless markets. Massage can offer pain relief to football players, dentists, postsurgery patients, assembly line workers, secretaries, and artists. Massage can offer pleasure, touch, and companionship to elderly shut-ins, infants, single mothers, ministers, gardeners, and hairstylists. Human touch, applied with caring and skill, can meet a host of needs from heartaches to muscle aches. When we reviewed the human needs that massage can meet, we did an exercise called "Massage is valuable because. . . ." To choose benefits that you want to offer your clients, look back at that exercise and refresh your memory about what you want to offer clients with your skilled touch. Your unique personality has some facet to it that may be your conscious or unconscious primary benefit, and the better you understand yourself and the needs humans have, the better you can serve your clients on multiple levels.

Marketing Motherliness

My favorite example of understanding and marketing your unique benefit comes from my mother. She saw how much I enjoyed my work and she decided to go to the school where I taught so that she could become a massage therapist. Since I was her teacher, she got this strange notion that her work and practice should be similar to mine. Long story short, her natural affinity for massage was different than mine, so after trying unsuccessfully to fit into my mold of work, she broke out and devised her own style and benefits.

In the case of benefits, mine were primarily about relieving stress in uptight business professionals whereas hers were much more about nurturing. It was hard for her to give much value to such an etheric benefit as nurturing but that was her true healing gift, and eventually she built a practice being, among other things, a "mommy" to motherless adults. Here she could shine, touching and stroking and caring in a way that many of her clients had never experienced from their own mothers, or whose mothers had died and were sorely missed. Most marketing books would not consider motherliness as an asset or a salable benefit, but for my mother, it was the perfect niche for her practice. When she retired from massage, I inherited some of her clients, and while a few stuck with me, most just disappeared. Does that mean my work isn't good or effective? No, it doesn't, but being motherly is not my strong suit. It's not my main benefit, and I could not provide her clients with what they wanted most from their massage, which was a gentle mother's touch.

Special Additions

Beyond the modalities or type of work you want in your practice, there are a few nuances to consider as you create your niche and design your ideal practice. These elements may be where you become a "specialist" and they could be the factor that will be most attractive to your target market. Being unique and different can make you memorable in a competitive marketplace, and when you know yourself, value yourself, and want to break into a certain market segment, having special additions can make all the difference in the world.

Do you have skills or training in such additions as guided visualization, hypnotherapy, biofeedback, hydrotherapy, stretching, fitness training, nutrition, healthy cooking, yoga, tai chi, crystal work, breathwork, or hot stones? Imagine building a practice around a uniquely desirable combination of services that clients are out there looking for. To amplify this concept, let's look at another industry for some ideas on the power and profitability of additions.

The Diet Expert

While thumbing through an issue of a fashion magazine, I came across an article on diet experts, people who work under the broad umbrella of the nutrition field. The spotlight was aimed on said experts who cater to those who want to be healthy (especially movie and music stars), and as I read, I was surprised that many of these experts had no formal training. Their "weight-loss wizard" titles were earned with gems such as recommending fruits, vegetables, lean proteins, and cutting down on fat. What made these people stand out from the crowd was not their sage advice, but the additions they tacked on to otherwise humdrum, anybody-knows-that information. What made these experts special was the amount and kind of attention they paid to their clients. Whether the diet expert had weekly sessions to discuss increasing metabolism rates, did hair sample analysis for mineral levels, designed a tailored eating program, or reviewed blood samples, the clients felt like they got more than they would get from a run-of-the-mill nutritionist. After all, who would you rather go to, someone who oohed and ahhed over your food journal, nodded sympathetically while you explained your turmoil over ice cream and then gave you a customized protein shake, or someone who weighed you and then handed you a load of frozen dinners and a calorie counter?

I marvel at the thought that a man with no nutrition training but with a strong background in "motivational psychology" can be elevated to diet guru status enough to be written up in a magazine, but he gave consumers the attention and additions that they wanted, and he has a waiting list of eight months for those who want his help.

While massage is a more tightly monitored industry than nutrition is, at least in some states, we would do ourselves a disservice to scoff at the marketing methods and the "additions" used by the people just mentioned. Your future clients want to feel special, be fussed over, be listened to, have customized strategies designed for them, be motivated and supported through life changes, and learn more about their bodies. Offering additions like an aromatherapy concoction mixed exclusively for each client, a specially selected chakra-balancing music sampling, or a computer-generated astrology chart that points out which area of the body needs more work at a certain phase of the moon may cause a few snickers or eye rolling, but if it fits your target market, it will help you build your practice.

Your additions in your ideal practice can run the gamut from having a bowl of fresh fruit and a bottle of sparkling water ready when your client leaves the massage room, to having a team of specialists working with you offering cholesterol and blood pressure screenings, back strengthening exercises, herbal remedies, or biofeedback training. As you ponder what additions, if any, you want to incorporate into your massage practice, consider the following categories of what you can include in your work or setting that can make you memorable and appreciated. In my experience of interviewing clients, the additions are what they seem to remember and talk about, even more than the massage itself, so think about what you can add that will enhance your clients' overall massage experience. This is just a short list of additions to consider. If you come up with something else that can build your perfect practice, by all means include it.

What Additions Do Your Clients:

- see—art work, equipment, wall color, certificates, reading material
- touch—oils and cremes, sheets, table, face rest, temperature, your hands
- hear—music, chanting, chimes, toning, silence, conversation, drums, ambient sound
- taste—refreshments, drinks
- smell—aromatherapy, body and breath, sheets, oils and lotions, candles
- feel—showers, hot tubs, pools, sauna, steam bath, mineral soaks
- learn—new skills, self-awareness, understanding of the body
- act on—exercise, stretching, posture, movement

Remember, what makes you different makes you memorable, and if you want to expand on your additions to draw a clientele that wants more than just a rubdown, creating an aura or atmosphere that is unlike your client's regular environment or unlike a typical clinical setting may hold a strong appeal.

EXERCISE: Special Additions

- Write down 10 services you can add to your practice that will appeal to your market and help differentiate you from your competition.

Your Ideal Setting

Another important facet in creating your ideal practice is deciding in what kind of setting you want to spend your work time. Do you want to do fast-paced, on-site work, moving quickly from person to person within an office or business setting? Do you want to work at one place, and if so, by yourself or in conjunction with other therapists, colleagues, or doctors? Going back to your last exercise about additions, what would that space look like, what kind of sounds or music would you hear, how would it smell, and how would it feel? In short, what can you do to your setting to create the energy and atmosphere that matches your work? Do you want to work at home, turning a spare room or space into your massage room? Do you like the variety of outcalls, going to offices or homes? If so, in what areas or neighborhoods? Do you want more of a spa setting, and can you set up your own day spa?

Do you want more of an alternative setting, especially more on-site oriented such as wildlife safaris, emergency sites, truck stops, motor home campsites, airports, convention centers, coffee shops, health food stores, seminars, psychic fairs, movie shoots, street fairs, festivals, and on and on? In this case, think about places you've always wanted to go, or careers you dreamed of having but never got around to, and think if you can bring your massage into those worlds.

If you are more into sports massage, can you see yourself in more sports-oriented settings like bird-watching hikes, dance companies, golf clubs, college or professional teams' training rooms, gyms, at an endless variety of competitions, boat races, fund-raising sports events, the Iditarod, and the like? Now that sports massage has become an accepted part of the Olympics, the Ironman Triathlon and other such events, the doors are open more than ever for massage therapists to find their place among world-class athletes.

What are some settings that make you happiest? Unshackle your mind from any limited options you may have and really think about who you are, what you want, and where you want to spend most of your waking hours. Then write down those ideas, uncensored and unedited, and notice what shows up.

Exercise for Ideal Setting

- Write down where you would most love to practice. Then write down the elements of what you would like to have in your ideal setting to make it safe, inviting, and available to your ideal clients.

Your Ideal Time

Now that we've considered space in the form of those settings, what about time? In a perfect world, what would be your ideal number of days to work per week, and ideal number of hours on those days? How many days a month do you want to work, and will that vary depending on the month? Some therapists I know are skiing buffs, so they work hard during the warm months, then take off for a month or more during ski season.

Time for each session also needs to be considered in your ideal practice. Do you like working for 15 minutes, 30 minutes, an hour, or more than an hour? This is a preference you will learn from experience, but given your inherent nature, you can probably make some good guesses here and now. If you are naturally slower, laid back, and methodical, anticipate that you may be more physically and energetically comfortable with sessions that go over an hour. If you are more brisk and efficient, you can probably be happy working 50 minutes to an hour. If you are downright speedy, like action and change, and enjoy the stimulation of a variety of clients, you may be more suited for the shorter sessions appropriate for on-site or chair massage, pre- and postevent sports massage, or working with chiropractors doing patient prep massage.

No one way is better or more admirable than another. The trick is to know who you are, accept yourself, and build your ideal timing around that. Forcing yourself against your inherent nature may be okay while you experiment with what works best for you, but over the long haul, being true to yourself is the best choice.

EXERCISE for Ideal Time

- On a separate sheet of paper, write down the ideal time structure that you would like to work in. Include answers to the questions posed above.

Reaching Skill #2: Choosing Your Ideal Client

After all the work you have done in the prior sections of creating your ideal practice, you probably have noticed some patterns emerging about yourself. Knowing these factors in your dream practice, you now can formulate the ideal client that would fit into that scenario. While these perfect creatures may not be roaming the face of the earth by the thousands, having a firm grasp on what kind of practice you want will produce enough of a generic client type that you can start to develop your marketing program around how to reach them and educate them to the value of your work.

One former student of mine needed only one client to make up her dream practice, and she finally found him: a world-famous singer who wanted a massage therapist to go on the road with him while he toured in concert. Not only was the pay marvelous, but she traveled all over the world, stayed in some pretty plush places, and saw sights she probably would have never seen. So, before you dismiss the idea of dreaming big, miracles have happened in the lives of many therapists who weren't willing to give up on getting what they really wanted.

In your ideal practice, do you want to work mostly with men, women, or both? Do you want to work with people in certain professions, people who are rich, middle class, blue collar, struggling artists, entrepreneurs? Do you want to work with pregnant women, new parents, newborns, kids, teens? Do you enjoy the elderly? Do you want people who are just learning how to take care of themselves and massage is their first step into raised consciousness, or do you want people who are very evolved, spiritually developed, compassionate, vegetarians, and so on.

One therapist I know required that anyone who wanted to be his client had to be an athlete or exercise regularly, and while he was charging $80 to

$100 an hour in 1985 when most people thought $40 was a lot, he had to turn many clients away. His work was good, but he had that added twist that made him different, and his exercise requirement created such a buzz and reputation that people flocked to him. He knew what he wanted, and the clearer he got about his ideal clients, the more he was able to find them, and they were able to find him.

Do you want to work with people who share your religion or belief system, or who share a common hobby, sport, recreational activity, or art? A common ground is a wonderful opportunity for getting some of your first clients, especially if you are new in town. On the other hand, do you want to work with people you want to be more like such as entrepreneurs, world travelers, adventurers, inventors, computer whizzes, business leaders, athletes, writers, musicians, actors, or speakers?

As with charting any course, knowing your destination is critical. The clearer your destination, the less time, money, and energy you'll waste along the way, and the more you'll get to enjoy the fruits of your labor. When you talk to others about building your practice, and you know what you want and maybe even know what's in the way of your getting what you want, people can be much more helpful if they have a specific task in mind of how to give you a hand. For some strange but wonderful reason, Americans fancy themselves as problem-solvers. If you tell them your problem is that you need one or two new clients who fit your target market, they instinctively take the problem on as their own and try to solve it for you.

If you want clients from a number of categories, that's fine. I think it is good protection for your practice to have at least two primary target markets. That way, if the economy takes a dive in one of your target markets, you will have a back-up. When I began my practice in 1984, my two main markets were wealthy, entrepreneurial couples and retired elderly women. The entrepreneurial couples were charged more, but mostly because they were difficult to schedule, prone to last-minute cancellations, and I was never quite sure I could count on them. More than a few times, I was met at the door by the maid of one client who handed me a check and apologized that the couple had to leave unexpectedly in their private plane. My "little old ladies," as they liked to call themselves, were charged a much lower rate, but I could count on them being there every week for their massages. And besides, they were fun to talk to. When the economy took a tumble that affected a number of my wealthy couples, the little old ladies floated my monetary boat while I rebuilt my practice.

Preselecting a target market may feel a bit funny, but the reason we're doing this is because many business owners don't take the time or have the guts to either choose a market or limit markets in any way, especially if they are feeling desperate. One of the biggest marketing fallacies is that if you cast a bigger net, you'll catch more fish. Again and again, research in marketing and advertising campaigns has found that by casting a narrow net, businesses reach their most profitable market sooner. When you have the courage to select a niche market and appeal to it, amazing things can happen.

To summarize this point on choosing and understanding your ideal clients, remember that this is your life, and if you value your time, think hard about what kind of people you want to spend it with. What kind of clients will contribute conversations that will fascinate you, offer words of wisdom, give gifts, and show appreciation for your hard work? If each moment of your life is precious, how do you want to spend it with the people you work with? You probably will be spending cumulative years with these people, mutually sharing your daily lives. This relationship will motivate you to learn, and continue to improve your ability and competency. Do not take that lightly. If you wake up on work days looking forward to the clients you get to see that day, you virtually can guarantee yourself long-term success.

EXERCISE: Choosing Your Ideal Client

■ Write down a brief description of your ideal client using the demographic factors below. You can start the sentence with My Ideal Client is. . . . You don't have to use every element and you can add other elements that matter to you. You also can list a few additional ideal client profiles if you want to go after multiple markets. I'll give a few examples from my own practice to get you started. A little hint: If you have a hard time imagining your ideal client, think of who you don't want to work on and why, then write the opposite.

Example: My ideal client is a woman between 30 and 70 years old who is an entrepreneur earning $70,000 plus annually, and is involved in a sport or physical activity. My ideal client has previous experience with massage, wants sessions every other week for stress management "maintenance massage," and sports performance enhancement or injury recovery work, and lives within 15 miles of my home office.

Example: My second ideal client is a man between 45 and 70 years old who is an executive earning $100,000 plus and travels extensively. This ideal client has previous experience with massage, wants sessions monthly for stress management and relaxation, and lives within 15 miles of my home office.

Example: My third ideal client is an elderly widow who is retired. She wants weekly sessions for a variety of small aches and pains, for conversation, companionship, and touch.

Client Demographics

Male and/or Female	Primary need
Profession	Type of work
Income level	Perception level
Age	Massage experience
Education	Frequency of sessions
Marital status	

My ideal client is . . .

Congratulations! You have just finished one of the hardest parts of this book. You now are unlike most people in this world who waffle around, aren't sure what they want, aren't even sure what they don't want, and never have nailed down a dream on paper. Virtually every success book ever written emphasizes the power of knowing what you want and writing it down. That way, when the door of opportunity is opened to you, sometimes for just a fraction of a second, you can say to yourself, "Yes, that's exactly what I want!" and step into a life that makes people mutter about how lucky you are. This book isn't about hope or luck; it's about knowing what you want, and doing what it takes to have the practice and life that you love.

Reaching Skill #3: Finding Your Ideal Clients

During this time of transition for our profession, we still face issues of lack of trust, value, and misperceptions about massage. Many people genuinely want to receive massage due to its growing popularity, but because of the very personal nature of massage, they still want some form of referral to reduce the risks of literally placing themselves in a stranger's hands. Most traditional marketing is anonymous; advertising, direct mail marketing, posted flyers, and the like do not reduce the worries of the buyer that the massage being advertised is going to be a good experience. In addition, therapists face risks as well by blindly marketing to an unscreened populace. What both clients and therapists want are personal referrals that are prescreened and safe. With this factor in mind, one of our best ways to find clients is through a process I call Mutual Marketing.

Mutual Marketing

The foundation of mutual marketing is built on three fundamental questions you can ask to build your successful practice. We will go through each of these questions thoroughly.

Three Key Questions

1. Who is my target market?
2. What small businesses already serve my target market?
3. What do I have to offer that business to get my hands on its customers?

We just covered the first question, Who is my target market (or ideal client)? Now we will look at the other two, What businesses have your clients? and What can you offer those businesses to get their referrals? The answers to these two questions will vary with each massage therapist because target markets will be different, but thousands of possibilities exist for working with small businesses. Embrace the thought process here and you will start opening your eyes to all the ways you and your clients can safely and easily find each other.

What Small Businesses Already Serve My Target Market?

This is where the fun and creativity starts. Somewhere out there, one or two small business owners have been working, perhaps for years, and they already have a client list that matches your target market. If you can find that one business, or even two or three of them, you can, in essence, knock on one door and have your whole practice waiting for you behind it.

Why do I advocate partnering with a small business for your source of personal referrals? Because it is one of the fastest, easiest, safest, and most controllable ways to access new clients through a source that vouches for your trustworthiness and value. If you are new in town, your friends and family don't know anyone who can afford massage, or your handful of clients aren't willing, able, or keep forgetting to refer you, who else would be willing to help you build your practice? Someone who can mutually benefit from marketing your service of massage.

The act of crossreferring customers has been used from huge corporations to sole proprietor businesses, and for where massage is now, it is time that our profession starts making better use of this wonderful resource of clients. I remember one of the first times I saw this crossreferring principle in action with a small business. I had just arrived at a friend's house, and she was finishing up some paperwork with a dusty looking man who turned out to be a chimney sweep. My friend had been thinking about getting her chimney cleaned but she had been putting it off. Then she got a coupon in the mail that offered a free, one-month membership at a local gym if she used this particular chimney sweep. The crossoffer did two things. One, it motivated her to finally get her chimney cleaned since there was a deadline on the gym offer; and two, of all the choices she had, she made a decision to choose this particular chimney sweep just so that she could get the gym membership. Also, she figured if the gym was willing to risk its reputation by being associated with a chimney sweep, he must be pretty reputable as well. As she paid him for his work, he gave her a pass card that got her into the gym. I was intrigued. There was no obvious link between chimneys and gyms that I could see, but the crossreference got her to take action, choose this chimney sweep over all the others, and when she went to the gym later, they had a chance to sell her a regular membership. The chimney sweep probably paid nothing to the gym, it didn't cost the gym anything but a pass card, and both businesses helped each other out with virtually cost-free marketing.

The beauty of massage over virtually any other service business is that it is in the enviable position of being associated with almost any kind of business for this type of crossreferral. Since massage is viewed as a luxury service, a medically beneficial service, an avenue for sports enhancement, and as part of the good life, among many things, we can partner with any small or big business.

With its broad and valuable appeal, massage can be linked with a huge number of seemingly unrelated businesses to the benefit of that business and to you. Small businesses are always in competition for customers, and they are in need of an edge over other similar businesses. They advertise and market, and spend a lot of money keeping their doors open, so if you can help bring in new customers or keep their current customers coming back, they will help you build your practice by giving you direct access and trustworthy referrals to their customer base. Small businesses are the ideal mutual marketing partners because you can give them a strong incentive to help you, they help screen potentially dangerous clients, they vouch for your value and trustworthiness, and as you grow your practice over time, you can refer business in their direction as well.

Choosing Your Ideal Mutual Marketing Partner

You can approach virtually any type of business to be a mutual marketing partner but some businesses will be able to help you more than others. When considering businesses to approach, consider the following questions.

Do they already serve your ideal clients or target market?

Do they have a good, linkable association to the needs you want to meet? For example, if you want to be a sports massage specialist, approach businesses with sports-oriented products or services.

Are they located in close proximity to your home or office?

Are they amenable to partnership projects?

Do they have a wide sphere of influence or contact in the community?

Can they benefit from partnering with you?

Example: In using the reaching skills we have covered so far, when I start with the skills of knowing myself, and mixing my passions and interests with the needs of my target market, it is a natural fit for me to want to work with golfers. I love golf, most people who golf can afford massage, and golfers seem to keep hurting themselves and I keep needing to fix them. If I wanted a clientele of golfers, I would consider partnering with a golf instructor.

EXERCISE: Selecting a Potential Mutual Marketing Partner

■ To select a potential partner, think about who you are, what kind of clients you want, what needs you want to serve, and what businesses already serve your target market. Then take out a piece of paper and label it My Ideal Mutual Marketing Partner. Then look at the different categories below and think about what businesses would be best for you to approach to work together. Keep your mind open and write down any business you can think of with which you'd like to work. Don't edit yourself; just write.

Factors to Consider for a Mutual Marketing Partner

Types of Businesses

Service

Product/Manufacturing

Nonprofit

Government

Business Image

Conservative/Traditional—elder care lawyer, accountant, banker

Professional—white collar, real estate agent, sports agents, wedding planners

Informal—golf pro, travel agent, dance schools, florist, pet-sitter

Manual—blue collar, landscaper, pool cleaner, building contractor

Outrageous—bungy jump, sky dive, white-water rafting

Customer Base

Large—serves your main target market and your secondary ideal client profiles

Narrow—serves only your main market

Contact Frequency

Regular repeat—maid service, pool cleaner, gardener, hairstylist, tai chi class

Occasional repeat—travel agent, restaurant, nutritionist, herbalist, yoga teacher

Seasonal repeat—golf pro, tax preparer, landscaper

One time only—spa builder, real estate agent, moving company, photographer

Impulse buyer—novelty store owner, jeweler, boutiques, antique dealer

Emergency buyer—electrician, plumber, roofer, contractor, computer repair

Customer Needs

Basic needs—grocer, baker, water delivery

Essential service—barber, carpenter, mechanic

Preferred service—personal trainer, esthetician, interior decorator

Nonessential—dog psychologist, tanning salon, riding stable, diaper service

Novelty/Impulse—psychic, rock climbing gym

Contact Value (how much the customer spends per contact)

$1 to $100—winery, restaurant, book store, kayak rental, parasailing

$100 to 500—camera shop, shoe store, building supply store

$500 to 2,000—bicycle shop, computer store, home furnishings store

$2,000—car dealer, RV sales, boat sales

Contact Quality with Business Owner

Low personal contact—telephone, e-mail, employees handle customers

Medium personal contact—acquaintance, small background knowledge

Intensive personal contact; occasional—agent, broker

Intensive personal contact; regular—manicurist, tutor, piano teacher

A few businesses that already may have your ideal clients

Tanning salons

Yoga classes

Nutritionists

Athletic trainers

Dance schools

Symphonies

Sports agents

Real estate agents

Travel agents

River raft tours

RV sales

Antique furniture

(Who goes into the homes you want to work in?)

Art supply store

Jazz club

Sailing club

Golf club

Jewelry store

Motorcycle store

Art gallery

Contractor

Bicycle shop

Skateboard park

Skydiving school

Landscaper

Computer store

Interior designer

Architect

Exercise equipment store

Florist

Restaurants

Pet store

Bridal shop / tuxedo rentals

Microbrewery

Sushi bar (shiatsu)

Stadium unions such as road crews, concert crews

Operas

Church groups

Singles clubs

Recreation centers

Rodeos

Travel clubs

Retreat centers

Seminars

Associations

Philanthropic organizations such as Lions Club, Rotary Club, Kiwanas

City recreation classes

Gardening Clubs

Walk around your town and look at businesses. Go through your Yellow Pages. Visit your Chamber of Commerce. Be open to ideas.

*Wedding Party—
Massage and
Makeover Party*

SALON NAME
ADDRESS
PHONE

HOLD A MASSAGE AND MAKEOVER
PARTY FOR YOUR WEDDING PARTY!

LET OUR TEAM OF SPECIALISTS MAKE
YOUR WEDDING MEMORABLE

RELAX YOUR WEDDING PARTY WITH
SOOTHING MASSAGES BY (YOUR NAME)

LOOK YOUR BEST WITH MAKEUP AND
HAIRSTYLING BY XYZ SALON

OUR TEAM IS HERE TO HELP MAKE YOUR
WEDDING EXTRAORDINARY!

Figure 4–2   You can partner with hundreds of businesses to reach new clients.

EXERCISE: Choosing a Mutual Marketing Partner

- ■ Write down 10 businesses you can partner with. Be creative and think about what businesses would be viable partners to work with in reaching your ideal clients.

What Do I Have to Offer a Business to "Get My Hands" On Its Customers?

The third key question of mutual marketing basically asks, "What do I have to offer small business owners so they would be thrilled to refer me to their customers?" You have a number of options and they can vary, depending on the business owners' needs. You can trade massage with the owner or staff for referrals, ask for referrals as a personal favor, or offer some form of massage promotion that they can use to meet their highest needs.

You can concoct all sorts of promotions, gift premiums, and even rewards of massage that will make that business gain and keep customers; be more appealing than a competitor; and essentially create a deal in a customer's mind that would be hard to refuse. There are many ways you can do this, and as we go through the upcoming examples of this process, be creative and see if you can come up with other offers, deals, or ideas that will have small businesses thrilled to be helping you as you help them.

Please notice that, as compared to many other businesses, the offer of giving your partner access to your clients is not included as one of the options. Due to confidentiality issues, do not give anyone access to your client list. You can tell your clients about the great landscaper or nice restaurant you are doing a promotion for, but don't give out your client information.

How to Create a Mutual Marketing Partnership

The first thing to know about any business, including yours, is that there are some universal needs to be successful. The more you understand the needs your mutual marketing partner has, the more you can tailor your offers to meet their needs. Businesses need to:

- ■ attract attention to bring new customers in the door.
- ■ find a way to stand out from their competition.
- ■ make a sale once a customer is in the door.
- ■ bring the customer back again.
- ■ upsell current customers to spend more on higher volume or quality.
- ■ have current customers refer other qualified buyers.

When you are considering potential partners, look for businesses that are motivated to work with you. They could be facing new competition, losing market share, wanting to get in touch with missing customers, trying to attract attention to get people in the door, or needing an incentive to close a sale.

The Shoe Store

One of my massage clients is a business consultant, and he told me a story that illustrates the importance of understanding what needs a business really has. He was consulting with the owner of an upscale men's shoe store who ran the store with her daughter. Their sales were slipping from previous levels and they weren't sure what to do about it. When he asked the mother and daughter what they perceived was needed to turn the store around, they gave different answers. The daughter's primary goal was "to get customers in the chair." Her mother's goal was to "sell shoes." They realized that the daughter had spent a lot of time and energy getting people into the store, and even sitting in the chair to try on shoes, but that was when she stopped the selling process. She had met her goal, but it was the wrong goal. When she was in charge of the store, people came in as she'd planned, but they didn't buy.

So, if you knew that the goal of the owner was to get people in the door, into the chair, and then make a sale, what could you offer her to get access to her upscale customers?

To get people in the door, she could run an advertisement or send out a coupon saying that if people bought a pair of shoes, they could get a free foot reflexology, either on-site on a particular special sale day, or by booking a later appointment with you. She could hand out discount coupons for your massage as a "thank you" for visiting the store to create good will and

Figure 4–3 By helping other businesses, you can also reach your ideal clients quickly and easily.

"buzz." If she wanted repeat sales over time or more shoes sold in one visit, she could give out a "frequent buyer card." If the buyer buys three pairs of shoes, he gets a certificate for a free half-hour massage or a half-off price for a full hour. If the owner wanted her current customers to refer their friends, she could offer a frequent buyer card to the buyer and any friend to purchase enough shoes for a free massage.

In all of these cases, your name and contact number would be given to these upscale buyers. In this way, you have been introduced to a strong market, been associated with an upscale store, gained trust by association, shaped perception, and gained a one-stop-shopping avenue for a strong source of direct referrals. You have helped a small business handle a serious problem and you get pre-qualified referrals for minimal cost, if any. Now that is smart marketing!

If promotions such as these don't work for your circumstances, ask to leave your cards or brochures in the store for a trade of massage, or just as a favor. It is amazing how much others are willing to help, if only we ask.

If you think that mutual marketing requires giving away a lot of massage for free, it doesn't. Some promotional setups can work better if you give away a few massages to get access to your target market, and many successful therapists have benefited greatly from a few well-placed and well-timed donated massages.

The Five Levels of Mutual Marketing

Working with a business partner can be a very involved relationship, or it can be fairly distant. There are many ways to work with a small business owner, but we will cover five levels of interrelationship so that you can consider what type of connection would work best for you. Each level of relationship has variations on a number of different elements. These elements are the:

- actions you take.
- actions your partner takes.
- marketing tools you use.
- benefits of your joint projects to your partner.
- benefits of your joint projects to yourself.
- drawbacks of each level of project.

Level 1: You get a mailing list of your partner's customers and take it from there.

You can mail out a marketing postcard, card, letter, flyer, or coupon.

You may or may not mention your partner in your marketing piece.

Benefits to Business

payment for the list

trade massage for list

goodwill or favor to you

Benefits to You

your message reaches a large number of prospects quickly

minimal expenditure of time and money to reach your target market

Drawback to You

> prospects unscreened, and it's harder to prove your value or create trust

Level 2:   You get a mailing list plus a personal endorsement from your partner

> You can mail a marketing piece such as a letter on their stationery, or use quotes or endorsement from the owner; the ad copy reflects their business

Benefits to Business

> pay/trade/good will

> you pay to market for them when you mention them in your letter; this gives them attention, association, and free advertising

Benefit to You

> you reach a large audience quickly and cheaply; and with the endorsement, you gain more trust and value by association and personal referral

Drawback to You

> If you are working without full licensure, you create a risk for you and your partner and therefore shouldn't use endorsements

Level 3:   You create a marketing piece with their endorsement, but they distribute it

> They can send your marketing piece as a special mailer, include it in with billing or invoices, regular mailer, newsletter, or promote you on their website

Benefit to Business

> get to use image of massage and "good life" associated with their business

Benefits to You

> direct access to qualified customers in your target market

> less expense to you since they do the distribution

> more interaction with partner, with more possibility of personal referral

Drawbacks to You

> some elements of the marketing process may be out of your control

> may be slow

> your marketing message still requires your prospect to make the decision to buy a massage

> your partner's incentive to refer you is low; minimal needs are met

> words on paper are no match for hands-on experience of your work

Level 4:   You sell massage packages and promote your partner's business by offering the bonus of their service free or at a discount

> *Example:*   The customer buys five massages and gets a free, half-hour golf lesson

You get your partner's client list and write and mail a marketing piece offering your joint package deal, call the client list offering the package deal, or e-mail the client list offering the package deal

And/Or

Your partner distributes your marketing piece at the business site, as an enclosure with an invoice, or through their own mailer or other means

Benefits to Business

they stay in contact with current customers without "selling"

if you pay, they market cost-free

their offer can reinitiate a business relationship with former customers

their offer can be converted to a better sale with upselling

they gain good will with their customers for making a valuable offer

Benefits to You

you get money up front for package deals, a good short-term strategy

it gets people under your hands to demonstrate cumulative value

people who experience your work are more willing to rebook and refer

your partner is closely involved, which means more personal referrals

Drawbacks to You

purchasing a package of massage without testing your work may be a leap for some, and it requires a decision to buy

the agreement of the bonus can cost money if you pay for your partner's service or product

if your partner is not good at marketing, or can't resell or upsell and gets no benefit from the deal, it may be difficult

there is a lower return percentage, but each lead is more valuable and committed

Level 5: Your partner uses massage certificates or events to promote their business

"Buy 5 golf lessons and get a free massage or discount coupon for massage"

Massage has wide appeal to broad markets and can help generate their sales

Since the image of massage draws many types of people, it can be used in broadcast advertisements with an image of you working; in ads to promote a sale or event with on-site massage at business location; and in ads offering gift certificates or discount coupons in exchange for X number of repeat sales (within X amount of time), X number of dollars spent, X amount of service time booked, and X number of referrals to new customers

Massage image or promotion is used in direct mail promotion to customer list

Massage image or promotion is used in direct mail to broad purchased list

Massage image or promotion offered in store only

Benefits to Business

new marketing angle for advantage over competition

massage appeals to a huge range of markets and attracts everyone

massage is easy to associate to their product or service for good ads

massage creates strong association to the "good life"

promotions can attract new clients, missing clients, create loyalty

gets attention, novel, different, unique, creates a buzz, gets people in

gets people to buy

gets people to become regular buyers

your partner gets money up front for package deals

gets people to upgrade the value of their purchase

Benefits to You

you reach your narrow target market and ideal client quickly

your association improves your market's perception of massage

you reach prospects you are more able to trust, with one level of screening

the association with your partner decreases odds of harassment

the client's decision to buy is removed; they don't have to have value proven beforehand

the promotion gets people under your hands quickly

your benefits of massage are more evident from your work than other forms of marketing

getting a chance to prove your work leads to opportunity to rebook

if you are new, a big promotion gives you a lot of experience trying out techniques and learning what you like and don't like

it gives you a fast learning curve. If no one rebooks, you can find out quickly what's wrong

Drawbacks to You

you may have a lot of work up front with little short-term return. This is a long-term strategy.

you can become resentful of doing free or discounted work if you're not careful

promotional work won't pay off if you don't have good rebooking skills

EXERCISE: Making an Offer to a Mutual Partner

■ Look at your list of potential mutual marketing partners. Pick one partner from your list that you think would give you the best access to your ideal client or target market. Then review the five levels of mutual marketing and create three offers to make to your partner for a mutual marketing project.

Partner: _____

Project 1: _____

_____

_____

Project 2: _____

_____

_____

Project 3: _____

_____

_____

Gaining Trust First

As a concept, mutual marketing is actually very simple. Many other businesses have been using partnership marketing for years. Companies around the world have realized that if they share each other's customers, their profits will increase because they do not need to spend as much money finding and advertising to their target markets. Some massage therapists have taken the first step toward mutual marketing by putting up cards or signs in other businesses such as gyms or health food stores, but we are now ready for proactive marketing with direct recommendations from small businesses, not passive, easily ignored pieces of paper. Since massage is enjoying a growing, widespread, positive public perception, your job of finding a mutual marketing partner will be much easier than it would have been even a few years ago. Finding a mutual marketing partner may take time, or you may build a successful partnership with the first business you approach.

One important element of creating a mutual marketing partnership is trust. Before any of these ideas can be implemented, you must create a professional relationship with your potential partners. You can offer your mutual marketing partners free massages, do on-site work in their offices, or do whatever you must so they know your work is of the highest quality. Don't expect them to trust you on your word that you're good. You'll have to prove it. Then, once you have established their trust, you can work on numerous projects together to build both of your businesses. Trust, depending on the past experience of the other person, may be easy to build or could take a while. Trust cannot be forced, and don't take it personally if the other person seems too distrustful of you or your offer.

Being an Equal and Professional Partner

Since this is an official business agreement, it is important that you discuss your arrangements and agreements clearly and get them down in writing. While it may be tempting to work under the table with your bartering arrangements for tax purposes, realize that if your mutual marketing partner gets audited, a trail can lead back to you. If you have not declared or paid taxes on your bartering, the consequences can be serious. I strongly suggest that you draw up a contract: one, so that you can be clear about what it is you agreed on; and two, so that you are treated in a professional manner. You are a professional in your field and you can be a great asset to another business, so approach a potential partner as an equal and handle your relationship as a peer.

To make the most out of your partnership, talk with your partner about what needs the business has and strategize together about various crosspromotional projects. Before you even meet, have some interesting options for how to promote their business first, and they will be much more open to any kind of working relationship. If you are fortunate, you will be able to partner with a business owner with good marketing skills. However, many small business owners may be good at what they do, but may not be good at marketing. To maximize the value of your time, energy, and investment, you may need to help your partner realize how to make the best use of your joint projects.

For example, if I were to partner with a golf instructor, I would go the extra step to make sure she was following up with the leads she got when we did the "Buy five massages, get a half-hour golf lesson free" project. Golf instructors, like most professionals, would rather be golfing than marketing, so if I want to make it a win-win project, I would consider helping her with encouragement or reminders to follow up on the leads we generated. This may not be necessary, but if you get many valuable clients from your partner, do what you can to maintain and forward the relationship. One good partner, as I have learned, can provide you with the majority of your clients without you ever having to market again, so invest well in the relationship.

Client Net Worth

If you are going to do any form of marketing beyond the 10 X 10 method, you will be making a more serious investment of time and money. When you consider marketing methods such as mutual marketing or more traditional forms of reaching prospective buyers, eventually you must gain or profit more than you spend, otherwise you can put yourself out of business. The reason that I like mutual marketing so much is that you can reach large numbers of your target market inexpensively with a very high potential for a good return on your investment. If you are a new therapist starting out, you will probably have more time than money, and many of these projects can be set up to take time, but with little money spent.

As you evaluate your use of mutual marketing, I'd like to introduce a term at this point that I call client net worth (CNW). Client net worth is the sum of what one massage client is potentially worth to you financially over the lifetime of your working relationship. This net worth is critical to know because it will determine how much you are willing and able to spend, or give away to get a client.

While the income you anticipate earning from each client will start off as an estimate, if you plan to do numerous marketing campaigns, you will need to sit down and figure out what it really costs you to land a new client. However, if you follow the principles in the Bare Bones Marketing section, all you need are a few good clients to build a practice. You may have only to do a few marketing campaigns, then let the rebookings and referrals do the rest. For now, though, let's work with some general numbers so you can see the value of one client and why it is worth getting him.

Client Net Worth Examples

Let's take some of my first clients, a couple I had been massaging since 1985. I started by massaging the husband, a former boss of mine, every Friday. Then I moved to working with him and his wife every Friday, and then every other Friday, until I broke my wrist last year and had to give up my practice. Over the span of time I have known them, I have earned around $46,000 from them. Adding on the income from some of the people they have referred, that brings their CNW closer to $50,000. Do I make them a priority, hold my Friday nights open, and treat them well? Do I go the extra mile, play with their dog, wait a few extra minutes while he takes a shower after his massage before starting her massage since he doesn't like getting dressed when he's oily? Do I bring in special aromatherapy oil for her since that makes her feel special? Of course I do. Do I listen to her discussion of what was on the television talk shows that day without giving my opinion? No, I have to draw the line of customer service somewhere.

My point is, I serve, pamper, and care for my clients in every way that I can, and in this case, the CNW of those extra miles I walked have resulted in more than $50,000 in sales with no advertising expenses. For many businesses, advertising is a huge expense and takes much of their budget, but if you can retain a client of this caliber, you can save your marketing and advertising expenses, and have each return visit be much more profitable.

Doing Client Net Worth Math

Depending on your target market, you may do mostly weekly, biweekly, or monthly massage, and since the average American moves every five years, let's consider that in the equation. Let's say you get a new client who comes in once a week for $60. He is out of town for summer vacations, Christmas, and assorted other trips, so out of the 52 weeks of the year, he comes in 45 of those. This comes to $2,700 a year. If you only work with him for three years, his CNW is $8,100 ($60 a session x 45 sessions a year = $2,700 a year X 3 years = $8,100 CNW).

Let's say you get a client who comes in every other week at $60 a session, and she comes in 26 times a year. Her yearly worth to you is $1,560, and if she stayed three years, she'd gross you close to $5,000. If she stayed with you for 10 years, her CNW would be $15,000 not including price raises. That's a lot of money, and if it only costs you one free gift certificate to get that caliber of client, do you think it's a worthwhile investment ($60 a session X 26 sessions a year = $1,560 a year X 3 years = $4,680)?

If you do top-quality work, give excellent customer service, and really take care of your clients in the way they like, they should become regulars, if that is the kind of practice you have. More clinic-oriented practices won't have multiyear client rebookings, but many practices have a foundation of long-standing repeat clients. We'll talk about how to build a repeat client practice in the chapter or rebooking, but for now I simply want to emphasize the value of rebookings and referrals for CNW so when I give unusual ideas later, you'll understand my rationale.

Mutual Marketing Examples

Mutual marketing can happen in any type of business, and if you know who you are, what needs you want to meet, what kind of work you want to do, and the potential profitability of your mutual marketing projects, you can get to work. If you still want more ideas, I will go through a few examples below to show mutual marketing in action.

Partnering With a Travel Agent

Let's say your target market consists of upper-management executives or older, wealthy women. If your specialty is more for pain reduction, then ask yourself, when are these people sore, tired, and otherwise in need of your services? One possible answer is when they have been traveling. The next question is, what small businesses serve them when they travel? An answer to that would be a travel agency, and a potential mutual marketing partner could be a travel agent. So let's look at some of the ways you can work with this one, well-connected mutual marketing partner.

The first thing to do is establish what needs a travel agent has. At this point, travel agents are in serious trouble. Airlines are cutting the percentages that agents get for bookings, and airlines are giving travelers incentives to book online or directly through the carrier, leaving out the agent altogether. As a partner, a travel agent needs to get new customers, but the primary need is retaining current customers. Therefore, your offer would need to include some promotion that rewarded the agents customers for using her services instead of booking their flights themselves.

Using Gift Certificates

To meet the travel agent's needs while getting rapid access to her customers, you can use the level five strategy and give away free massage as part of a promotion. One way to do that is to print a stack of numbered gift certificates and give them to the travel agent, along with some brochures or educational materials. Let her know who your target market is and ask that she gives the certificates to them. Give her some of the following ideas on how to increase her business by using your certificates, but also let her be creative.

Travel Agent Promotionals

There are number of ways the agent can use your certificates to promote both of your businesses simultaneously. One way is for the agent to use the certificates as a promotional: buy a cruise from me and you get two massage certificates; book 10,000 miles in three months and get a free massage after your long flight; or buy a vacation package to Hawaii and get two massages for the price of one, or one massage free. If you do outcalls and the recipients of your gift certificate are a couple, try to massage both of them. Your odds of returning for two paid sessions are higher.

Another way is to piggyback on ads. If your travel agent uses advertising to promote travel specials, ask the agent to include your name or offer in her

Bring the Magic of the Islands Home With You

Purchase 2 round-trip tickets and resort package to Hawaii with XYZ Travel and receive 2 free massages from (your name) upon your return

XYZ Travel
Address
Phone

Figure 4–4   Travel agents can connect you to numerous target markets.

ad or promotional literature. This gives you valuable exposure, offers piggy-back marketing for you, and even if people don't buy from the travel agent, you still get exposure. If massage is offered as a free gift for purchasing travel specials, it creates a valuable premium for her customers. This differentiates her from other agents and may bring in new or repeat business.

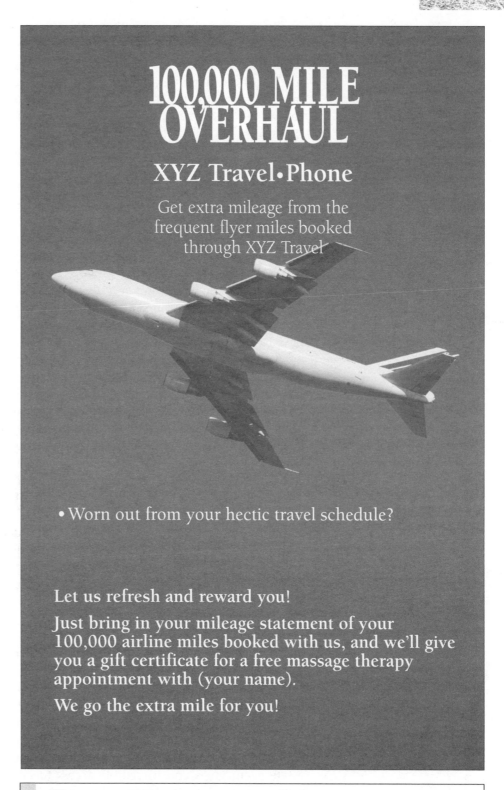

100,000 MILE OVERHAUL

XYZ Travel•Phone

Get extra mileage from the frequent flyer miles booked through XYZ Travel

• Worn out from your hectic travel schedule?

Let us refresh and reward you!

Just bring in your mileage statement of your 100,000 airline miles booked with us, and we'll give you a gift certificate for a free massage therapy appointment with (your name).

We go the extra mile for you!

Figure 4–5　Help your partners improve their business by using massage promotions.

If she is a great resource for repeat clients and you want to continue the relationship after your initial project, keep giving her free massage gift certificates that she can use to build her business. This increases her incentives to send you quality prospects and refer you often since she will benefit when you massage her clients. If you are trading massage for her referrals, figure out a formula for how many massages you will give her in exchange for a set number of referrals. Keep accurate books and keep up your end of the agreement without reminder, and she will think she really got lucky. The lucky one is you because if her clients expect to pay $75 or more for a massage because they are used to massage prices at hotels or resorts, your profit from this venture can be substantial. You have not had to pay for expensive advertising, you created trust by word of mouth, and you helped someone else. I believe this makes it a win-win experience.

If you think you can convert the certificate receiver into an ongoing client, this strategy gives you the opportunity to build a practice fairly quickly. Remember, doing a lot of free massage will increase your new client work load initially, but it ups your odds of repeat customers. And, you don't have to do it forever. If you need cash right away, this arrangement won't work because this is a long-term, profit-building process. If you want money right away, you might presell the certificates at a discount for volume to the agent. That way, you have some money and she will prequalify the prospect better since it costs her, too. Be creative, meet her needs, meet your needs, and you may never have to market again.

Real Estate Agents

Let's look at another scenario of the level five promotion strategy. Let's say you want to do stress management massage with employees of a large company that is growing quickly and hiring people in your area. Using the same key questions, ask yourself what small businesses already serve your ideal client or market when they are stressed, and think about what you can to offer those businesses to get access to their customers.

In this case, you have multiple windows of opportunity. People who sit in offices or work at computers all day often have sore necks and backs, risk carpal tunnel syndrome, and otherwise perpetually need massage. However, if they don't value massage much, don't consider massage as an option, or are so wrapped up in their work that they don't notice they hurt, they can be difficult to market to. In this case, your marketing focus needs to narrow to a smaller window of opportunity where you can identify a small business that serves this market in a shorter time frame. One time frame to consider is when there is a break in their normal routine, such as when they are moving. Their physical and emotional stress will be greater at that time, their need for massage will be higher than during their normal routine of life, and they will be dealing with a small business through which you can easily access them.

For this example, let's consider a real estate agent as our mutual marketing partner. If a large company is bringing in many new employees, it may be using a specific agency to help relocate its people. Getting access to a real estate agent gives you incredible access to all the new employees moving into your area. In this scenario, the agent already has the relocation business and needs no promotion, so what you have to offer him is either massage in exchange for his referrals, or he may promote you as a favor to you and his clients.

On the other hand, there may be an agent you would like to work with who is trying to entice prospective homebuyers to choose him over other agents, and he needs an edge over his competition. To gain him as a mutual marketing partner, go to his office and offer gift certificates that he can give to people who buy a home from him. The agent can use this angle in his advertising or promotions to slant to upscale customers, using the gift of massage to create the image that by using him, the prospective buyer will have an easy, relaxing experience during the highly emotional and volatile time of home buying. His marketing can use images of massage that gives the new home owner something to look forward to. They can imagine that after the deal closes, the boxes are moved in, and the moving truck has gone, in comes the massage therapist with a bottle of chilled champagne or some other gift, complements of the real estate agent, and massages the worn out movers.

Another less complicated or involved way to work with a real estate agent partner is to have him give to his current or prospective customers (courtesy of you) a plastic map of the local area with a star marked over your office, and a gold foil label at the bottom of the map that includes your name, address, and telephone number. New people in the area will need to learn their way around, and will probably use the map all the time. They will see your name, and be more inclined to call you to schedule an appointment. The main benefit of a map is that, unlike business cards, they are difficult to lose and are usually kept in one place such as the glove box.

Preemptive Strikes

One of the biggest benefits of working with a real estate agent is that you get first access to many new people moving into your town. In a highly competitive market, this is a preemptive strike, giving you an edge over anyone else in the area because it gives you first contact and creates a loyalty similar to imprinting on newborns. You may be their first friendly contact in a new area, creating a unique attachment and commitment. One of the major tenets of marketing is that being first in the customer's mind is crucial for success. Those who come second either have to have a better product or service, a better price, or some other unique advantage to take the customer away. And even then, people often will not switch.

Finding a Real Estate Agent

If you want to work with a real estate agent but don't know which one caters to your target market, pick up a home sales or rental magazine, look in the real estate section in your newspaper, or look at the homes or neighborhoods you think your target market is likely to be interested in. Then notice who is selling or renting the homes or apartments, and approach the agent to suggest ways of working together as mutual marketing partners.

Finding New People in Town

If you want to find new people in town but not work through a real estate agent, pick up the business section of the paper and watch for the days when new executives in the area are welcomed. Send them a 2-for-1 coupon or some other promotion, and introduce yourself. With the demise of the Welcome Wagon in many areas, it is harder to find new people in the area, but you can go to your local Chamber of Commerce for lists of new residents. This method does not give you the screening that a mutual marketing partner can offer, but if you like to be the first massage therapist they meet, this avenue is worth considering.

Welcome to Your New Home

After the stress and strain of moving, let us soothe your tired muscles with a pampering massage!

Your Name
Address
Phone

Try our 2-for-1 massage special before (expiration date) and let us welcome you to the neighborhood!

Figure 4–6 Real estate agents can refer you to new people in the community.

Hot Tub Dealer

Depending on your target market, a hot tub dealer also can be an excellent source of referrals. The concept of relaxing in a hot tub is a good association for a massage therapist and would be a natural fit for a partnership. You can promote both businesses by offering gift certificates for outcall massages for the dealer to give to buyers to go with their first soak in their brand-new backyard hot tub. Bring a complimentary basket of fresh fruit and sparkling water on ice from the hot tub company and really make an impression.

Advanced Marketing Alternatives

As massage becomes more mainstream, avenues of marketing previously unavailable are now open to us. Although we still need to establish trust and can benefit most from direct referrals, we have some alternative methods of marketing that may be a bit uncommon for massage therapists to use, but they work for other businesses and are worth considering.

Mutual marketing can be very effective in having others help you get access to their customers, but you also can be a customer resource through your own client list. Since it is inadvisable to give anyone else direct access to your clients, don't sell or give away your list. However, you can help both your partners and clients by giving indirect access to your clients through you. You control the connection so your clients are protected. And if you're a smart marketer you'll recognize your list's value.

Crossreferring Your Partners

If you really like playing marketing games, you can branch out your joint ventures in a number of directions. You can take on the role of a mutual marketer with other businesses, acting as a trusted referral service. You can make referrals for the new people in town who were referred to you by the real estate agent, and introduce them to hand-selected contractors, carpet cleaning services, pool cleaners, maid services, restaurants, and so on.

Branching out in this way can generate passive income, or if money is not part of the equation, it can build up a fortune of good will, trust, loyalty and crossreferrals back to you. As with your own partners, you can charge a referral fee, take a percentage cut or a finder's fee, get free or discounted products or services in exchange for your referrals, and so on. Believe me, no advertisement or traditional marketing can buy any of this!

For a slightly different twist, let's say there is a maid service that works in a neighborhood where you have a few clients, but you want to get more in the area. And let's say a new client from your real estate agent partner in that neighborhood comes in for a massage, and during the course of your conversation you learn your client is looking for a cleaning person. You could then tell your client about this cleaning service. Once your client has contracted with the agency, you could go in, talk with the owner, say that you referred that client and you have other clients in the neighborhood, and you would be interested in becoming a marketing partner. In this scenario, you gave the cleaning service a client first, and now, they may be willing to partner with you for access to similar caliber clients. You both serve the same neighborhood, and you help give each other qualified leads. Again, do not give anyone direct access to your clients; their privacy is tantamount. If you feel it would be risking anything, don't use this option.

In the case of the hot tub dealer, you may notice while you're outside giving the massage that they have an old deck that looks worse because the new hot tub looks so good. If one of your partners is a contractor, you can make a referral. And, now that they are out in the backyard a lot, are they going to want new landscaping? Do you have a landscaper you can refer? Of course you do because your pool cleaner partner knows one. In essence, your small promotion with the hot tub dealer now gives you the ability to get a new client, refer your partners, and benefit in multiple ways from your hard work and ingenuity. Again, your referral to the contractor or landscaper can be for a fee, as a favor, or priority service when your roof leaks one stormy night.

Is this thinking making sense? Is it exciting? Can you think of other spheres of influence or mutual marketing partners? Remember, because massage is gaining popularity and is viewed by many as a luxury or high-cost service, you can be perceived by partners as having a high-value service worth partnering with. If you bring in good leads to, say, the real estate agent, then it is appropriate you get a finder's fee. This type of passive income earning is not for the faint of heart, but if you are willing to set up the structures of paying crossreferrals, it can help save your hands and body from massage being your sole source of income. If you are concerned about charging for your valuable referrals, then just give them away for good will, but I consider this type of crossreferring ethical, and it is certainly legal. This is how the big kids play, and while it may take a sweaty palm or two in the beginning while you get used to this kind of joint venture, it can be worth your while.

Cross-selling Bonuses

If you like marketing, but some of the prior ideas are too big of a step, you can take some smaller steps to maximize the value of your client list. One way of making the most of your client list is to gather up free items, discounts on products and services, and other goodies from your partners and give them away. You can give them to your current clients or you can use them as an enticement to help potential clients make the decision to buy. In the prior example about the gym and the chimney sweep, the free gym membership is what sealed the deal for the chimney sweep. He offered a valuable cross-selling bonus that caused my friend to take timely action and choose him over his competition.

If you become good at making mutual marketing partners, you can gather some incredible bonuses to give to your clients, use for sales incentives, or to enjoy yourself. In every case, your partner benefits because you are giving access to your clients who are likely to take the bonus you give and become a regular paying customer for your partner. To gather up bonuses to give away, consider again who you are and what you like, what your ideal clients would value, and what needs of theirs you can help serve. With those in mind, think about what businesses provide that you and your clients value, and consider what they would be willing to give you to get access, albeit indirectly, to your clients.

Sample Bonuses You Can Offer to Your Clients

Buy one, get one free coupon for a restaurant

Free drink at the local juice bar

Certificate for organic wines

Coupons for lessons at a local riding stable

Subscriptions for health newsletters or magazines

Free month at a weight loss clinic

Free tune up for their bicycle

10 percent off on ski lift tickets

Free session at tanning salon

Free yoga classes

Free martial arts lesson

Free tai chi class

Consultation with nutritionist

Free herbal product, bath salts, or oils from bath and body shop

Free vitamins or discount from local health food store

$10 off on health-related book or specific title, at local bookstore

Free consultation with a homeopath, naturopath, osteopath, chiropractor, and the like (this is a more unusual direction to go, but could lead back to some crossreferrals to you).

Free first day of a . . . seminar, training, class

EXERCISE: Using Cross-selling Bonuses

■ Write down five bonuses you can gather from mutual marketing partners, either to give as gifts to your current clients or to use to market to new clients.

How to Get Cross-selling Bonuses

There are a thousand variations of cross-selling bonuses from businesses that will want your clients, and they will give you freebies or big discounts for the chance to get your clients in their doors. It is cheaper for them than advertising blindly, and if you have a strong list, the businesses you approach will be more amenable. If you are smart and determined, you can gather a load of desirable bonuses that will help get you clients. You can say something like, "I'm a massage therapist, and I have wealthy, health-conscious, active clients. I want to offer them bonuses and gifts, and make them glad they're my client. I'd like to promote your business or service to them in exchange for a discount or free introductory offer from you. Once they are in your door, you can upsell them or follow up to after-market. Since they fit your target market, I thought you'd be interested." If the person you are talking to can't see the value in what you are saying, try somewhere else or go higher up. A manager may not think this is smart, but the owner who pays the advertising bill will be thrilled.

How to Use Your Bonuses

Once you get some bonuses, you can use them in more traditional marketing pieces such as a letter to a mailing list you got from one of your partners, or you can give them to your current clients to keep them amazed at how wonderful you are. If you've lost contact with some former clients, your new bonuses can be a good excuse to get back in touch. It's better to open a letter with, "I just got a wonderful gift that I would love to share with you as my valued client," rather than just saying, "Hey, where are you?" You also can give your new bonuses to your other mutual marketing partners as "thank you" gifts, incentives to remember to refer you, and just to stay in touch.

Bonus Packages

Bonuses even can be gathered in packages among multiple partners. If you have been working with a nice restaurant and a floral shop, you can do a holiday special by offering a package containing a dinner for two, a dozen red roses, and an in-home massage. Your partners advertise the package to their customers at their place of business or through a joint mailing, and you market it to your current clients. Any expenses are shared, and you all benefit from the unique angle you have used to stand out from your competition. For a little thinking and some good communicating, you just may have gathered yourself enough clients from one project to start your whole practice. Beats putting up a business card in a gym, doesn't it?

Drawings

If you enjoyed working with the restaurant and florist, you can crossrefer in another way by offering give-away prize drawings around special occasions or holidays. If you have an office, each of you can put up a sign announcing a package or single-bonus giveaway to be drawn on a certain date. The sign can give all the contact information necessary for all the partners so in case people don't want to participate, they at least start to associate you with your partners and the image they represent. A month or so before the drawing, you can put out a bowl to hold the business cards to be drawn. If your clients don't want their name on a list or privacy is an issue, have blank cards with only their first names that can go into the mix. If one is pulled, you will know who it is. Not only do you each get a long period of free advertising and recognition but also you can follow up all of those cards with other marketing materials, if you choose.

Media Events

If you really like marketing games and want even more exposure, team up with the restaurant and florist and any other business that fits your market, and give something away to needy people over the holidays. You can make it a public event by saying that for every holiday package sold, you will donate a set amount of money to a local charity, or you can give away your own products or services. If the restaurant catered a dinner for a shelter, you can give massage to the cooking staff who is pulling together dozens of dinners, or you can massage the recipients themselves. Either way, send a press release (that's in the next chapter) to the local media and get coverage of your donations. The media love holiday stories that are unique, touching, and different from the same old stories they ran last year, and you have a great shot at television and newspaper coverage. Since massage will be the most unusual partner in the promotion, figure out how to do an on-site or hands-on demonstration for the cameras so they can get some interesting photos or footage. Your promotion will create interest and good will in your target markets, and even if a resulting story or article does not directly hit your target market, it can be great for future press releases, other promotional material, and good stories you can tell your clients.

Try It; You'll Like It

I realize that many of these marketing ideas are not yet commonplace in the massage profession, but they are strong tools that have been used successfully for years by other small businesses, and we should use them for our own success as well. Once you consider the possibility of using bonuses, cross-selling and single- or multipartner promotions, you will start to see opportunities everywhere. Now that you know how to think this way, if you are willing to get out there to try even a few of these ideas, you can build your dream practice in ways that will amaze you.

C H A P T E R 5   *Reaching Tools*

CHAPTER
OBJECTIVES

After reading this chapter, you should be able to:
- design a professional business card.
- design a professional brochure.
- describe three ways to distribute your brochures.
- create a gift certificate.
- identify uses and sources of promotional gifts.
- discuss the benefits and drawbacks of having a website.
- describe the difference between reference and action marketing tools.
- explain the key elements of an action marketing piece.
- explain the uses for postcards, letters, flyers, and surveys for reaching new clients.
- explain the benefits and methods of testing marketing products.
- write a professional press release.

Reaching New Clients

Building your dream practice requires that at some point in the process, you reach out to people with the intention of booking them as paying clients. This may sound obvious, but if you look at a lot of marketing and advertising, you'd never know what the product or service is, or what the campaign was all about. If you are going to use any marketing materials beyond a basic card, have a good purpose for them, think about how you are going to distribute them, and evaluate whether you will get a good return on your investment.

When you choose your marketing tools to reach out to others to build your practice, there are two factors that are important to consider: speed of reaching people and control of who gets your marketing message. I wish I didn't have to start what should be a basic chapter on marketing tools with a warning, but during this transition time in our profession, we still face issues of safety for practitioners, thereby forcing more controlled distribution, depending on your risk and circumstances. In addition, public misperceptions, ignorance, and lack of understanding and value for our services makes our marketing message fairly complex.

Since my goal for this book is to have you succeed in your practice, we will cover some of the safest ways to reach new clients while keeping in mind that time is of the essence for making a living with massage. What we will aim for is a balance between speed and exposure while designing marketing tools that still create trust, establish value, positively and accurately shape public perception, and motivate and guide a person to book an appointment. This will take more levels of thinking than other professionals have to deal with, but for where our field is today, it is vital that you understand the many functions your marketing materials need to serve beyond just getting your name out in the public eye. I wish that we could all work safely and easily, and just use the marketing tools and techniques available to, oh, say, plumbers, hairstylists, or even tax preparers. But many of us can't yet. Due to issues of safety and the huge variances in the Perception Continuum, we need to be a bit more clever and savvy in how we reach out and what we say to people with our marketing tools.

Marketing tools have one primary purpose: leverage. Marketing tools give you the opportunity to reach new clients more effectively in person, and to reach more clients without having to be physically present. The more risk you face with exposure, the fewer marketing tools you will be able to use, the more tightly you must control your marketing distribution, the more you must be present to reach others, and the more time it will take to build a practice. Every factor of risk must be weighed for the cost of time and money in building your practice. I have a practice where I go to my clients' homes and work out of my own home. My risk is very high if my marketing gets into the wrong hands. Because of this, I choose not to use marketing that reaches large yet anonymous groups of people quickly, so building a practice is a slower process. On the other side of this equation, though, I spend nothing on office rent, and saving that monthly expense is financially more valuable to me than large or rapid market exposure.

The other risk that therapists face is working without all the necessary pieces of paper, especially a local business license. Unfortunately, this is still a difficult, unpleasant, expensive, and sometimes almost impossible process for many qualified practitioners in our profession. The marketing drawback to not having your pieces of paper is that faster and broader exposure through marketing tools and media become risky and inadvisable, and you lose leverage in reaching your market. If you need to pay a few hundred dollars for the Continuing Education Units needed to maintain your state license, or need to bite the bullet and go through that annoying vice squad check-up process, then do so; it will give you the freedom to market yourself more fully, and will more than pay for itself because you are able to reach more people.

Basically, the less you have to protect yourself, the more you can have other people, media, and written materials speak for you. The more leverage you have through mutual marketing partners and marketing tools, the more quickly and easily you can build your practice. Also, the less you have to protect yourself, the more types of marketing tools you can use, with materials ranging from powerful business cards and informative brochures to complex, multibusiness partnering projects with television ads, large promotional events, and mass mailings.

Written Reaching Tools

Among your best options for marketing materials are written tools, which for most therapists are your safest leverage for the least amount of money with the highest potential of return on your investment. Written marketing tools can be broken down into two categories. I call the first category Reference Marketing Tools. These are passive marketing materials that educate potential clients, enhance their perception of you and massage, create a compelling reason to use your services, and give contact information. Reference marketing tools include business cards and brochures, or educational pieces that go along with gift certificates.

I call the second category of written materials Action Marketing Tools. These are proactive documents that inform the reader about you and your services. But they go an important step further by giving the reader a specific action to take, usually right away. Action marketing tools can include a package of a letter, brochure, and special offer coupon to mailing lists; table tent cards; pads of tear-off page information cards; time-limited coupons in a multibusiness booklet; or classified ads in the publications your ideal clients are likely to read. I encourage you to look at direct response ads such as direct mail, infomercials, coupon books, and other marketing pieces you see around you on a daily basis. If you like them, look at what they include, especially if you've seen them before, because if they have been around a while, they are probably working. Muscle marketing gives you more speed and direct control in building your dream practice, and in order to reach new clients in as many ways as possible, consider the following written reaching tools.

Reference Marketing Tools

Business cards

Brochures

Massage menus

Gift certificates

Promotional gifts

Resumes

Articles

Website

Action Marketing Tools

Coupons

Direct mail—letters, postcards, surveys

Flyers

Business reply cards

Table tents

Business proposals

Both

Ads—Telephone book, newspapers, magazines

Press releases

Signs

Creating any written marketing piece means thinking about, crafting, and pulling together a variety of elements that can be mixed and matched, depending on your needs, your budget, the amount of space you have, and the purpose of the tool. Whether you are writing a six-panel brochure, creating a folded business card, or designing a quarter-page magazine ad, you will want an image and message that is attractive to your market, and tells the reader what they need to know to take a next step in becoming your client. In this next section, we will cover the Muscle Marketing business card and the key elements of written reference and action marketing tools.

The Muscle Marketing Business Card

The Bare Bones business card from the first section of the book included just your name, title, and contact number. A simple card can work well if you are talking to many people yourself and simply handing it out in person. However, when your card is distributed by others, posted in public places, or received as part of a package mailer, it is helpful to have a stronger graphic presentation that represents you and your services in your stead.

A good business card uses graphics, print fonts, color, white space, and well-crafted words to portray an image of you that is appealing to your ideal clients. Bold colors and robust shapes give a feel much different from pale pastels and curlicues, and it will take some thinking and probably some expert advice to create an impression that suits your style while appealing to your market. Logos, photos, type of paper, and layout all affect your professional image, and need to be chosen to create trust and value and shape the perception of the person who sees it.

I remember going to a meeting of professional public speakers and exchanging cards with a group of colleagues. Professional speakers can command very high fees, but I was struck by one woman in our group who wanted to break into a higher speaking bracket. Her cards were printed on her home computer's dot-matrix printer on flimsy paper. Her graphic representation was incongruent with the impression she was trying to create, and if I were a large company looking to pay $10,000 for a convention speaker, I would take one look at that homemade card and assume she wasn't up to the task. She may have prided herself in printing her own cards, but they were so unprofessional that they were a detriment to her business. If you are going to make one financial investment into your marketing, put it toward your business card. You will be judged by it, and it will affect what people think of you and are willing to pay you.

Go to a graphic artist or high-quality print shop for the details that are too numerous to cover here, but consider these points before you go in. Business cards are what people use to find your information to contact you, so make your card easy to keep and easy to see. Avoid cards that are oversized because they are hard to store in wallets or card holders, and usually end up getting thrown out. Many graphic artists are really frustrated fine artists, and while they may want to make a marvelous piece of avant garde art for you or want some wild symbolic logo on your card, remind them that you need a practical card, not an oddity or an art piece.

Business cards can contain many elements and be laid out in numerous ways. Some options are:

Text
Your name
Title (remember, you can make it up!)

Monica Roseberry
Speaker/Author

Outstanding Room Only
xxxx
Walnut Creek, CA 94596
800-707-3462

monica@marketingmassage.com
www.marketingmassage.com

| *Figure 5–1* | To help people remember you, use your photograph. |

Office or work number

Home number (get a second line if you need to)

Voice mail number

Toll-free number

Cellular phone number

Pager number

E-mail address

Street address (only if it's safe)

Business name

Slogan

Massage menu

Website address

Fill-in appointment times

Graphic Elements

Map to your office or location

Logo

Photo

Use of color for background, print, and graphics

Choice of fonts (type faces or styles)

Amount of white space

Paper—weight, texture, finish

Layout

Printed on one or both sides

Folded

Printed lengthwise or widthwise

The Elements of a Business Card and Other Written Tools

In the process of creating a business card, you will design and decide on many of the elements that also can go into any other written marketing tools. Therefore, let's take a close look at some of the primary elements of your card. In the first section of the book, we talked about your name, title, and access numbers, and how to handle having a business telephone in your home if you work at home or do outcall massage.

Beyond the access information are some other options to consider.

Your Business Name

A business name is fun to create. It can lend an air of credibility, professional stature, and give a creative way to tell about your special work. A business name is not required for our profession, but if you are going to use one, be careful. First, you have to make up one that will represent your business accurately while appealing to your target market. Second, you have to make sure no one has already registered, trademarked, or service-marked the name. Before you spend money to have cards made, research online and at your county business registry to see if the name you want is already taken. If it's not taken locally, then file for a fictitious business name with your county. Look in the front of your telephone book in the County Government Offices section under fictitious business names (FBN) for further help. If you want to open a business bank account, have checks made, and so on, you will need an FBN document proving that you have paid for the name and have listed it in a local newspaper. When your name goes into the paper, it gives other businesses the time

| Figure 5-2 My card from 1984. | Figure 5-3 Use both sides. |

and right to challenge you on using a name they may already be using. Don't print anything until the whole filing process is over. You'd be surprised how many people claim they are the first to use "In Touch" and other such names. Again, a business name is not necessary, but if you want one, go through the legal process before you print your cards or any other materials.

Your Graphic Representation

Having traveled this country with the intention of meeting massage professionals, I can tell you right now that if I see another business card with a pair of hands on it, I'm likely to scream. I'm just kidding; I've seen beautiful cards with wonderful logos, whether or not they were of hands. But the question is, how does the logo help your business? My personal opinion is that logos for business cards and printed matter are nice, but they won't help your business much. Since you are selling a service, what you are really selling is you, and the best graphic representation you can have is a high-quality photograph of you in either a headshot or an action shot. The photo can be used as the whole background of the card with the words superimposed, or as a distinct stand-alone element.

I no longer expect that people will remember my name or much about me after I have given them my card. I have had marvelous conversations with people and even written things on the back of their cards such as "Kate's party" or a date, but months later, the details have slipped my mind and I wonder why I kept the card in my desk. What people will remember most is a face, and if you are going to use an image, use one that will be hard to forget. When I set out on my crosscountry research trip, I made a new set of cards with my cell phone number and chose a new photo for it. I had an image in mind of being seen as friendly, fun, casual, a traveler, and someone approachable, so I chose a full-body photo taken on a vacation that gave the relaxed yet professional feel I wanted. My card stands out in any pile of papers. The photo reminds people instantly of who I am and I am proud to give them out. I took the photo and my contact information down to a large office supply store, selected a font, talked with the clerk about the layout, and for $90 they put together the text and photo, and printed them. Even nice cards don't have to be a big hassle or expense.

If you are going to use a photo and have a professional photographer take it, be careful in the image you want to convey. I was handed a card by a massage therapist who had gone to one of the "glamour" portrait franchises for her business card photo. While the picture was pretty, she had been doused in so much makeup and tarted up so much that the photo was inappropriately seductive. In addition, she never looked that way in "normal" life, giving a feeling of incongruency to those who met her and compared the photo to how she currently looked.

Whatever logo or image you use, have it represent you well, be consistent with it, put it on all of your written materials, and get people to become familiar with it. Repetition is important in establishing your business identity, so choose one image and stick with it.

Your Slogan

If you are going to do a lot of mass media marketing, you might consider using a slogan along with your image. Phrases such as the Army's "Be all that you can be" or Motel 6's "We'll leave the light on for you" are catchy, stick in people's minds, and give the audience a feeling or impression. If you want a slogan, there are two ways to approach creating one. You can pick a specific market or client profile you want to work with, consider the needs that market has, and address those needs directly or indirectly. If your market is comprised of people who are lonely, in pain, need to relax, or stressed, you can use phrases such as, Always There for You; Your Weekly Vacation; Touch You Can Trust, and so on. You also can create a slogan by thinking about who you are and what you want to offer. Choose a slogan that represents you and your work, and the people who see it who want what you offer will become your market.

Personally, I am not a big fan of slogans for massage therapists. Unless you are highly specialized and have a narrow target market, you may choose a slogan that inadvertently might turn away potential clients who see your materials but think you won't be right for them. For example, you may decide on a sporty theme, slogan, and look for your marketing tools, but even if you are willing to have elderly widows as clients, your marketing tools likely will turn them away since they don't have sporty needs. In addition to the risk of shutting off various markets, your slogan may be misinterpreted by people who are at different levels on the Perception Continuum. My suggestion is either to create a professional but generic image for general marketing, or to have multiple cards and marketing tools specific to your various markets, and distribute them with controlled dissemination. If you are like most therapists who need to appeal to multiple target and "flanker" (or side) markets for enough people to fill your practice, be careful that your slogan does not close doors on viable clients.

Massage Menu

If you will be handing out your business card personally, what is on it can spark questions and conversation that can give you an easy opening to tell more about yourself and your work. Having a massage menu on your card that lists the kinds of work you do can give you the chance to talk clearly about your services, whether you hand out your card or someone calls who got your card elsewhere. Offering multiple options shows that you know how to do more than one rote routine, educates others that there is more to massage than their one preconceived notion, and gives more options to say yes to. If you want to list more than two or three modalities, print them on the back of your card, otherwise your text becomes too small to read and looks too crowded together.

While I highly recommend having a massage menu, keep in mind that one of the marketing mistakes that massage professionals make is believing that the general public has awareness of and value for their particular massage modality and specialty. Of the some six billion people on this planet, the vast majority of them have no understanding of different bodywork styles. It can cost you clients if you think people will want to book an appointment for a session of a bodywork modality that you have spent thousands of dollars studying when they have never heard of it. If you are going to list your specialties, you can put down specific bodywork modalities, but be prepared to explain them. Since education is one of the most important forms of marketing you can do, a menu gives you the opening to do so. If you have to choose between a snappy but meaningless logo and a menu, go for the menu.

Finally, the more informally you market, or the more risk you face, the more important your card becomes. If you were to have only one tool, consider a folding card that can include many educational elements in a small but keepable size. It can act as a mini-brochure to be given out in any setting. Somehow, handing out brochures at a friend's party seems a bit gauche, but handing out cards is acceptable protocol. As with any marketing tool, the more you have distributed, the better your leverage is for building your practice. Remember, most successful therapists I have interviewed only used a card to build their practices, so give this tool the respect it is due.

Brochures

A brochure is a common staple for most small businesses and can be an effective tool for building your practice. Brochures can educate your clients about your services, further develop your business image, say things about you that you wouldn't say yourself, and give an air of professionalism to your practice. Even if a brochure won't necessarily close a deal or convince someone to buy your services, having them around can create a feeling of trust in you. However, before you decide to spend the time and money on a brochure, consider first how you will distribute them. Where and how you will distribute your brochures will determine its content, so let's consider a few possible uses for this marketing tool.

Ways to Use Your Brochure

Distributed by you directly to a new prospect

> Give out at promotional events—health fairs, expos, partner projects

> Give out at speaking engagements—demonstrations, classes, seminars

Distributed directly by those who know you

> Include with gift certificates—given by clients, family, friends, marketing partners

> Give to mutual marketing partners to distribute at place of business

> Have in massage room for clients to pick up and give to personal referrals

> Give out at networking meetings

Distributed indirectly

> Mail to mutual marketers list along with letter

> Put out in public places

Depending on where your brochures are distributed, they either will be picked up by someone who has no other concept of you, or you or someone else will broaden the receiver's view of you by speaking further on your behalf. If most of your brochures will be given out by you or those who know you, the factor of trust is much easier to establish. This lets you focus your brochure's content on establishing your value and leading the reader to the decision to buy from you.

In this kind of scenario, imagine that one of your friends or clients hands over your brochure to a friend and says, "She's great! You have to get a massage from her!" The friend looks down at your brochure, opens her mind to the possibility of getting a massage because of the strong recommendation, and then starts to do a quick once-over of the page. How does your brochure need to look to make her want to read it thoroughly, and what can you say about yourself and your work that will convince her to call you?

Designing Your Brochure

More space on a brochure may tempt you to load in many more elements than your business card, but resist. Your brochure's primary purpose is not to tell your whole story but to act as an engaging introduction to get the reader to the next step of the buying process; to contact you. Just as a resume is designed to create enough interest to get to the interview stage, your brochure needs to capture the reader's imagination with enough information to go forward but without bogging down in too many details. As with your business card, you can consider the following factors to include in your brochure, along with a few new elements.

Contact Information

    Name

    Title

    Telephone numbers

    E-mail address

    Street address

    Business name

    Website address

Marketing Message

    Slogan

    Headline

    Services—massage menu, description of modalities, special offerings

    Benefits

    Testimonials

Graphic Elements

    Map to your office or location

    Logo

    Photo

    Illustrations—charts, graphs, anatomical illustrations

    Use of color for background, print, and graphics

    Choice of fonts—variety, print size, bullet points

    Amount of white space

    Paper—weight, texture, finish

Layout

    Size—page size, number of panels, panel size

The Look of Your Brochure

Playing a song on a piano requires that you play notes in a particular order. What makes those notes sound beautiful or chaotic is the amount of space left in between the notes, and it is the silences in the piece that create the flow, emotion, and movement of the song. Run all the notes together and you have noise; separate them too far apart and the song is lost. Laying out your brochure follows the same rules of music. The printed elements have movement and flow because of the empty space around them, and the placement of the words and artwork gives the piece a visual rhythm.

If you want some ideas for your brochure's "look," go to the bookstore and look at the magazines that your target market is likely to read. Look at the advertisements and see what advertisers to your market have done to draw in the reader. Notice the amount of empty space, the placement of elements, the imagery used, and pay attention to which ads capture your eye. Even though ads are used more to invoke feelings and use more imagery than a brochure might, you can learn a lot about choosing the look of your brochure from them. Whether you have a sheet of colored paper photocopied and folded, or an 11 X 17 glossy fold-out with gorgeous photographs, consider your business image and your target market's preferences before you choose your look.

Creating Your Marketing Message

Beyond the elements that we covered with the business card, brochures give us room for more text that can be used to inform your potential clients about how and why they should book with you. While there are as many different client types as there are people, it is helpful to understand that there are different words that reach certain segments of your market more effectively. When people are reading your words, they are basically making buying decisions, and there are three common frames of reference from which they make their decisions.

A "people person" typically makes buying decisions based on what other people will think and they have a high need for external approval. These are the "me too" kind of buyers who will jump on the nearest bandwagon, fashion, or trend. One way to think about marketing to these people is to think about what they wish they had when they were in high school. They wanted to be popular, to be liked, to be in the in-crowd, and to belong. Many of their buying decisions today are based on trying to get what they never got in high school. For these "me tooers," feeling connected and trusting is important. They search for chemistry and a relationship based on mutual good feelings. Your words need to let these buyers know that you are accepting and welcoming, yet exclusive. You may offer them the opening to belong to your small group of clients or even to your personal mission.

Another type of buyer is the "scientist." These people make many of their buying decisions on an unconscious, emotional basis but consciously, they want to understand logical rationales to back up their decisions. While "people persons" usually work in service jobs, the "scientists" usually work with things. As our profession conducts research and studies on the benefits and efficacy of massage, we gather the evidence that these people need to consider including massage in their lives. If your primary market is made up of "scientists," your marketing will need to address their desire for rational, logical data before they choose to get massage from you. Your words need to be concrete, specific, and results-oriented. Even your graphics can be scientific with official-looking charts and graphs, or anatomical illustrations.

A third type of buyer is the WIIFM buyer. Their buying decisions are based on the "what's in it for me?" principle. Control of any situation is important for them, and often, they are entrepreneurs. They don't care about what other people think of them, and scientific data isn't that important to them. What matters is what you and your massage can do for them. Pay careful attention to the benefits and advantages that you offer WIIFM buyers because this is what they care about. If you work with a lot of entrepreneurs, choose words that will convey clearly how much you can do for them.

If you know what type of buyer your ideal client is, you can use slogans, words, graphics, and other elements in your brochure to engage that personality type. If you don't know what draws your target market, cover your bases by either being generic in your brochure or appealing to all three types in the different panels or pages.

Besides having different ways of making buying decisions, your brochure readers are on different levels of the Perception Continuum. Within the continuum are two overall stages that affect whether your words speak to the questions and concerns in their minds. One stage is known as "product acceptance," wherein the reader is in the lower levels of the continuum, and needs to be educated about massage, and its value and benefits before even considering booking with you. The second stage is called "brand recognition," wherein your readers want a massage, but they don't know or trust you personally. In this case, your brochure needs to give the details about you and your massage skills so they can decide whether or not they will choose you over your competition.

Mixing these factors together, you can figure out what you need to say to convince your readers to call or book an appointment. If you are not sure which category your prospects fall into, use the space allotted in your brochure to appeal to all three categories and buying stages. One paragraph can emphasize the growing popularity of massage; another can emphasize that massage has been around for centuries and its methods are tried-and-true; and a third can emphasize to the WIIFM buyers that they can design the session according to their needs. Introduce the value, benefits, and descriptions of your massage to the uninitiated, and introduce yourself almost as if writing a resume so that the readers can become familiar with you and choose you as their massage therapist.

Answering the Unspoken, Frequently Asked Questions (FAQS)

Besides taking into consideration the buyer types and stages of acceptance for choosing your words, you also may consider using your brochure to answer questions that your prospective clients may have. Questions I have heard range from, "Do I have to take off all my clothes?" to "Are you going to turn me black and blue like that person up at the mud baths did?" After hearing many questions over the span of my practice, I still am surprised at some of the misperceptions people have about massage, and what interesting fears they have. For example, a common fear I have heard in various forms is that the person is afraid of becoming "hooked" on massage and will become, in essence, a junky to an expensive addiction.

I also have learned never to assume that a prospective client has the slightest idea about what to expect from his or her first session. In the first year of my practice, I would leave the room while my client got on the table, and I would come back to find people lying down on the table fully clothed, lying buck-naked on top of the blanket, or lying face up with the back of their head falling through the face-rest hole. I learned quickly that I could not assume anything about what people know about getting a massage.

There are many people out there who would like to try a massage, but they have many unspoken questions that prevent them from ever trying one. If you can identify and answer their unspoken questions and fears in your marketing material, you are more likely to be seeing them soon as your clients.

Common FAQS
Trust Questions

> Do I have to get undressed?
>
> Is this therapist safe?
>
> Does massage hurt?
>
> Will I be too relaxed?
>
> What if I get "hooked" on massage?

Value Questions

> Is this worth my time and money?
>
> What can I expect for this fee?
>
> What if I don't like their work?
>
> Will this fix my problems?
>
> How long do the benefits last?

Convenience Questions

> Is this going to be worth the hassle?
>
> How much time is this going to take?
>
> How frequently do I have to get massage for it to do any good?
>
> If I'm oily, will that ruin my clothes?

Establishing Your Benefits and Advantages

As you look at the prior questions, one way to answer them is to give information that tells about the many benefits you offer. Even if you don't answer every question, if you give your brochure reader really good reasons to come see you, they at least can make the decision to talk to you personally, or to book an appointment and get the rest of their questions answered later. Massage professionals can offer many benefits, and we can distinguish ourselves from other therapists and services with unique advantages that will help convince the reader to get a massage, and get it from you. Consider these possible categories of advantages as enticements for your brochure reader.

> Your background, training, experience, specialties, massage modalities
>
> The advantages you offer that are different from your competition's
>
> The benefits your clients will gain by seeing you
>
> The problems your clients will avoid by getting regular massage from you
>
> Your unique character and gifts

More specifically, the benefits and advantages you list in your brochure may include some or all of the following points.

> 1. You cost less than . . .
> 2. You cost more, but here's why . . .
> 3. You have a higher quality of . . .
> 4. You offer more customer service
> 5. You offer education with your service

6. You offer a 100 percent money-back guarantee.

7. You offer bonuses.

8. You give long sessions.

9. You offer more choice, selection, and options (width).

10. You specialize in a particular area or illness such as carpal tunnel, fibromyalgia, sports injuries, and neck pain (depth).

11. You specialize in and incorporate a nonmassage skill (hypnotherapy, hot tub, spa treatments, isolation tank, crystal work, light therapy, shamanic trance work, sweats, stress management, and more).

12. You have a specialized background such as you used to be a nurse, physical therapist, athlete, or counselor.

13. You can relate to and accept people who are overweight, clean and sober, survivors, or phobic with an I've been there, I know approach.

14. You do outcall.

15. Your location is easy to find with lots of parking.

16. You work more hours, late hours, early hours, and weekends.

17. You offer a full list of referrals to other service providers for a particular specialty or need.

18. You cater to a specific group and draw on your interests or background to service the frail and elderly, active and elderly, children with diseases, people with AIDS, executives, women in menopause, entrepreneurs, telecommuters, infants, soccer moms, golfers, tennis players, and so on.

19. You have worked with famous people.

20. You arrive on time.

21. You reverse the limitations of aging.

22. You change how people feel or you effect some kind of change.

23. You are Nationally Certified, AMTA, ABMP member, licensed, 1000-hour grad, and the like.

24. You have a bodywork specialty.

25. You promise performance enhancement of different types.

Your Services

Educating your reader about your different services continues to give them valuable information about why they should book with you. You can use your brochure to tell people about how your massage is applied, what each modality is designed to do, what results can be expected from each service, and how your services can be combined in various ways. The massage menu from your business card can be expanded to tell more about the value and application of aromatherapy, Reiki, reflexology, deep tissue, acupressure, spa treatments, assisted stretching, postural assessment or whatever else you offer.

Testimonials

Somewhere along the line of establishing your value in other's minds, there comes a place where you risk having your marketing sound unpleasantly like bragging. While clients want the best there is, we have a weird cultural rule that tooting your own horn too loudly is not a good thing. We love athletes who break records and wow crowds, but too much hot air, taunting, or arrogance and we turn our backs. To be able to go further in telling about your benefits and expertise without turning people off, use an age-old marketing tool, the testimonial. Having other people say nice things about you is totally acceptable, and readers usually are more inclined to believe a claim if a group of strangers make positive statements agreeing with the claim. You can get testimonials from current clients, family, friends, fellow massage students, colleagues, or anyone to whom you give massage.

Photographs or Illustrations

When a person first looks at your brochure, what is most eye-catching is usually the artwork. What people see in your photographs, drawings, and illustrations can intrigue them enough to read further or to put your brochure down. Your artwork needs to capture and maintain interest, tell about you and your work, establish your image, and help build trust in you. Gaining trust may or may not be difficult given your target market, but understanding how to build trust with images is important. One of the tenets of marketing is what is called the Law of Familiarity. The gist of this law is that people trust what is familiar to them and distrust what is unfamiliar. The most common perception of massage is what people see in advertising for resorts, hotels, and other products or services that use massage to associate the product to being part of the good life. I have seen television ads that use the image of massage to sell candy, trucks, auto financing, and pizza. Typically, the image of massage is either of a person lying on a table receiving some form of work that looks like traditional Swedish or the person is getting seated massage.

Your modality or specialty may be quite different in intention and application from Swedish, but since the law of familiarity states that people buy what is familiar, you might consider using a photograph or illustration of yourself working with a Swedish-style application, or using a nonaction photo. If you are selling to an uneducated market, it becomes even more important to use images that they are already familiar with and probably have good feelings about. Once your brochure reader has made contact with you to learn more about your work, you can further educate about your specialty where the law of familiarity is less critical. In my experience, I have found that most of us are marketing to prospects who are still in the product acceptance stage. If the image you are portraying is too far off from their limited perception, they won't make the leap to becoming your client.

If you are marketing to a more educated buyer who knows about different types of massage, then you may choose imagery that emphasizes your differences from other more common massages. Being different, exotic, or artistic can be important when you face a great deal of competition and your market is in the latter part of the brand recognition stage. This is when people become the bored "been-there, done-that" buyers, and they want something exciting and new to try, and to tell their friends about. Currently, there are very few people who are in this tried-it-all, now-what category, so unless you are working directly with many clients very experienced in receiving many types of massage, stick with the familiar to build that all-important trust.

Producing a Brochure

Brochures can range from simple and inexpensive information pieces to elaborate, graphically stunning works of art. If you are on a tight budget, you can create and print a brochure on your home computer using a simple graphic layout program and beautiful preprinted paper stock. Or you can trade massage with a graphic designer and printer to get a beautiful end product. You can even buy preprinted brochures made by others for massage professionals if they appeal to your target market. If you are tempted to cut corners on a brochure, it may be better that you don't have one at all. A poorly designed and unattractive brochure with misspellings and bad grammar actually can drive away business just as a good-looking and informative brochure can help create business. Your talent and abilities as a massage professional are judged by your representation on a piece of paper, and if you can't afford a quality representation, stick with your cards and direct contacts until you can make a brochure worthy of your practice. Think of your brochure as an investment. It may cost you money up front, but it can pay for itself quickly and has the potential for creating profit well beyond what it initially cost. Your brochure can be a valuable form of leverage, so take the time to do it right.

Gift Certificates

Gift certificates are powerful muscle marketing tools. Unlike other pieces of paper you use to market, gift certificates have real value in the mind of the holder, and they are not likely to be lost, misplaced, or thrown away. Getting gift certificates into your prospective clients hands can be done quickly through your mutual marketing partners if you are in a fast building phase, or you can get them out more slowly through direct sales. Gift certificates can come in many shapes and sizes, but they need a few elements for them to work well. Since the odds are good that some of them will be mailed to gift recipients, have your printer create pieces that can fit inside a standard size greeting card, or create an envelope and certificate package that the gift-giver would be proud to send. You can buy a box of nice envelopes, measure one, and have your printer set your insert paper size to fit inside.

I recommend that you use your gift certificate as an educational piece. If the receiver is dubious about getting massage, you would be smart to print some of your other marketing elements on the back of the certificate to coax them to call to set up an appointment. While some people unscrupulously have exploited this knowledge and sold certificates knowing they won't be used, it is a shortsighted view of how to make a living with massage. Solid practices are built by happy clients returning and referring others, and the more people who come in to get a massage from you, the faster you can rebook them. Due to abuses of gift certificates, it is now illegal in many places to put expiration dates on them, and scams that involved selling certificates with fast expirations are not only unethical but also illegal in a growing number of states.

Your certificate needs to include these subject lines.

A Gift of (whatever you have sold: a one-hour massage, a hot stone treatment, or the like.)

From

To

Your name

Your contact information

The date (optional)

A GIFT OF MASSAGE

TO: _____ Jane Doe _____

FOR: _____ A one-hour aromatherapy massage _____

WITH: _____ Your name, Title _____

FROM: _____ John Doe _____

DATE: _____ February 14 _____

Your Business Name
123 Main Street, #22
Anywhere, USA
800-555-1212

For an extra bonus of 20 minutes, please book by:
Date: <u>March 22</u>

Figure 5–4   Gift certificates can be a powerful tool for building a practice.

Beyond that, you can include any of the elements from your other marketing pieces to get recipients to call. If it is illegal in your area to use an expiration date, entice the gift certificate recipient to call quickly by offering a special incentive if they book by a certain date. You can give away extra time, a promotional gift, or a product or service from one of your mutual marketing partners. If your certificate is being given out by one of your partners, or through a promotional ad or coupon, put a code on the certificate so that you know which of your marketing ventures are worth your time and effort.

As we talked about in the client net worth section, reaching new clients with discounted or give-away gift certificates can be one of the fastest, least expensive, and most effective forms of marketing you can do. Gift certificates remove the whole issue of the decision to buy, and let you prove your value and create trust the best way possible: by putting your hands on your new client.

Promotional Gifts

Reaching new clients through the printed word does not have to be limited to a paper medium. Muscle marketing is designed to get you into people's awareness, and to give them reasons and ways to contact you. Since paper can be easy to lose or throw away, having your name and contact information on novelty items or gifts greatly increases your odds that someone will be able to find your telephone number when they realize months after meeting you that buying a gift certificate for a coworker would be the perfect gift. Surprise, your number is on the coffee mug that this guy picked up at a health fair booth where he met you, and your contact information is right there in his kitchen cupboard. Cost of mug: negligible. Value to you: the price of one massage, and the ability to rebook and gain referrals from your new client. Now that's a good return on your investment!

Depending on your target market and what's appropriate, you can give out sample bottles of massage oil with your label on it, bath beads or soaps in a container with your name on it, candles, incense, crystals, meditation books, inflatable travel neck pillows, those plastic maps you gave to the real estate agent, coffee mugs, golf visors, massage tools, or anything else that when people look at it everyday, they think of you. Of course, if you have a mutual marketing partner with products that you can put your name and number on and give away, you have the opportunity to crosspromote both of you.

Small Promotional Items

If bigger gifts cost more than you can afford in the beginning, use pens, bookmarks, restaurant tip cards, laminated reflexology cards, preprinted sticky notes, memo pads, coasters, jar openers, key fobs, golf tees, and other promotional items. If these promotional items mean you get a new client, book one additional massage, or create a referral because your client had your telephone number handy, these freebies more than pay for themselves. You can find companies that specialize in promotional items by looking in the Yellow Pages under Advertising Specialties. Visit their stores or get their catalogs, and let your mind run wild with great ways of keeping yourself at the forefront of your prospects' or clients' minds.

The Walking, Talking Billboard

With the growing acceptance of massage across the country, many people are poised between the stage of wanting to get a massage but not knowing who to get one from. Of all the ways you can get yourself recognized by those looking for you, wearing clothing that indicates you do massage can be one of your most effective forms of marketing. You can design your own T-shirt, polo shirt, denim long-sleeve shirt, baseball cap, tote bag, or other wearable item that can lead to seemingly miraculous and coincidental moments when people ask you if you do massage. Even if you buy predesigned shirts from massage product companies, use this inexpensive and fun form of marketing. You can introduce yourself in any setting with your wearable message, and for goodness sakes, have your cards with you for those who want to follow up.

Resumes

Reference marketing tools sometimes only have an audience or target market of one. If you want to cultivate relationships with massage colleagues, medical and health practitioners, joint venture partners, or other individuals who can be a valid source of referrals, it may be appropriate for you to give them your professional resume or curriculum vitae. If you want to teach a class, speak for a group, get a booth at a health fair, or otherwise need to show your massage background, you most likely will need a resume as part of the package you submit. Writing a resume takes thought and effort, but having a good resume in reserve means you can get it out quickly when opportunities come your way. Many books cover the details of writing a resume, and if you are planning to get a massage job in addition to or preparation for a private practice, definitely get a book or professional resume writer to help you.

Website

A website about your business on the Internet can be a good form of marketing, or it can be pretty tepid. The first drawback is that while the Internet is highly touted for its many benefits, it is frequently used for pornography and you must make your website very clear that the type of massage you are advertising is nonsexual. If you want to give out a telephone number for people to reach you who have visited your website, I strongly suggest that you get a voice mail number to screen your potential clientele. A number of my colleagues who have Yellow Pages ads that say "professional therapeutic massage—nonsexual only" still get harassing calls, so I make the assumptive leap that if callers can't get it that an ad actually says what it means in the Yellow Pages, they probably won't pay attention to what you say on your website either.

The second drawback to a website is that it is a fairly passive marketing tool for reaching new clients. It is great for having current clients or partners use as a reference to tell their referrals more about you, but it is not usually an active marketing tool. In other words, don't think that just because you put up a website you will get tons of new customers. Anyone doing a blind search for a new massage therapist on the Internet will have to wade through numerous porn sites, and if trust is an issue, it will be very hard to convey your professionalism when your site comes up sandwiched in between Lovely Girls Massage and sex toys. It is unfortunate, and it makes the Internet a somewhat inhospitable place for advertising a practice.

That said, if you choose to have a website, you can use it more for the rebooking and referral stages of marketing. All of the elements that go into your brochure and resume can go on your site in an expanded version since page space is not an issue. You can include your massage menu, information about yourself and your background or training, information about your work, client testimonials, more photos, and links to your marketing partners' sites. Then, when you give out your card at a party, you can point out that anything else they want to know about you is on your website, which is easy since your URL is printed on your card. In addition to your card, brochure, gift certificate, or promotional gift, having a website gives another air of legitimacy and lets people research you if they want further evidence of your value and trustworthiness.

For the rebooking function, your website can have an on-screen calendar with time slots open for appointments that lets your current clients book with you online. Your client can see what's open, request a time slot by means of e-mail, and get a response back as often as you check your site. You can answer at any time of day without waking clients up with a telephone call, especially if you respond at two in the morning. I know a number of massage therapists who maintain practices in multiple cities, and having a website where people could book appointments instead of making long-distance telephone calls would be quite handy.

For a more interactive website, you can have viewers sign up for an electronic newsletter, leave information on how you can reach them to talk to them in person, or fill in an electronic survey of their opinions and preferences about what kind of massage benefits they are looking for. They can take a guided photo tour of your office, watch a video of you working, listen to audio or video testimonials, study an anatomy lesson about how massage affects muscles or relieves pain, or anything else you can think of that would engage your web visitors and convince them they should call you for an appointment.

Action Marketing Tools

Reaching out to new clients is, for most therapists, a fairly well-controlled process. Giving out reference tools such as cards, brochures, gift certificates, and promotional items is done primarily by you or those who know you. These are your safest tools to use to build your practice and may be all the tools you need. Reference tools remind people of you and give them direct access to reaching you, but they have some drawbacks if time is of the essence for you. The first drawback is that they can take more time for you to disseminate. The second is that they provide little or no incentive for the recipient to make the buying decision faster. To leap these two tall buildings in a single bound, we can employ, ta da, Action Marketing Tools! Action tools are various forms of marketing that are distributed rapidly to larger groups of people through more traditional means such as direct mail, and they include time limitations, and often, a bonus or discount for responding in that time period.

Just as in the story of my friend who wanted to clean her chimney, she didn't get around to it until she got a coupon in the mail that offered her a free month's gym membership if she used the chimneysweep service by a certain date, so, too, can you spur prospects to take immediate action to book with you. The purpose of action marketing is to get a potential client to take some form of action when seeing your marketing tool. That action can be to call a telephone number for a free gift, schedule a free consultation, book an appointment, write in for a coupon, come by your office, or pick up a gift certificate from one of the places you are holding a promotional.

If your target market is in the product acceptance stage, the action they feel most comfortable taking would be to learn about the value of massage. It may take you a number of small, safe steps to educate them before they are ready to book. If most of your target market already accepts massage and is simply looking for a trustworthy practitioner, you can skip some of the small wooing steps and be more direct in your approach toward the goal of booking your first appointment.

Types of Action Marketing

Numerous ways exist to reach your market with some form of action marketing. Simple flyers can be posted in select locations with tear-off telephone numbers on the bottom; postcards can be sent to a large number of people on a rented mailing list; or elaborate, multipage promotional kits can be sent to a select group of people referred by a marketing partner. Regardless of the cost, length, or sophistication of your marketing materials, there are some basic elements that should be included in every marketing piece. These include the headline, body copy, call to action, and closing.

Headline

The first part of any action piece is your headline. This is what draws readers in and convinces them to read further. A weak headline means your piece gets filed in the round file while a strong headline captures enough interest to have your offer considered. Your headline must convey a powerful, self-serving, desirable benefit for your reader. It can focus on what the person wants, doesn't want, or wants to avoid. It can motivate the reader to action with the promise of pleasure, the easing of pain, or both. It should be educational and promise information that will lead to a result they want, and if they continue to read, there will be a payoff for their time and attention. Essentially, you need to write a headline so that the reader can't help but want to know more. Given where massage is during this time of transition, your headline and the rest of your material would better interest and educate your reader by being informative, logical, pragmatic, objective, definitive, scientific, analytical, measurable, and strategic. Since you are trying to present yourself as a trustworthy professional, don't be vague, cute, ethereal, or obscure. What may work for marketing more established products or services doesn't apply to massage yet, so stick to the basics.

Body Copy

Following the headline is the opening paragraph and body copy that gives the payoff promised in the headline. Much of the work you have done for your reference marketing tools can be used directly in your action marketing tools body copy. We will go over a few new elements here, and you can mix and match your reference elements and the following elements, depending on your goals and the amount of space you have. Your body copy can have:

A promise

Clear and detailed facts about you, your work, your advantages, and so forth.

Explicit benefits and reasons for buying

How you will take away their risk by providing guarantees

Endorsements or testimonials

Gifts, bonuses, deals, or discounts for acting by a specific time

All the necessary information to make a decision

What action to take once they've heard you out

These elements are important in selling any service business and they are especially important when selling massage. By including these elements, you clear the way for a faster and easier decision.

Promises. Promises are attention grabbers. Unfortunately, very few people take the act of making a promise seriously, so when someone does, we stop for a moment to see if they actually will fulfill it. With so much mistrust between the public and advertisers, anyone willing to stick their neck out and make a promise will get attention. With trust as one of the main barriers between massage therapists and our potential clients, making a promise may be potent way to make a case for your trustworthiness.

Specific and Measurable Results. You don't have to make any kind of promise, but if you choose to do so, you can strengthen it further by making it measurable as well as desirable. If your target market is elderly women golfers, don't just say you'll improve their game or help them feel better: say you'll add 10 yards to their tee shot and then tell them why. Tell them that massage can help them have better range of motion in their hips or improve their energy to last a full 18 holes because of better posture, breathing skills, stress management tools, and the like. Use your promise as a way to educate, or if you feel you can't back your promise, just educate. If you do make a strong promise, give a money-back guarantee and be ready to back it.

If your clients are executives, don't just promise they'll be more productive. Tell them they will be able to make faster, smarter decisions with better mental clarity from improved blood flow to the brain because you will release the compressing muscles in the shoulders and neck. Describe how your stress management techniques or relaxation audiotape you give as an added bonus may help aid sleep at night so they will have two more productive hours in a workday.

While these are just examples, if you know your target markets, you can make similar types of claims. Just don't exaggerate. If you don't know your target markets well enough to make such specific promises, then read magazines, trade journals, join associations, search the Internet, or interview people in that market to learn what their needs are and start with more generic claims. You can make an educated guess, but if you are wrong about what your market needs and you sell a solution to a problem they don't have, you'll waste valuable time and resources by marketing the wrong message. I remember trying to sell to high-level executives by telling them I could reduce their stress. It seemed logical and valuable to me, but I wasn't having much luck. I finally decided to ask a friend and powerful executive why my marketing message wasn't working. "If I let go of my stress," he said, "I'd fall apart. My stress is the only thing that holds me together so I'm afraid to let go of it." The thought of a long, luxurious, stress-reducing massage had no appeal to him, and he guessed it probably wouldn't appeal to his colleagues, either. So, if he were to get a massage, I asked, what would he want and why? It turns out what he really wanted was a quick, energizing, oil-free massage that could let him work more hours. So much for that assumption! If you want to save yourself money and time, do some research first; then you will know what your market wants and needs, and you can make a compelling offer that can meet those needs.

Guarantees. Of all the things that will make your marketing stand out from other massage therapists, I recommend that you offer a guarantee so powerful that all risk is removed for your prospect trying your work. Many people have had bad experiences or heard horror stories about the brute who pummeled his way through a bruising massage, or the talkative divorcee who yapped about her ex-husband the whole session. These prospective clients are worried that you may not be worth their time or money, and that worry may stop them from booking an appointment. Whatever new clients may be wary of, I tell them that I give their money back if they aren't happy for any reason. My guarantee relaxes and relieves them, and it impresses them knowing I am that confident in my work. If you are willing to give a guarantee, make it a prominent feature in your marketing piece. It will be novel, unexpected, and very welcome. The purpose of a guarantee is to reduce the risk in the decision to buy and to give you leverage in convincing someone to try your work. A guarantee helps establish trust. Even if your prospects are not initially convinced of the value of your work, you take away their risk until you can prove it.

Protecting Yourself from Guarantee Abuse. A guarantee takes away the risk of the buying decision for your client, but it puts you at risk for wasting your time with a scammer. There are ways to protect yourself in your guarantee, so do not hesitate to use guarantees. After all, if offering a guarantee doubles or triples your client base, and two or three people scam you for a massage over the years, are those lost three hours worth all those clients with their net worth, plus their referrals? Of course they are! No marketing or advertising program is going to be effective 100 percent of the time, so don't be tight, cheap, greedy, or come from scarcity with your guarantee. Instead, come from abundance, be a service and quality fanatic, make every facet of your work top of the line, let your clients know what you do for them, and if your work is worth it, a guarantee will pay off big for you.

Your written guarantee in your marketing materials can bring clients in the door, and to protect yourself and provide good customer service, reiterate your guarantee during your premassage conversation. This gives your client as well as yourself an "out" on the guarantee. You can state that you give a money-back guarantee, and if after the first half-hour he is not happy, he can leave without paying. Then, at the half-hour mark, ask him if he is happy with your work and would like to continue the massage. In that way, if he really doesn't like your work, he can simply get up and go. Or if he is scamming, he can't change his mind at the end of the session. In the best case, he can give you feedback on what would make him happier. Either way, you have protected some of your time, and if you learn quickly what makes your new client happy, you will be able to do better work.

Endorsements and Testimonials. Having other people promote you is a wonderful way to be more direct in leading people to action than by having the words come from you. Somehow, it is more acceptable to have a client or marketing partner say, "Jane Doe is the best massage therapist ever! Run, don't walk to get a terrific massage from her!" Endorsements have a bit more push to them than a testimonial. Usually a testimonial just says that you're great or gives examples of how you helped, but an endorsement tells the reader they should take some sort of action. It's a subtle difference, but having your endorsers tell your potential client what to do next can be a decisive statement.

Who endorses you may or may not be a factor in your marketing. I have seen endorsement statements followed by data ranging from "Mary C., California" to full names, job descriptions, and photos. Admittedly, I am a little wary of the minimalist endorsers, and I wonder if someone just made them up. The more information you give about your endorsers, the more legitimate they seem. If you are aiming for a narrow target market such as, say, horseback riders and competitive show jumpers, then you want endorsements from like-minded people, preferably those who have won a few ribbons or are notables in the sport. People trust people who are like themselves, and who face their problems and needs, so pick your endorsers to match the market you want to reach.

Offers. Before you make offers to bring in new clients, think about the purpose of your offers. If you have a long-term strategy and want to have clients come back on a regular basis, then you want a multimassage package offer that demonstrates the cumulative value of your work. If you need larger sums of money to buy a washing machine and dryer, then create a multi-massage package offer that asks for payment up front with a discount for each session, or buy a package of 10 and get one free. If you want to get people in the habit of referring their friends to you, make an offer where they buy a massage and get a gift certificate to give away. I will cover a number of options for creating offers, but first you have to think about what you need most so your offer really can help your business.

Factors to consider include money, time, repetition (number of sessions), frequency of sessions, your needs, and the clients' needs.

Package Deals. Money and time are two pieces of your offer strategy. If you don't have a lot of time to build a practice, then make offers of lower prices to get new clients in the door. When time is not a factor, your offers don't have to give as heavy a discount. The next factor in your strategy then becomes repetition or number of sessions purchased. Package deals mix and match money, time, and repetition in a variety of ways depending on the desires and needs of you and your market. For example, if your need is to create long-term, repeat clients, one of the best strategies you can use is to offer discounted package deals that bring in clients for at least three massages. This gives them a price break, gives the experience of the cumulative effects of massage, generates value in their minds, and proves your benefits.

Years ago, my mother ran a package deal in a local coupon book offering a deal of three massages for $99, paid up front. The coupon ad ran once and it gave her enough clients to fill out her practice. She traded massage with the woman who created the coupon books so no money was spent, and when she gave me one client who needed deeper work than she could do, I built a big part of my practice on that person's referrals. Mom did a lot of $33 massages initially, which was hard for her, but enough clients stayed with her after their initial three massage to make the promotional offer more than worth it. Honestly, given the amount of money most businesses spend advertising, the fact that we get paid to advertise (which is what a package deal is) should make us clap our hands in joy.

You can do all sorts of variations on this, ranging from simple two-for-one offers to selling a set time slot for an annual fee up front with good discounts. For example, the person agrees to massages every Monday at 2:00 P.M. If he can't be there, he can send someone else. If no one shows up, you get the hour off but keep the fee you charged up front.

Time Bonuses. Another offer element—time—can be used as a low-cost, high-value bonus. Again, consider your needs first. If you want people to value your price but you want to get them in the door, you can send out coupons, mailers, or ads offering a free extra half-hour for the price of one hour. You can offer one free massage when they buy four up front at your full price, or if they don't have that kind of money, you can offer a free massage after they've had 10 full-price massages in a row. If you want your clients to come in with a particular frequency, you can offer a time bonus of a free half-hour if they get four massages within a month. If you have slow days, you can offer an extra 15 minutes for massages on Tuesdays, or between the hours of 11:00 A.M. and 2:00 P.M. A different take, if you want referrals, is to give a free gift certificate for your client to give to a friend after she has come in for four sessions. As you can see, the possibilities are almost endless. You can play with these factors to get needed cash up front, keep customers for the long term, train them how frequently to get massage, get them familiar with and ready to pay your full price, or whatever else it takes to build your dream practice. Any time you consider making an offer, ask yourself what you want and to what your market will be drawn. People may differ in their opinions on this topic, but in my research, it seems to be more beneficial than not to be generous with time up front. Time is a flexible asset. It is your cheapest, most effective benefit to offer, and it can pay off handsomely.

Combining Guarantees, Bonuses, and Gifts. The most desirable and irresistible combination to buyers is a total risk-free trial proposition or guarantee, along with a bonus or gift just for trying you out. For example, you can do a money-back guaranteed three-massage package deal, offered at a discount, along with a free consultation from a feng shui expert, a personal trainer, or a nutritionist. Packages such as these will separate you from other therapists you are competing with, can lead someone in your direction, or remove a barrier to a person making a commitment for massage. Your guarantee removes their risk; your offer or deal moves them closer to a decision; and your marketing partners' bonuses or gifts create a tremendous advantage, link you positively with people or businesses already known and trusted, and create a high perceived value with little or no cost to you. Somehow, this seems to beat standing around at a networking meeting handing out brochures.

Deadlines. What makes your action marketing tool effective in bringing people to you rapidly is a deadline by when they will lose the opportunity to take advantage of your deal or offer. People are funny about getting to things, even things they want to do. Having a deadline moves your offer into a more active part of their awareness, with a conscious or unconscious time clock ticking down to move them to action. After all, if it weren't for deadlines, taxes would never be paid, tulip bulbs wouldn't get planted, and books would never get finished. The possibility of losing out on your good offer is one of the most powerful forms of leverage you can use to get your buyer out of the easy chair and over to the telephone to call you.

How to Close Your Action Marketing Tool

Let's finish up this section on action marketing tools with how to close the piece with the purpose of "opening" a potential relationship. One of the biggest mistakes marketers make is that they don't treat their ad, coupon, or letter like a sales call, and don't close the piece by asking the prospect to take some kind of action. If you make a call, send a letter, or leave a flyer, conclude the process by taking your prospects by the hand and leading them to take some kind of action.

Imagine that you are talking to a woman who got your name as a referral and she has called you to ask about your work. At the end of the conversation, after you've explained your benefits, your type of work, and the like, would you just hang up? Of course not. You'd go to the natural completion of the conversation by asking for the opportunity to work with her, and ask whether she would like to book an appointment or take some other kind of action. If you treat your marketing tools like a sales conversation, you need to close with the call to action, telling your readers explicitly what to do.

Possible Actions for Prospects to Take.   Depending on the level of trust or value your readers have of you, your marketing tool can lead them directly to booking an appointment, or toward a smaller, less committed step. You can ask them to drop by your office to meet you for a free consultation, or to pick up a free gift, coupon, or certificate. You can ask them to attend a speech or seminar, or ask for a less risky, more educational step like calling you for a brochure, questionnaire, newsletter, resume, or a free tape you offer about massage or something related. Whatever action you ask for, do what you can to get them to respond right now, before they put down your ad, letter, or whatever you sent, and they forget about your great offer.

This final element of asking the person to make a decision is where marketing becomes selling, and it is where I have seen massage therapists become the most uncomfortable. Images of used car salesmen and other negative selling stereotypes often are associated with getting a person to make a decision to buy. If those images make you uncomfortable or resistant, you will need to call on your higher self, and greater purpose or mission, to remind you of why you are marketing massage in the first place. Going back to the first attribute, the desire to serve, you can remind yourself in moments of self-doubt, fear, or discomfort that you have an incredible gift to offer, and you can endure a few minutes of conversation or lines of type to get to the joy of helping others with your touch.

As human beings, all of us face the fear of rejection, and at the closing moment of any marketing or selling, we have to look someone in the eye or hear a voice on the phone that says "yes" or "no" to the personal gift being offered. If we were selling tires or refrigerators and people did not like them, the rejection would not be personal. However, with massage, we are selling ourselves and our touch, and being rejected can feel personal and painful. If you never ask a person to make a decision to get a massage from you, you will never be rejected or have to feel that pain, but the odds are high you also will do very little massage, which can be even more painful. All your marketing culminates in the final act of giving a massage, and since that is the backbone of your dream practice, I encourage you to go with the more direct action marketing tools to build that practice quickly.

Putting It All Together

Creating a marketing tool of any type takes knowing the purpose and goals of the piece, and combining the many elements we have covered into a viable piece. Depending on your needs, budget, skills, or the skills of those who help you, you may decide to create coupons, postcards, letters, surveys, newsletters, flyers, or other types of tools to reach out to new clients.

Postcards

The primary benefits of postcards are that they are not as intimidating to write as long letters because of their limited space, and they are relatively cheap to print and mail. And since your recipients don't have to open an envelope, there is a higher likelihood they will at least turn the postcard over and read your eye-popping headline. Postcards also give you the benefit of doing three or four mailing in a row to the same recipients. This makes them more effective, since your mailer and advertisement message often doesn't even register in a person's consciousness until about the third or fourth time it is seen.

Letters

Letters can range from a simple one-sided sheet of paper to thick, multipage documents that resemble magazines. Letters can have pages of text and use various means to attract the reader's attention including circling important words with red ink, using yellow sticky notes to highlight sections, small note cards that fall out of large documents, and so on. If you ever want to study the ultimate in letters and mailers, take a look at the packets from Publisher's Clearing House. Postcards to mail in, stickers to lick, scratch-off dots, highlighted lines, personalized photos with your name written on a big check, all boggle my mind as I look at what goes into these elaborate, clever, and obviously very effective marketing tools.

While postcards are good as quick attention grabbers, letters are better if the recipient is actually interested in massage. A letter can give enough information on its own to make a sale. If your very informative letter reaches a person who has been looking for a massage therapist, the amount and quality of information you give can build trust enough to have them call and book an appointment.

To create an effective letter, use the elements we covered, be unique in your look and message, present your most important material early in case your readers only give you a few seconds to catch their interest, and tell them what to do once they are done reading.

Letters can be enhanced by their envelopes, and how your envelope looks will probably determine whether or not your letter even will be opened. Handwritten addresses make your letter look more personalized, and you can print your offer and deadline on the outside so the recipient will know what you offer as they sort through their pile of mail.

Letters Sent Through Mutual Marketing Partner Mailing Lists

Before you create a mailer, learn as much as you can about who you are sending it to. If you do decide to send a mailer, you will have a much better chance of understanding your recipients if you send it to your mutual marketing partners' mailing lists than to a blind or rented list. Whether you pay, trade for, or are given mailing lists, do your best to get your partner's endorsement to personalize your letter.

Golf Pro Example

Let's say there is a golf pro who already has a large clientele of students that matches your target market. You don't want to do a bunch of free massages, but when you ask him to be part of the process of contacting his student list, he balks a little bit because he "hates selling anything." In this kind of scenario, you can offer a free golf lesson as a bonus for signing up for a certain number of massages. In this way, you can benefit by your association with him and establish yourself as a golf massage specialist by offering those who book and pay for X number of massages, a half-hour lesson with the golf pro. You then either pay nothing, or a discounted or full price for that lesson. The true benefit to the pro is that he gets the opportunity to regain contact with former students, and sell them a series of lessons if their half-hour lesson shows how rusty their golf game has become. If he has been out of touch with many of the people on his mailing list, your direct mail letter is a way for him to get back in contact with former customers without having to pay a dime. All he has to do is give you his mailing list, provide a few free lessons (unless it actually is worth it for you to pay for them), and turn those free lessons back into paying clients.

Nineteenth Hole Golfers Massage Special

Improve your game!

Purchase a package deal of five golfer-specific sports massage sessions and receive a bonus of a half-hour's free lesson with (golf pro)

Your Name
Phone

Figure 5–5 Partnering with a golf professional can open many doors to potential clients.

While you're at it with the mailing piece, go to the golf club salesman and ask for some discount coupons for equipment to include in your mailer. In fact, you can ask the golf store or salesman to cover the cost of your printing and mailing since the golf pro's list of people is prequalified. Then, go to a ritzy or new golf course with slow sales and get coupons for their greens fees to include in your direct mail piece. In exchange for access to the list of the pro's clients, you get their mailing list, and coupons for their greens fees, restaurant and bar, or clothing items from their pro shop. Now the club salesman will really want to pay for your mailing because you have access to a whole new list of golfers. And your golf pro has a whole slew of potential prospects you've rounded up. You send out your mailer and as extra insurance, post your flyer, card, or brochure prominently at the club, give a bunch to the golf pro and the golf club proprietor, and you've pinpointed and reached your exact target market for nothing except some creative thought, good communication, a few telephone calls, and the time spent writing your direct mail piece. I could go on and on with variations in just this example, but you get the idea of what this one direct mail letter can do for your practice.

Flyers

The purpose of flyers, comprised of many if not all of the elements of action marketing, is to get your prospects' attention, create interest, and lead to some form of action. Flyers can be easy to make, cheap to print, and fast to distribute. If your environment is not friendly, flyers are out of the question, but for "above radar" businesses, flyers can be an effective tool. They can be given to mutual marketers, sent to a mailing list, or posted in a place frequented by your target market. Since your flyers will be seen by a large number of people, it is important you make it good-looking, eye-catching, and professional. Changing it often means that people will see it and not be as likely to overlook it as they would be if it was the same flyer up month after month.

The drawback to flyers is because they are inexpensive to make and can be put together quickly on a home computer, they don't have the same cache or image as other forms of advertising. For example, you would rarely see a flyer posted for a doctor, dentist, psychologist, or physical therapist advertising those professionals' services. However, it is more common to see flyers for manicurists and hairstylists since flyers are acceptable for many service businesses. Since massage can be both a personal and professional service, you will need to determine who your market is and what you are offering to determine whether or not a flyer would be congruent with your target market's perception of your services.

Surveys

Another possible way to market is to use surveys. One use of surveys is the more traditional method of sending questionnaires to current and past clients to get information that can be used in testimonials or for research about how to improve your practice. However, a second use is to send surveys to prospective clients, using them as a marketing tool. Instead of telling your prospect what you do, ask them what they would want from a massage experience. You can say something along the lines of "I am a new massage therapist in town and want to know what you want and expect, or like or dislike, about massage." The people who take the time to answer your survey or questionnaire are good candidates for further marketing pieces, and, of course, you can learn a lot from what they have told you. If you are new at massage, this is a fast way to gather information about your target market, and it replaces guessing with knowledge of what people want so that you can create marketing material more effectively. Even if your recipients don't respond to your survey, it lets them know of your existence, and that may be all you need to make a sale. In addition, the fact that you have marketed with a survey tells them that you actually care what they think, and that customer service and value is important to you.

A word of caution here: don't believe everything people say in response to your survey. Studies in the marketing and advertising world have shown repeatedly that what people say they want is often different from what they are willing to spend money on. However, surveys are a great way to start your marketing research and can teach you a lot about your market.

Distributing Your Marketing Tools

Since the purpose of marketing tools is to give you leverage in reaching more people quickly, it makes sense that the more places your tools are distributed, the better your leverage is. There are almost endless ways to distribute your marketing, so look at the world around you and see where you can get out your message of massage.

Getting Mailing Lists of Your Target Market

If you are going to be mailing marketing tools to potential clients gather mailing lists from various sources and then screen them so that you don't waste time and money sending materials to people who live too far away, or the like. You can rent lists, borrow lists, trade massage, or do your research and create your own list. Lists can be gotten from:

- mutual marketers
- associations
- magazines
- list brokers (look in the business Yellow Pages under Mailing Lists)
- library (ask the reference librarian for the SRDS mailing list directory; then call and ask for free catalogs to see what scope of lists they offer so you can tightly narrow your search to reach your target market)
- Yellow Pages listings by profession (addresses are usually included and ZIP code maps are in the front pages)

Or create your own list. Buy contact management software to document names and addresses, and make notations about which direct response ad was sent.

Advertisements

Most of the marketing tools we have covered so far are designed to be educational, informative, and persuasive. These tools are going to be distributed mostly by you, those fairly closely connected to you, or to narrowly targeted markets. In combining your needs for safety, speed, saving money, and reaching your target market as accurately as possible, we have stayed away from the more expensive, risky, and uncontrolled tool of advertising.

Because of where the profession is at this time in the general public's perception, advertising to mass audiences has been a less common tool for building a practice. This is now changing, and if you are in an area where massage is well accepted and competition is high, you might find value in traditional advertising.

Designing an ad takes many of the thoughts and elements with which you are now becoming familiar. The difference is that your message now has more exposure. Whether you are creating a telephone book advertisement or a television infomercial, you still need to get attention, create interest, offer the audience something they want, and give them the reasons and information on how to contact you. You won't need much help making a telephone book ad, but if you are going into television, radio, the Internet, magazines, and other more expensive mediums, get some help. Mistakes can be costly. While you design the message, seek help if you are unfamiliar with the medium. Again, before you go into any marketing, start with the end in mind; set clear goals of what you want for your practice, what markets you want to serve, and what to say to introduce prospective clients to your touch.

Testing Your Marketing Factors

So, after all is said and done about how to create an effective marketing tool, how do you know if it will work? The only way to really know is to test it using definitive and measurable means. Testing will show you which headline is effective, what offers or bonuses appeal to your market, what graphics catch people's eye, or what tools people actually read and keep. Before you invest in any marketing medium, verbally test out elements such as your slogan, headlines, or key phrases on everyone you can. Watch people closely to see how they respond. If they look confused at your message or offer, go back to the drawing board and streamline your words. Continue to practice your material and get feedback until you think you may be onto a message to which your market will respond. Then, and only then, should you put out the time and money for marketing tools.

We have introduced many elements you can include in your marketing tools, and if you use a tool more than once (which you may not need to!), you should test those elements individually. Factors to test include your price, your slogan, your offers, your rationale of why the public should buy, your benefits, and your guarantees. If you use presentations or public speeches, test different elements on a live audience; if you use printed materials, play with your packaging, look, and message. Don't assume anything in your marketing. Let your clients tell you what they want. You can test printed materials not only for content but also for the frequency and timing of distributing them. Depending on your goals, finances, and time, you can do a mailing one time a week for three months, a monthly mailing featuring different offers, or send out a quarterly newsletter giving advice or health tips, coupons for a massage series, various offers, and anything to have them become familiar with you.

If you will be doing frequent marketing, you will have more opportunity to test your factors, but if at all possible, test one factor at a time. I realize that testing may not sound like a lot of fun and most businesses never actually test their marketing. So why would you not test? First of all, you'll never have to deal with failure, being wrong, being disappointed, or looking bad. It may be less ego damaging to guess what will work with your market, but if you are going to put any significant time and money into marketing tools and projects, test them to see if you are on the right path.

When I was new in my practice, I got a referral to a woman who lived in a very wealthy, small community. After driving through the tree-lined streets past stunning mansions and manicured lawns, I decided that I wanted to have more clients in this private community. I figured that since they had their own private post office, I could make up a flyer, and give it to the postmaster, and he would put it in their mailboxes. Being a bit cash-strapped at the time, I cheerily made up my own hand-drawn flyer with a goofy looking cartoon character giving a massage as a way to announce my services. Needless to say, I got no clients from that marketing endeavor, but I learned a few lessons. I tell you this story to let you know a basic rule of marketing and life: successful people fail much of the time; the difference between them and everyone else is that they just get up and keep on trying. In that instance, I failed to get clients, but I learned a lot that helped in the future, so it wasn't wasted effort. Even with marketing projects that get a small response, be careful how failure is defined. If a flyer or coupon only gets one or two new clients, that one response could be viewed as a failure. However, as I have seen and experienced, those few clients became the foundation of a practice that ended up leading to long-term success.

Have no ego attached to your marketing, and don't presume to know what will draw in clients, keep them coming back, or make them leave. Our industry is so new that we don't have the luxury to look back on successful marketing campaigns, or myriad books of examples and data the way other professions can. We still don't have national consensus on what to call ourselves as a profession, so we have a long way to go in fully understanding how to market this field.

Even with my college degree in public relations and advertising, and with all the study I have done in marketing, none of what I talk about here is "the truth" about marketing. The best you and I can do is make educated guesses about why people buy massage, then use that knowledge to appeal to them in some form of marketing. Why people buy massage in Florida may be very different from why they buy it in California or France. With that in mind, the only way you can really know what marketing will work for you as an individual and for your target market in your corner of the world is to establish a goal for your projects and tools, test them out, observe your results, notice what works and what doesn't work, make changes, and try again. Maybe that's why a massage business is called a "practice."

Public Relations and Publicity

Reaching out to new clients also can be done through one of the best forms of exposure that money can't buy: public relations. Having the press, media, magazines, or television tell your story or talk about your massage work is priceless coverage. Stories about you and your work simultaneously give you the three fundamentals of marketing: creating trust, establishing value, and shaping perception. A half-page newspaper story on the massages that you did at a local fund-raiser or soup kitchen can tell thousands of people you're legitimate, you're available, you're good enough to make the papers, and you're located at such and such a place.

While your direct marketing is done for the purpose of booking an appointment, the primary purpose of public relations is to gain credibility or credentials, and create a reputation, name recognition, and legitimization. Good public relations can direct people toward you and toward the final action of booking clients, but you won't always be able to control what a journalist says or whether your contact information will be included in the story. Even if a story does not lead directly to sales, you still can make good use of it by using reprints of the piece for sales letters, ads, newsletters, handouts, or to hang on your office wall. Since most everyone likes to have a brush with celebrity, no matter how local, send copies of the story to your current clients to validate their own choice of you as their massage therapist. If you want new clients, include, along with the copy of the article, a special deal that for every two or three referrals that come your way from your clients during the next month, you'll give your current client an extra half-hour, a free massage, a bouquet of roses, a nice dinner out at your marketing partner's restaurant, or whatever else you can make up to take advantage of your public relations story.

What Media Reach Your Target Market

Even in an area as broad as publicity, you still can aim directly at your target market. If you have a fairly good idea of who your target market is, you can start to research which newspapers, magazines, or newsletters your clients read; what radio stations they listen to; or what television stations or shows they watch. When you have identified those media, narrow down your target further by aiming at the sections of those newspapers or magazines that would be interested in your story. Massage is not hard, front-page, or breaking news, but it can go into the Lifestyle Section, Business Section, Sports Page, or anywhere you can slant a story.

The Purpose of Articles

When I started writing magazine articles, I had a meeting with a publisher early on who told me a secret that changed my writing style forever. He was kind of a crusty old goat but he knew what he was talking about, so I listened. "Do you know what the purpose of your articles are?" he asked me, fixing me with a hard stare. "Um, to inform the readers?" I guessed, trying to sound logical. "No," he said, "that's not the reason we publish your stories. The only reason we run good stories is to keep the reader on the page long enough to see the advertisements around your article. Your job is to make sure people see the advertisements." I was both horrified and relieved. If my main job was to just keep people reading, then all the other rules didn't matter. I threw off my new writer inhibitions and became an opinionated, outspoken, tongue-in-cheek kind of writer, and I quickly built a loyal following for my column. I broke many rules to keep people reading, and because I knew what my real job was, I worked very hard at figuring out what would keep people's interest.

When you approach any form of media for publicity, you will be light years ahead of others if you know up front that the main reason you will get a feature story or air time is because you have a story that will keep the audience's attention long enough to see the ads. The reason a publication will print a story about you or a television station will send out a crew is because you have a story that is novel, unusual, interesting, informative, or entertaining. The media do not publish stories for your sake or income: they do it to sell toothpaste. You can resent this idea or you can use it. You can shun publicity or you can learn to think like a news producer facing a boring lineup of stories that needs a kick to grab the audience's attention. Massage is still a very novel topic, and a clever marketer, which you are becoming, can get tons of free publicity by coming up with great story angles to promote to the media.

What Makes a Good Story

If you want to use free publicity, ask yourself what makes your work interesting, different, unique, or remarkable. Do you have a touching story about working with elderly shut-ins? Have you done chair massage at a disaster site? Are you doing on-site work at a business that is in the news, or working on volunteers at a local political campaign? Are you giving massage to the local high school or college sports team? Have you donated free massage as a raffle prize for a prominent local charity? Have you invented a new massage product or style, written a book, or done a research project on the benefits of massage on lowering blood pressure? Do you use a hot, new item, or work with angels? Did one of your clients drop 10 strokes off his golf game or hit a hole-in-one the day after your massage? Ask if you can tell the story and then share the glory!

Local Community Angles

Editors in local newspapers and magazines love to get new and uncustomary stories, and since many people are curious about massage, you could be the perfect antidote for a boring news day. One of your easiest doors to get through is with a local community angle. Did you get the first massage license in your city? Do you have a photo of yourself doing an on-site massage on that city's chief of police? Have you hit an anniversary of serving your community, whether massage related or not? Are you and a marketing partner doing a marathon massage giveaway with every customer coming in getting a free chair massage, and every customer who buys your partner's product means a hundred dollar donation toward building a local library, school, or firehouse? If you read your local paper and see what local issues you can do a promotion in conjunction with, you can land yourself stories that will make you and the editors mighty happy.

Industry Spokesperson Angle

One way to get a steady flow of publicity is to consider declaring yourself an industry spokesperson. Craft a story about the history of massage in your town, or become a futurist and create a valid piece on the role of massage and holistic health for the future. Follow news stories and debates on hot topics and offer slants from your industry's perspective. Will health coverage include massage? How many doctors now offer massage as one of their services? Does massage help carpal tunnel syndrome, asthma, or relieve the pain of arthritis in the aging population? If you offer enough story ideas, even if they aren't all used, after a while the paper will start calling you as the local expert when massage shows up in a story that is making news.

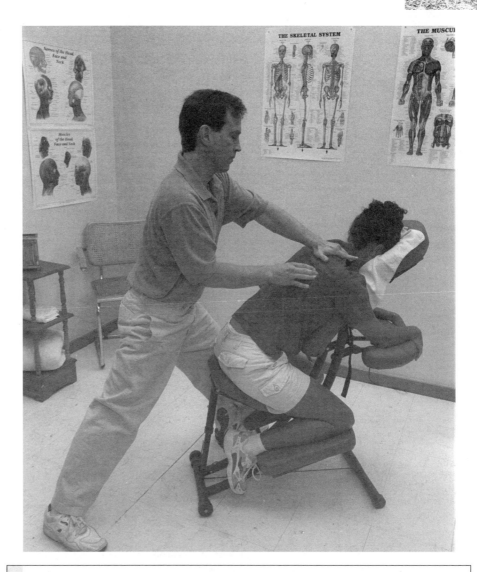

Figure 5–6   Chair massages at a public event is an excellent way to educate the public and promote your practice.

Trend Angles

Newspapers like scoops and trends, and they can turn around on a story idea a lot faster than magazines that sometimes have lead times of six months or more. Angles on consumer-related stories are often of interest, so use them. Have you helped a client an HMO turned away? Do you work with women with breast cancer undergoing chemotherapy and is breast cancer a growing concern in your area? Do you help stressed out employees who have been downsized? Are your soccer moms' kids getting knee injuries and concussions? Do you cater to an ethnic minority new to your community? Or are you facing discrimination in getting a business license because you do massage? Then go to the paper, tell your story, and get help and community support.

Keep Your Eyes Open and Let Others Do the Writing

If you are not a great writer, that's okay. Publicity stories are usually written by journalists and professional writers—not by you—so don't let writing stop you. You just have to keep your eyes and mind open, and figure out how you can slant massage to almost anything for a good story. Fortunately, massage is so versatile and multifaceted that your story options are myriad. Submit story ideas, and don't let "no's" stop you. If one story doesn't capture the imagination of the editor, send in a different story with another angle. Even if you never get a story, you will have learned a great deal about doing your own marketing and that can be invaluable.

The Elements of Writing a Press Release

If you have a hot or newsworthy item, you can call an editor in charge of the department you think your story would fit into. Or if it's not a rush, write him or her a press release. Whether you want to be interviewed on a local radio show, have a television news crew do a shoot, or have a writer come out, you should send out a professional press release. A press release is easy to write, and is not intimidating if you follow these simple, logical steps.

1. Write in a simple, uncomplicated style. Make your story idea clear and easy to understand.

2. Double-space your lines, and use a large, easy-to-read font. If your page looks too crowded or hard to read, an editor will toss it.

3. Make no mistakes. If you don't write or spell well, get help. A friend may help you or you can go down to the local college and put up a notice for a writer, journalist, English major, or the like to help you out.

4. Make your press release look good. Print it on good paper with a good printer. If you don't have a good printer, take your diskette to a photocopying store, a friend, or marketing partner and print it there.

5. Use white paper with black ink. The editor may want to copy your release to some other department that can follow up on your story or make copies for a committee that reviews story ideas. Colored paper copies gray and murky, so stick with white.

6. List a contact name and telephone number where your editor or assigned writer can call you. Answer your telephone professionally with your name and have a message machine with a professional message.

7. Put a dateline at the top of the page with the date you mailed your press release and the city from which you mailed it. Sometimes a story idea may sit around for a while, and if an editor comes across it without a date, he won't know if it's two years old or brand new, and into the trash can it goes.

8. Even if you don't have formal stationery, use a professional letterhead format that includes your name and address, and type NEWS at the top of the page.

9. Start with your most important information. Grab the editor's attention quickly using some of your tactics from your other marketing tools. Leave less relevant information for the end of the release.

10. Don't overhype your story. Give real information: who, what, when, where, and why. Don't use a lot of adjectives such as great, the best,

superlative service, and the like. Give facts the editor can use, especially if he has to convince other people to run your story.

11. Write a short, simple, respectful note to go with your release. It can say something like Dear X: I thought you might be interested in the enclosed. Sincerely,

12. Mail your press release.

13. Wait a few days, then follow up with a one-minute telephone call to the editor. You only need to say who you are and that you are confirming that he received your release.

14. If the paper, magazine, or station runs your story, send a "thank you" note. Most people don't, and being an editor can feel like a pretty thankless job. Continue your standard of going the extra mile and giving outstanding service, even with news editors.

Press Releases for Television Coverage

If you want television coverage, entice the targeted show's producer with visual elements and images she can show the viewers. If possible, send photos with your release that give her an idea of what the cameras would focus on. Can you get a camera crew into the locker room of the local sports arena for a demo on one of your professional athlete clients, or do you work with your county's only isolation tank? Do you have an unusual setting such as an outside garden, work for the circus, or have a client whom you've helped recover from an accident that dominated the headlines a year ago? Are you doing on-site massage at your client's office for the employees as a Christmas gift to them? The media always need new holiday stories so give them a great piece in advance that they can do with you. Television shows and newspapers are including more soft pieces with feel-good stories, so you might as well be in one.

If you decide you want to use publicity to promote your practice, there are a few factors to keep in mind. One, since we still have to consider privacy for clients and those we touch, only do stories with people who are willing to be seen on camera. Two, you may need to educate your producer about the issue of legitimacy. There is still some titillation to the word massage, so be clear with the news producer that you don't want any double entendre or sexual overtones. And three, we still need to promote massage as a profession. Publicity may or may not bring you clients directly the way our other marketing methods do, but remember that every time you make the news or reach the public about the many great benefits of massage, you continue to shift thousands of people up the Perception Continuum. Many of us are able to practice today because of the work that other therapists have done to pave the way to the growing acceptance we enjoy today, so keep in mind that publicity represents and benefits not only you but also the rest of the profession.

Sources for Press Releases

The best place to go for getting your story told is to publications you know and read, or television and radio stations you watch or listen to. Pay attention to the types of stories they run, the tone or attitude of the writer or producer, and custom tailor your story for that individual. I got my very first magazine article accepted, sight unseen, in a two-minute conversation with the publisher because I had studied his magazines for many months until I found a story angle I knew he couldn't resist. That one story led to a column and many more articles, and it started because I understood what the publisher wanted. Find columnists, writers, or television shows you like, figure out how you can give them a good story that matches their style, and then make your pitch.

If you want to do stories but don't know where or to whom to send them, go to your local library and look up *Bacon's Publicity Checker*. This tells you where to send releases for all categories of story-takers. It includes information on papers, editors, columnists, wire services, magazines, and trade publications. You also can look in the book entitled *Working Press of the Nation* for other sources. Staff changes at newspapers and magazines can happen without notice, so make one final call to the front desk beforehand to make sure you have the correct information, name, spelling, and address for where to send your press release. Don't be afraid to try this great form of marketing. Publishers always need good stories, so introduce yourself, pitch an angle, and see what develops.

Public Speaking

According to statistics, public speaking is the number one fear American's face. More people are afraid of speaking than they are of dying. If you don't like public speaking, then don't use it as a means of marketing. You'd be better served doing a promotional project at a gym or the local fire station where you can let your hands do the talking. However, if you have the gift of gab and you enjoy the spotlight or the stage, consider using public speaking as a form of marketing. The mere act of standing up in front of others helps to build trust and shape positive perception, regardless of what your message is.

Figure 5–7   Public speaking can introduce you to potential clients quickly and easily.

You can approach speaking a number of ways. If you have a topic that you love talking about, then craft a speech and promote that topic. If you want to speak but aren't sure what to talk about, call the groups you want to speak for, tell them who you are and what you do, and tell them that you would be interested in speaking to their Monday evening group. Since you want to tailor your talk to the specific needs of the group, you need to know what the group would like to know about massage, and if they have an interest in holistic health. The contact person you are talking to may not have a good topic idea at the moment, so be prepared with a generic backup one, such as how massage can benefit this tennis club, philanthropy group, service group, or whatever.

Friends, family, and even clients who belong to groups such as the Soroptomists, Lion's Club, and Rotary Club can help get you in the door and design your speech for the group. Even if you don't know anyone in a group to approach, realize that if they have regular meetings that need a speaker, the person in charge of getting speakers is often desperate to get somebody in for the meeting next Thursday.

The art of writing and delivering a speech is too broad for this book, but if you want to be a speaker, give seminars, or teach, think about:

Who you are and what you enjoy talking about.

What your audience wants to know that can improve their lives and/or entertain them.

What purpose you have in giving a speech.

How you can get new clients from the group without your speech sounding like a sales pitch.

Be forewarned: public speaking can be addictive. It is fun, engaging, and challenging. If you find yourself enjoying telling people about yourself and your work from the stage, public speaking could be your ticket to a full practice, and maybe even a career path toward teaching and seminars.

Ethernet

Finally, despite all the marvelous marketing tools for reaching clients we have covered so far, this final one is my favorite. I call it the Ethernet because this form of marketing is about getting your communications and messages to your current and future clients through the invisible, mysterious ethers. Ethernet marketing has no form or substance, no concrete tools. Basically, your message is carried only by the power of your intention. I know it sounds a little woo-woo, but I have played with the power of intention for a very long time, and I am amazed by its force. If I need time off but am totally booked, clients magically call to cancel. If I need extra clients for my car registration fee, I just put the request out there in the Ethernet and the telephone starts ringing with people I have never heard of calling for an appointment. The more I use the Ethernet, the more I learn to trust it.

Sow Your Seeds

There are two points I want to make about using the Ethernet. One is that you must have done your homework and laid your groundwork for it to succeed. When I send out my intentions or requests and people call in, they say things like they got my card from a friend, saw me in a class, or met me at an event. I have been sowing the seeds of success for a long time and only after that do I get to reap the harvest.

Have Clear Intentions

The second element about tapping into the Ethernet is to have very clear and specific intentions about what you want. Saying you want to have lots of clients doesn't work. Saying that you want to have 15 clients a week programs the Ethernet to go out and get you what you want. If you have ever done a search on the Internet, you know that the more specific you are, the more quickly and easily you can find what you are looking for. Type in the word "book" as a search word and the system isn't very helpful. Type in the book's title and what you need shows up almost instantly. As we close this section on how to reach your new clients, remind yourself again of who you are, what you want, and why you want to serve these people.

The Ethernet works in ways I do not understand fully, but I do know that you can jam the power of the Ethernet by sending out mixed messages or unclear intentions. The old saying, "Be careful what you ask for, you may get it" holds true on the Ethernet as well. If you are ambivalent about success or are afraid to get out there and try your hand at life, you can put out all the slick brochures and ads you want, and people won't call. Success comes when you can handle it, so the more you practice success with visualizations, affirmations, or role modeling, the more the Ethernet can connect you with the target market that wants you and needs you.

CHAPTER

6

Rebooking Skills

CHAPTER
OBJECTIVES

After reading this chapter, you should be able to:

- identify the five moments of decision for rebooking clients.
- describe four factors of personal presentation that can affect rebooking.
- deliver premassage instructions for a new client.
- discuss the importance of managing boundaries.
- describe four elements to ask about during verbal checkins.
- explain the importance of handling a drape properly.
- describe seven moments of transition during massage.
- explain the six levels of client participation during massage.
- describe how to handle the separation stage of a session.
- describe how to deal with a dissatisfied client.

Rebooking to Build Your Dream Practice

Marketing for a massage practice has two primary functions. The first is to get new clients; the second is to keep them. Successful practitioners know that the true secret to a long-term career in private practice is in the second function of marketing that centers around rebooking current clients. The practitioners who had to give up their dream of a long-term massage practice probably made the unfortunate but common mistake of assuming that once a client was in the door, their marketing was done. Nothing could be further from the truth. All the work that was done prior to getting a new client onto the table is only a small percentage of the true marketing that builds and maintains a satisfying and financially successful practice.

The majority of your marketing is done during your session, and the following pages will take you step-by-step through the key elements of what it takes to serve your clients in such a way that they not only rebook but also will refer. As you may have noticed in the prior chapters, marketing to reach new clients takes time, effort, and money, and quite frankly, the less you have to focus on that function of marketing, the better. It is far easier to keep a client coming back than to get a new one, so let's look at what it takes to keep a client.

179

The Five Moments of Decision for Rebooking

The marketing strategies for rebooking current clients utilize the same basic principles as those we have covered for reaching new clients. In both cases, your marketing is designed to shape your clients' perceptions about you and massage continually, instill value that your massage is worth their time and money, and prove that you are trustworthy to touch them.

Once a person has booked an appointment, there are a number of instances where you have key opportunities to market. These instances are what I call the Five Moments of Decision. They are times within your whole encounter with your new clients when they are most likely to evaluate you and your work, and when they make conscious and unconscious decisions whether or not to rebook. While every minute with your client is important, we are going to cover what to do and say during:

Moment 1: Before your new clients arrive

Moment 2: The moment of arrival

Moment 3: During the massage

Moment 4: At the end of the massage

Moment 5: After the client is gone

Moment 1: Before Your New Clients Arrive

Getting new clients in the door is the first step to rebooking them. This may sound obvious, but having a booked appointment is no guarantee that your new clients will show up. This is especially true if they have received gift certificates for a massage but have doubts or fears about getting one. Your new clients may have made an initial decision to book an appointment with you, but sometimes it may take a little extra effort to get them in the door.

Marketing before your new clients arrive centers around building trust, and setting accurate and appropriate expectations for the massage. If you have enough lead time before your new clients arrive for their first session, there are many ways you can demonstrate your professionalism and let them feel good or safe about their decision to get a massage from you. If you sense hesitation during your initial conversation, prepare for the possibility that you may need to alleviate first-timer's anxiety if they have concerns about getting a massage. Even though your new prospects may have booked an appointment, they still may have unspoken fears or resistance, and it is your job to ferret those out and dispel them. Your new clients may be afraid of nudity, touch, have had a prior bad massage experience, have body issues such as scars or deformities, feel fat, feel intimidated, or worry about a host of other concerns you never may have considered. Creating trust at this moment should be your first priority.

To help ensure that your clients show up for their appointment, you can:

■ send a welcoming note with a confirmation card and a map to your office.

■ telephone the day before with a confirmation call and ask if they have any questions.

■ send your intake form and policy form to demonstrate your professionalism, and let them accurately and totally fill in the forms without rushing or feeling like they are wasting massage time filling in paperwork.

- send a suggestion list for how to prepare for their first massage including an explanation of what to expect, how to make the most of their massage, and so on.

- send your brochure, a copy of a newsletter if you have one, copies of articles about the benefits of massage, or whatever you can think of to help build value and trust.

- send a coupon for a free gift with your confirmation card, especially those mentioned in earlier chapters.

There are other ways to stay in touch before the first appointment but, in essence, make your new clients glad they are working with you before you ever touch them. Obviously, most people who book an appointment are willing and ready to be under your hands, but it is wise to be prepared for a little extra marketing, just in case. If all goes well, at the appointed day and time, you will get the opportunity to market again, this time for the second Moment of Decision, the moment of arrival.

Moment 2: The Moment of Arrival

The second moment of decision in rebooking occurs when your new clients show up for the first session. Impressions made at this point are especially important in establishing trust between you and them. If your new clients have never met you before and only talked with you on the telephone, they already have some impression of you. The first time they see you, they will quickly reevaluate their first impression and start to solidify their second impressions. You have about one minute to make the second, more lasting impression, and your job is to make it a good one. To rebook these clients, it is important for you to shape their future decisions now because once a person's mind is made up about you, other data that may be contrary to the initial impression may not be considered or even noticed.

Two of the most important factors you will be judged on are your personal presentation and your environment if a client is coming to see you at your home or office. In the section discussing professionalism, we talked about what you can wear and how you can present yourself in order to make your new clients feel comfortable and at ease. We covered what people see visually when they meet you, and in this chapter, we will go a step further and go over how people use their other senses to evaluate you and your space.

What Your Clients Hear in Your Personal Presentation

Sight is probably the primary sense your clients will use to judge you on their arrival. After that, what they hear, smell, and feel will make an impact with varying degrees depending on which senses are more attuned and sensitive. Concerning sound, we are evaluated on our voice and our words. Volume, pitch, rate of speed, accent, speech patterns, grammar, choice of words, and other elements of verbal communication are all part of what your new clients hear when they first meet you. However, unlike our physical appearance, judgments that affect trust and value aren't as rapid or as strong, but there are still some points to consider in verbal communication.

At the moment of arrival, how you greet and talk with your new clients can either set them on edge or relax them in preparation for the session. The basic rules are to speak professionally and clearly, refrain from foul language,

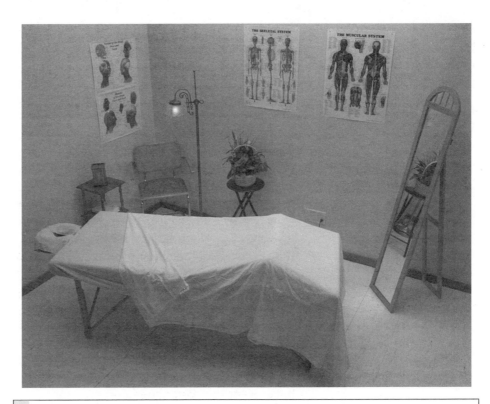

Figure 6–1 Prepare your massage setting to be comfortable, clean, and restful.

don't use bodywork jargon or acronyms, and use your voice to show that you are happy they are there.

Above all, your job at this moment of arrival is to make your clients feel safe and welcome. Perhaps one of the best ways to do that in your opening minutes together is to let your clients hear the sound of their own voices, not yours. Nervous chatter, trying to tell your life story in the first few minutes, or needing to demonstrate your massage prowess by telling them how great you are just don't set a good precedence or create the right atmosphere. When you do all the talking, it tells your clients that the upcoming session will be about you, not about them. People take the time and pay the money for massage so that someone will take care of them for at least one hour out of their lives, so ease their minds immediately that they are the focus of attention. I know I've said this before, but of all the complaints I have heard from clients about their massage experience, having massage therapists who talk the whole time about themselves and their lives tops the list. If you want to be head and shoulders above your massage competition, let your hands do the talking, not your mouth. Clients who want to rest and relax will appreciate this immeasurably, and if they are happy, they are more likely to rebook and refer others to you.

What Your Clients Smell in Your Personal Presentation

I really dread bringing up the next topic, but as a teacher, I faced it enough times in the classroom and would be irresponsible not to mention it. The topic is cleanliness, and while it would seem common sense that a professional show up for work clean and bathed, with brushed teeth, and basically smelling fresh, not everyone does. Perhaps this wouldn't be a big deal if our work was sitting alone in front of a computer, but a massage therapist is often mere inches from a client's nose; so please, show up clean and wear clean unwrinkled clothes.

Along similar lines, wash your hands before each massage. As a teacher, I sent more than a few students back to wash their hands when I happened to be outside the school's bathroom door, heard the toilet flush, and then saw the student immediately emerge without my hearing the water running in the sink. Ick! Beyond issues of cleanliness and hygiene, this is a marketing book, and if your client is within earshot of your bathroom and/or sink, they may be listening to hear if you are scrubbing up well. Clients have every sense tuned to whether or not they will be safe with you, so at least let them know that they can rely on your hands being clean. If your clients somehow figure out that you start your massage without washing your hands, especially after you've been to the restroom, I can guarantee they won't rebook. Would you?

Another sense of smell that clients encounter when they first meet you is your breath. As best you can, keep your breath smelling fresh. If you can't, don't breathe heavily on your clients. I had the unfortunate experience of receiving a massage from a person who seemed to have a great fondness for garlic. While this may not have been so bad, she insisted on taking deep cleansing breaths and blowing her garlic breath all over my face, especially during her opening grounding at my head. Did she do good work, help my sore muscles, or ease my pain? I have no idea. All I remember is that garlic breath and I vowed I would never go back.

If you have an office or work at home, keep mouthwash, a toothbrush, and toothpaste handy. If you do outcall and can't brush, sugar-free gum is the next best thing. Americans have been trained by advertisers to believe it is natural to smell minty fresh, so if you want Americans as your paying clients, know that this is important to them.

Perfumes, colognes, strong aromatherapy oils, pet odors, cigarette smoke, and other such smells are a final factor to consider from your clients' perspective. Given how close you are to your client's nose, much care needs to be taken around scents, and it is best that you have a scent-free body. That way, you don't have to deal with people's allergies, sensitivities, and whatnot. If you really like certain scents, you can have them in the form of incense, room sprays, or in your massage oils, and you can use them if your client is okay with it.

Having been environmentally sensitive for a brief time in my life, I can attest to the fact that nothing can give me a migraine faster than certain perfumes or synthetic air fresheners; and millions of other people are the same way. Save your signature scent for a night on the town, and leave it out of your practice time. Your goal is have clients come back, and since individual smelling preferences range so much, keep yourself neutral and everyone else happy.

What Your Clients Feel Externally in Your Personal Presentation

At the moment of arrival, your clients' sense of touch is probably used the least to evaluate you, well, besides taste, which is not a factor unless you offer food and drinks which might not be a bad idea. The sense of touch and the primary kinesthetic sensations your clients will experience at the moment of arrival will be during your greeting, and there are definitely a few factors to consider. The first factor is how you touch new clients in greeting them. In the beginning, a professional handshake is recommended. People evaluate others based on their handshakes, so be prepared. Have clean, oil-free hands, and when you take your client's hand to shake it, hold it firmly but not too hard. You can demonstrate your amazing hand strength later when you dig that big muscle spasm out of the levator scapula, but don't give it your all in a handshake. The best way to apply pressure is by pressing your thumb into the hand, not squeezing with your fingers from the bottom. A firm grasp with solid pressure tells your new clients that you have confidence, whereas the proverbial "dead fish" handshake can make some people's hair stand on end. Somewhere between the dead fish and the vise grip is a nice, welcoming handshake that can quickly help build trust and rapport.

For new clients, a handshake should be the extent of your physical greeting. Massage therapists are typically a huggy bunch, and some people think a hug is an appropriate greeting. However it may not be right for a new client. Not everyone is comfortable with hugs, and for people who are standoffish, a hug from you would make them very uncomfortable. Even among massage therapists, not everyone is up for a hug at any given moment. Despite the natural inclination to do so, hugs are not something to do without permission. Maybe after you've seen a client for a while, a hug would be an appropriate and wonderful gesture, but for the first-timers, keep your touch to a handshake at the outset or respond in kind if they go to hug you first.

EXERCISE: Shaking Hands

- If you are in a class or group, practice shaking hands with everyone in your group. Experiment with different handshakes, and how it feels to give and get them. Discuss with your group what you felt and noticed. If you are reading this book on your own, try to shake hands with as many people as you can in your daily life and notice what you feel. Pay attention to how people respond to you and how you respond to them because of their handshake.

What Your Clients Feel Internally in Your Personal Presentation

Finally, your personal presentation culminates in how your clients feel emotionally, or internally, about you. All of your hard work preparing for that first moment together should shape your clients' internal feelings that they made the right choice coming to see you. If you have thought ahead about what will make your new clients feel comfortable, at ease and safe with you, you will have done marketing that is extraordinary. If you can see yourself from your new clients' eyes, hear yourself with their ears, and otherwise imagine what it might be like for someone to come to a massage therapist for the first time, you will have compassion and insight for their hopes and fears about who you will be. Presenting yourself as a professional, and radiating a loving, caring attitude during your very first moments together will set the stage for the rest of your first session, and, hopefully, for many more to come.

Gaining Rapport

Beyond presenting yourself with confidence and competence, there is a more interesting but complex way of presenting yourself so that your clients feel safe and sure about working with you. It is a concept I first learned in a seminar on Ericksonian Hypnosis, then added to it with material from the book *Unlimited Power* by Anthony Robbins. The concept is called Matching and Mirroring combined with Pacing and Leading. The gist is that if you want someone to really feel at ease with you, match or imitate their posture, movements, gestures, words, and the like. The more you act like them, the more they will like you. It is a natural instinct to be drawn to people to whom we are similar, and if you want to gain incredible rapport and trust with your clients, make a few subtle changes in your self-presentation so they feel that you are similar to them. Matching and mirroring creates a sense of familiarity and connection because most people think they are pretty wonderful, and if you are like them, you're wonderful, too.

This doesn't mean that you give up your personality or mimic people. It means that you pay attention to them, notice how they stand, move, talk, laugh, dress, maintain eye contact, and so on, and then just be a bit more like them. When you greet your new clients, shake their hands with close to the same amount of pressure they exert, move at the speed they are walking, talk at about the speed they are talking, and watch the magic happen. If this concept makes you uncomfortable, you don't have to use it, but if you actually pay attention to how you are with your friends and family, you will see that you probably already match and mirror others. It is a natural human behavior, and if you learn to use it consciously, you can quickly help your clients feel at ease.

The concept of pacing and leading is a little different. Its premise is that humans can lead each other more easily if they are already in step with each other. If you have taken a walk with a friend, you probably ended up walking with the same basic speed and direction, and maybe even ended up in step with each other. If one of you veered a little in one direction, the other person most likely followed that subtle change.

This is important when you are encountering your new clients for the first time, and you want to lead them to a relaxed and peaceful state. If you have a client who sat in traffic for an hour while driving to your office, and he is agitated, waving his arms while he talks, is speaking rapidly, and breathing quickly, be prepared to change. If he encounters you all mellow and relaxed from the last massage you just gave, there will be a subtle form of friction between you. If your behaviors and states are too different, it will be much harder to lead him to a relaxed state. In this case, your job is to pick up your pace a little, speak at about the same speed, move your hands (not quite so fast or big), and otherwise pace him. Once you are in sync with him, you can start leading him into a more relaxed state using small changes. Slowly soften your voice, deepen your breathing, and reduce the size of your movements. If you are in sync, he is likely to follow your lead. Again, we do pacing and leading all the time as well, but having conscious knowledge of it lets it be a powerful tool. It helps reduce friction and mistrust between people, and creates a great beginning connection during the second moment of decision.

EXERCISE: Pacing and Leading Before a Session

- Pair off into groups of two and choose a Partner A and Partner B.
  Partner A acts as the client, coming in from a hard day of work, talking loudly, waving arms, and complaining about the traffic and a stiff neck.

Partner B acts as the therapist. Partner B welcomes Partner A with a greeting of similar volume and expression. The two talk animatedly about Partner A's day and about the upcoming massage. Slowly, over the course of a few minutes, Partner B starts to lower the volume, speak more slowly, make smaller movements, and otherwise gradually guide the client into a state more conducive to massage.

The partners then switch roles and repeat the exercise.

Your Massage Space and Surroundings

Rebooking clients also requires that they feel safe and comfortable, not just with you, but in your massage space. It doesn't have to be fancy, but it must feel safe. If you have an office at home, or in another establishment or building, shape your clients' perceptions and gain trust by being impeccable in your cleanliness, order, and ambiance. You want to portray your professionalism in your surroundings and part of that is done by removing anything that might create a sense of incongruence with your image as a professional. Your new clients are taking in every detail of your environment to determine if it is going to be safe for you to touch them. One detail overlooked by you could create a distrust that you will have to overcome, if you can.

Are your sheets threadbare? Are there mascara stains on the face rest cover? Does the table squeak? Is your laundry basket overflowing? Is there cat hair all over your pants? Do you have a dirty coffee cup on the counter? Is the bathroom dirty, out of toilet paper, or have a burned out light? I've seen this and heard about worse, otherwise I wouldn't mention it. You need to know that your new clients will transfer everything about the hygiene and cleanliness in your environment to your work whether you deserve it or not, so be meticulous.

You could have done all that work to crosssell to another business to get some new clients, but because there was a hair on the pillow or your blanket smelled stale, they won't be back. If you're lucky, they won't tell the person who referred them and damage other potential clients from that source. Unfortunately, you won't know who hygiene matters to until they leave and never come back. Or, even if they do return, they may not refer others because even if your setting is tolerable for them, they know their friends with allergies won't enjoy having your pet dog in the room or whatever it is that borders on questionable. Again, think from your clients' point of view. Imagine what it is like to come into your environment, and ask yourself if they will feel like it's an environment they will enjoy and come back to.

Marketing at the Intake

The initial face-to-face contact will be a critical time in your marketing strategy. If this person is a referral, create a common bond by mentioning the person who gave the referral, saying you will be sure to send a "thank you" card. This strengthens your association to the referrer, enhancing trust, and telling your new client that you know you are accountable to someone else for your behavior. In the other direction, it also makes the client accountable to that person. Since you will be in contact with the referrer, the new client is more likely to be on good behavior.

Your Verbal Intake

Before your clients get on the table, you need to do a verbal intake. If you had a chance to send them your written intake form before they arrived for the session, this can save you time and give them the opportunity to have thought carefully about what it is they want from you. If they have not filled out a written intake form already, have them fill it out before you begin your verbal intake. You also can fill it out for them as you talk so you get a complete history.

The purpose of your verbal intake is to establish a match between what your clients want and what you offer. I advise that you do this as an initial free consultation. This gives you something else to give away for free, and it gets them to talk freely without getting antsy that they are losing precious massage time. The verbal intake makes sure it is safe for you to work on each person and lets you gather more information about what your clients want. Above all, the verbal intake is a time for you to help each client feel special, understood, and known. You are establishing a relationship with each person, and your intake time gives you the opportunity to see each as an individual, and to introduce yourself as a person as well as a practitioner. If they are coming to you because of some kind of physical pain that their doctors could not help them with, this is important to know. Many people who had doctors' appointments felt that no one listened or cared enough to really help. They were treated as symptoms, not as people. Unfortunately, because of limitations that insurance companies place on medical professionals, doctors and other caregivers have limited time to develop rapport, offer comfort, or get to know a patient well. Fortunately, when you work for yourself in your own private practice, you can take the time to listen and demonstrate that the person as well as the client is important to you. I genuinely like and appreciate my clients, and while our relationships have grown over time, their first intake session was where our long-term relationship became established.

The Written Intake

I highly recommend that you take notes during the time your client is talking to you. If you are filling out intake forms for insurance purposes or because you are working on a doctor's referral, follow their protocols. Your written notes can guide you and remind you about your clients' complaints and problem areas, and assist you if you are making notes for a lawyer if you are working on an accident case. Notes also give you a place to document improvements, note which techniques you have tried, and otherwise let you work in a professional manner.

While all of those are important reasons to take notes, this is a marketing book. If you don't want to take notes for any of the above reasons, at least take notes to look good. This may sound shallow, but when you take notes, you give the impression you're paying attention to this individual's needs and you are behaving in a manner that matches their perception of what a professional should do. Besides, there's nothing more embarrassing than coming in to see a client and not remembering which knee was acting up or which wrist was experiencing carpal tunnel syndrome. Even if you have taken notes, the best way to approach an update on your client is to say "It's been a while since I've seen you and your body may have changed. What can I do for you today?"

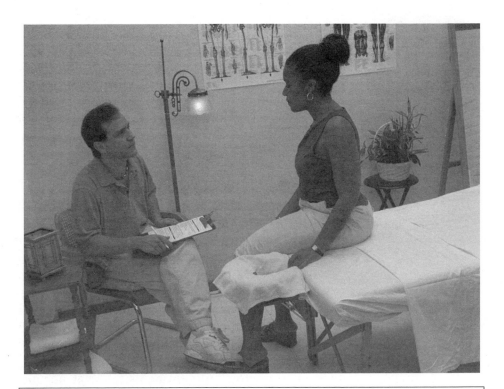

Figure 6–2 Doing an assessment and written intake lets you help your clients more quickly and effectively.

Give Your Clients What They Want

As we discussed earlier in the chapter on setting client expectations, you can find out what your clients want and expect by asking them. Ask what their goals are for the session, and what they want you to focus on or accomplish. Ask if there is anything from other massages they have had that they liked or that they don't want you to do. If they want to just relax and forget their day, don't spend 10 minutes trying to dig that knot out of a calf muscle. That's not why they are there. If the low back is bothersome, address the area immediately so they feel heard. In other words, listen closely to what your clients want and GIVE IT TO THEM.

Educate Your Clients

Much of marketing is really educating, and as you listen to what your clients want, educate them in what you do and what you offer based on what they need. Your education also can reveal if they have misconceptions, unrealistic expectations, or false notions about what you do or how they think you should work. For example, if a big guy has a sore low back and wants you to spend a whole hour using brute force and digging into the few muscles that hurt, you will disappoint him unless you educate him about a better strategy for working out low back pain. Tell him you would hurt him by working too deeply, too quickly, and for too long in such a small area. Teach him how the body works holistically, and explain that the problem may be starting from somewhere else such as an injured ankle or tight hamstrings that are making him compensate with his quadratus lumborum. Point to a muscle chart and talk about his body in intelligent, clear terms and you will be doing some of the best marketing you can ever imagine.

MARKETING QUESTIONNAIRE FOR NEW CLIENTS

Date: _____

Name: _____

Address: _____

City/State/Zip: _____

Home Telephone:/Work Telephone: _____

Birthday/Age/Sex/Marital Status: _____

Education:_____

Occupation: _____

How did you learn about me?_____

_____

_____

Have you had a professional massage before? _____Yes _____No

If yes,

   How long ago?_____

   How frequently did you receive massage? _____

   How many massages have you had? _____

   What kind of massage did you receive? _____

   What kind of massage do you want now? _____

   How often would you like to receive massage? _____

   Why did you leave your last therapist?_____

If no, what made you decide to get a massage now?

_____

_____

What are your primary reasons for receiving massage?

_____

_____

What would you like me to know so that I can best serve your massage needs?

_____

_____

The above client information is strictly confidential. It is used only by me to better understand and serve the need of my clients.

Figure 6–3   In addition to a regular intake form, consider filling out a marketing questionnaire on each client. They can fill out the form themselves, or you can while asking each question.

Why You Do What You Do

If you don't know much anatomy, I strongly suggest that you learn it. As I used to tell my students when I taught anatomy, the American culture associates anatomical knowledge to medical professionals. If you can speak the language of anatomy, your listener often will give you the credibility and esteem usually reserved for doctors. I'm not saying that you should diagnose, treat, or prescribe. I am saying you should know the body well enough to educate your clients about the anatomical principles behind your strategies and applications, or at the least, name the muscles you are working on. I educate my clients quite a bit, not only so they can understand what I am doing and why—and, therefore, value my work more—but also so they have a better idea of how to help themselves. Being able to talk about what you do and why in lucid, anatomical terms can be mighty impressive.

What You Can't Do

Occasionally, you will need to educate your clients about what you can do and what you can't do. If your new clients want massage you are not strong enough for, trained enough, or qualified to do, tell them that what they are asking for is beyond your strength, skill, or qualifications. Tell them what you can do and offer them other options to get the same results they're looking for, but if they want to go, let them leave without charging them. I have had clients who truly believe that "no pain, no gain" is the only kind of massage to get, and since that is not the kind of work that I choose to do, it is better for both of us that I let them go. As a marketer, I also do this because ultimately, they would be unsatisfied and unhappy. And, really, who wants an unhappy client?

What You Shouldn't Do

On the other hand, if there is something they don't want done, don't do it. Once again, I have heard stories from my clients where they have explicitly told a former massage therapist they don't want their feet done, their face touched, or their hairdo messed up, only to have the therapist do exactly what they were told not to do. In particular, one client told her therapist not to work on her feet. His response was, "Oh, I do great feet work, and I know you'll love it." Then, in spite of her protests, he proceeded to work on her feet, unleashing unpleasant memories and flashbacks. Needless to say, that experience was bad for her and she became very distrustful of all massage therapists because of this man's ego. She originally came to me because she had been given a gift certificate for a massage from one of my clients, and it took a great deal of promising on my part before she believed I would not work on her feet or otherwise trample on her boundaries.

The Premassage Spiel

The purpose of your premassage education is to instill trust, relieve fears, and set appropriate expectations. This education will vary depending on each client's experience with massage, but regardless of what they already know, you will want to prepare them for the experience they are about to have. If they have never had a massage before, I tell them my process from beginning to end so that they will know what to anticipate and what to do at each step. This preparation may seem obvious, but it can alleviate a great deal of anxiety and enhance the massage experience by letting them drift a bit more than they would if they did not know what to expect next.

If your clients have been to other massage therapists, their expectations will be different. They will have a preconceived notion of what you will do and how the session will go. Even if you do a good job, they might not have enjoyed the experience because something did not match their presumptions. On the other hand, if they had a bad experience with a previous therapist, they might be bracing themselves in case your work won't be of good quality. I tell new clients that I give a 100 percent money-back guarantee and do a reevaluation part way through, which alleviates their fear of being trapped. I have heard stories of how clients endured a terrible, painful, or unpleasant massage. When I asked them why they didn't just leave, they basically said, "I didn't want to hurt the therapist's feelings. I didn't want to be rude and I kept hoping it would get better." Giving clients the option to just walk away not only alleviates a host of different fears but also demonstrates your confidence in your own work, and confidence is catching.

A Word to the Guys

The subject of expectations set from bad prior experiences brings up a topic I feel needs to be addressed with a frankness I would rather not have to use. However, while I may catch some flak for this next point, my goal is to have every therapist who wants to work be able to succeed, so I will bring it up. Bad massages are often based on the fact that the therapist was not listening or paying attention to how their work felt. You must get good at this or it will cost you clients. Of the many unhappy stories I have heard about client injuries and crossed boundaries, tissue damage, or inflicted pain, almost every therapist involved was male. This doesn't mean that all men are insensitive brutes: I've trained hundreds of great guys with good boundaries and wonderful touch. However, the stories I have heard usually revolve around arrogance, egotism, an unwillingness to accept feedback, and a decided inability to have any notion of how their touch feels or is being received. Giving a great massage requires gathering information on all sorts of sensations and intuitions about what is happening to your client. If the empathetic ability to know how your work feels is missing or ignored, you will have a very hard time getting clients to come back.

Men, you have a bit of an uphill climb in building a practice anyway, and depending on the cultural stereotypes of men in your neck of the woods, you may face some issues about being manly in a field such as massage. I saw this issue with my male students, especially in the Bay Area of California. Many women did not want a male therapist because of a history of being abused or molested, they had a bad experience with a male therapist exuding sexual energy during their session, or they just didn't trust male touch, period. Some men didn't want male therapists either, fearing that someone would question their sexual preference, or their absolute worst fear, that they would have an involuntary erection or arousal while a man was touching them. The way I have seen male therapists compensate for these issues is to become very clinical, therapeutic, or reserved, or limit their work to modalities such as sports massage. In addition, some male therapists seem to think that by doing macho massage using lots of pressure, strength, and power moves, women won't think they're coming on to them and men won't think they're too "sensitive."

Again, having traveled and lived abroad for many years, I feel sorry for American men and the very narrow boxes of self-expression and touch they are allowed. My bigger mission of having every child raised with nurturing and loving touch means a shift in our cultural norms of male touch. If it can start with male massage professionals, we can be the grassroots of phenomenal change. For both male and female therapists to be able to touch in a nurturing, loving, caring, and therapeutic manner without stigmas and fears from ourselves and our clients is my dream.

Getting on the Table

Once the premassage conversation has concluded, expectations have been spoken, and questions answered, I then refamiliarize my client with my massage process. To do that, I say something like, "I am going to leave the room now to wash up, and while I'm gone you can go ahead and get on the table. I'd like to start you face down (or face up) and if you'd like, you can use this face rest so that you don't have to twist your neck. Most of my clients prefer to use the face rest, but if you don't want to, that's fine. Being comfortable is what's most important. It may take us a couple of tries until you are totally comfortable, but once we've got that figured out, you'll be set. If at some point you need to turn, scratch your nose, change a pillow position, or go to the bathroom, just let me know; my goal is to make this massage perfect for you and I want you to be comfortable at all times. I work best if you don't leave any clothes on and you will be covered by this top sheet the whole time, but if you want to leave anything on, that's fine. When I come back, I'll stand outside the door and call out to ask if you are ready; when you answer me, I'll come back in."

Throughout the conversation, I demonstrate what I am talking about. I pretend to put my face in the face rest and I lift the corner of the top sheet and point underneath. Even then, some people still lie down on the top sheet, and then we have to go through the little dance of getting them back off the table and under the sheet. If this is a person's first massage, the image they may have is based on what they have seen in magazine ads which often show the models lying face down with their hands folded under the chin. Your clients may have no idea of what a face rest is or how to use it, so explain it beforehand so you don't have to make them move too much when you come back into the room.

Also during this initial conversation, be careful not to use words that sound like commands; instead, give explanations. You don't know what this person has been through before, especially with the issue of undressing, so don't push the panic button with poor choices of words. I was working with a group of some 20 other massage therapists at a Palm Springs "ladies' day of beauty" convention event where the massage tables were crammed into a large room and were separated only by cloth curtains. Of all the conversations I overheard, ringing out over the top of all of them was a loud voice from a nearby therapist giving the command, "Just get naked and hop on up here." That pearl ranks right up there with such phrases as "Strip on down to nothing," or "Take it all off and I'll be back in a minute." Given that millions of people have been molested, you do not know what phrases their perpetrator used, so it is paramount that you craft a phrase for this moment in the massage process that is pretty much guaranteed not to bring back bad memories. I know this may sound a bit overboard to some people, but it is a reality I learned about in painful depth from many of my massage students, and it has created a sensitivity and awareness that I had not considered until I heard their stories.

I cannot emphasize enough how important clear communication is at this premassage juncture. Assume your new clients know nothing about massage, guide them through every obvious step of the way so they remain comfortable, and let them know your every move so they can trust that you won't walk in on them while they are undressed. Marketing includes all the little things you do to get and keep customers, and part of that is being sensitive and tolerant of your clients' issues of nudity. I've had little old ladies stride to the table with nothing on but a smile, and I've had young men very shy and protective about being seen nude. For the clients I have worked with who have left other therapists because the therapist just stood there and talked while the client undressed, mishandled the drape, or otherwise exposed them, this may be the one significant piece that makes or breaks a positive, long-term relationship.

If you work in a spa or other type of establishment, the facility may have a policy that you must help the client onto and off of the table. While the purpose of this is to ensure that the client doesn't fall off the table and file a subsequent lawsuit, it can be a good or bad experience for the client depending on how you handle it. Clients who have received massage from a practitioner who leaves the room while they undress and get on the table may feel uncomfortable with this more "hands-on" approach. Your job is to make them feel safe and cared for, and to position this step as a "special treatment" for the facilities' guests. I know this all may seem silly since once they are lying down you will see and touch much of the body, but being seen naked standing up is somehow quite different to most people. So regardless of your own comfort with nudity, be respectful of other's need for modesty.

EXERCISE: Creating the Premassage Spiel

- Think about the steps your clients will go through from the time of the intake process until they walk out the door or you drive away. Include:
  The intake process and what kinds of questions you will ask.
  The getting onto the table process, including undressing, and where you will be during that time.
  How you will ask for feedback during the session.
  Your closing ritual and when clients know the session is over.
  The getting off the table process, including where you will be during that time.
- Then divide up into groups of three and practice your premassage spiel.

Moment 3: During the Massage

Once your clients are safely on the table and comfortable, the massage comes down to two things: what you do and what you say. We are first going to cover a few key points about the application of massage, then thoroughly review what to say during this moment of decision.

Universal Massage Skills
It is mind-boggling how many different types of bodywork are available on the market today. Due to that, I cannot even begin to cover how to do your particular modality, but there are some universal factors that apply to almost all forms of bodywork, and understanding their importance can make a huge difference in whether or not clients rebook. These factors are:
- your opening ritual.
- types of touch.
- transitions.

- client participation.
- results of the session.

Your Opening Ritual

Opening rituals create a marvelous transition from your intake process to the actual hands-on work. I highly recommend that you have an opening ritual since it demarcates the beginning of the session with the pomp, flourish, or focus befitting the moment. You are taking your client onto a magical journey into the body and the moment deserves special recognition. An opening ritual can be anything you want it to be. Depending on your personality and that of your clients, it can be very subtle and short, or a time of great ceremony.

Massage is still a bit mystifying to some clients, and your opening ritual can give you some room to open their minds. For my fairly conservative clients, part of the fun for them of getting massage from me is the fact that I have a very woo-woo side that is far removed from their predictable daily lives, and my opening and closing routines give them a little taste of the mysterious. I will admit here that my opening and closing routines are very purposeful, and I have added an element of entertainment to them. My favorite business tycoon is Richard Branson, the eccentric owner of Virgin Airlines. His multibillion dollar secret is that most businesses, even airlines, are much more profitable if they understand and play up the role of being entertaining, whatever the business.

I have met some very successful therapists who put on quite an opening display, including smudging the room with burning sage, waving owl feathers, ringing chimes, laying out crystals, and other such rituals that are a big part of why people come to see them. These actions have their own value, but they also are quite theatrical and some clients just love it. It is not my intention to take away from the sacredness of more spiritually based rituals; they serve wonderful purposes, but they are also fascinating to the uninitiated and can be a big part of your draw. If you are a bit of a character and are known for being a bit, um, different, then the people who come to you based on your reputation may secretly be disappointed if you don't do something magical for your opening moments or throughout the session. If you're not quite so outlandish, create an opening ritual that suits you and your clients, and then stick with it. After a few sessions, the very act of your opening ritual is enough to trigger their relaxation response and they relax much more quickly.

My ritual serves multiple purposes. It includes an opening grounding where I rest my hands on the back or feet, followed by running my hands lightly over the sheet to bring awareness to the body from head to toe. This prepares me energetically and focuses me emotionally, all the while introducing my touch and creating the first impression that at least my touch is safe. I tell my new clients that I am introducing my hands to their body to build trust, sort of like a full-body handshake, and that I am feeling for temperature variances and subtle tension patterns. This, I explain, lets me know where to look first for possible problem spots, then strategize where I should concentrate my time. By revealing this as my intention, it tells them that I care enough to pay attention to their individual needs and that I will make the most of their time. I highlight these two points because I have dealt with many clients who felt that their prior therapist only did a routine massage and didn't spend time in the areas that had the highest need. This simple ritual and explanation sets the tone that my intention is to meet their needs and shows that I have some skills behind that intention.

EXERCISE: Create an Opening Ritual

■ On a separate sheet of paper, write down a description of your ideal opening ritual. Start with the purposes of the ritual such as what you need to do to create more trust, demonstrate your intention, or impress your client. Think about how you can convey your purposes with your touch, words, and movements. Run a few scenarios through in your head, find one you like, and write it down. If possible, have a few people in the group share or demonstrate their opening rituals.

The First Strokes. Once the opening ritual is complete, give the first strokes of your massage. Your first movements are probably your most important strokes because they create the final piece of your clients' first impression. Up to this point, they have heard your voice, listened to your thought process, sized up your environment, experienced your opening ritual, and evaluated you based on a million different little judgments. In my experience, all of those impressions are changeable at this point. If your first strokes feel loving, compassionate, competent, professional, or whatever it is they are looking for, you may be forgiven a host of oversights if your proof is in the pudding.

Types of Touch

The types of touch you use in a session vary greatly with the intention of the stroke, and you can use a combination of variables that fulfill that intention and affect your clients' experience of your work. These variables are the speed of your stroke, the amount of pressure used, the duration or length of the stroke, and its intention. A long, slow, deep stroke has a very different effect than a rapid series of light hacking or a steady, held direct pressure, and each serves a very different purpose. If your schooling has taught you only a few sequences to follow and ways to work, I recommend you start experimenting with how you can mix and match these elements for different results with your clients. The more you understand the impacts of speed, pressure, length of stroke, and intention, the more you can customize your work to your clients' needs.

Along this line, the complaints I have heard, especially from people who got massages in high turn-over settings such as cruise ships and luxury resorts, were that the therapist did a boring old routine with no variety and no stated intention. Variety is important in your touch, and I encourage you to think outside the box and experiment with these elements. If nothing else, you will prevent your own boredom in doing the same massage which I personally know has cost a few therapists their careers.

Pressure. Of all the variables, the amount of pressure is the one most likely to determine the satisfaction level of your clients. Pressure is not a variable to make guesses on. Stereotypes that big guys like heavy pressure and little ladies want light, fluffy work are dangerous to your return rate. The right pressure takes work to find, and entails getting feedback both from what your clients say and what your hands feel. In addition, your pressure needs to be adjusted constantly from body part to body part and from session to session. Too much pressure is painful or injurious, and too little pressure is frustrating and irritating.

Some therapists think they magically should know the perfect amount of pressure to use, or believe that they will lose face or client trust if they admit that they don't know what the right pressure is. To get feedback without losing face or trust, I tell my clients I'm not psychic, and while I am very good at figuring out the right amount of pressure, I cannot feel what they are feeling, so they need to let me know when my pressure is too heavy or too light. Feedback about pressure takes a bit to get out of some clients, and I have learned not to ask questions that can be answered with the word "fine." Questions that actually give you valuable feedback need to be specific. "Would you like more pressure?" or "It feels like you're tightening up; do I need to lighten up?" can teach you, over time, to trust your hands to the point you will have to ask for verbal feedback fewer times.

The opposite of the mute, lie-there-and-take-it client is the over-directing, pushy client. If you have a client who is demanding heavier pressure but you can feel under your hands that the tissue is resisting, be aware that they probably have so little body awareness you could push through to the other side and they would say it's still not enough pressure. Many people are out of touch with how they feel, and they need more stimulation than normal to the tissue and nervous system before it registers they have even felt your touch.

Be careful with clients like these, especially if they are new to massage. Since they aren't really able to feel pressure accurately, they will demand more pressure. If you comply, you will most likely hurt them. Having fallen into this more-pressure trap a number of times to assuage a client at the moment, I have learned that the aftereffects are not worth giving in to an insistent client. Education is the best way out of this bind. You need to tell people that you understand they want more pressure but your hands are telling you that you have gone as deeply as the tissue allows without tightening up, and if you work deeper, you will hurt them. If you are fairly new to massage and don't yet have the hand sensitivity that comes with years of practice, be careful with too much repetition in one place or forced pressure in any areas. You can hurt people that way and that's not why we got into the profession.

I prefer to do my education up front instead of waiting for a comment about pressure. I tell my new clients that it takes me some time to get familiar with their tissue and to figure out what their normal muscle tone feels like compared to areas of tension. I explain that while I am getting familiar with them, I will be using a lighter pressure than they might expect at the outset. I explain that once I have gained their body's trust, their muscles will relax more and I can work deeper without hurting them. This alleviates my need to prove anything in the first few minutes, which I have found myself inclined to do with new clients. When their tissue has relaxed, I point it out and then say that I can now go deeper if they would like me to. If they do, I gradually start adding pressure, asking for feedback as I go.

If you do the above but clients keep telling you they want more pressure, you will need to make some decisions. You can make a concerted effort to strengthen yourself, refer your clients elsewhere, or consider using or learning a modality that is effective without those clients expecting heavy pressure. Whatever you choose, don't let clients bully you into doing work deeper than you can physically handle. Building a dream practice means that you avoid as many hand, wrist, and body injuries as you can, and how you handle pressure either will lead to problems or to a long and fulfilling career.

Other Types of Touch. During the massage, you are touching your clients in ways different from your massage strokes. The other types of touch to consider that can strongly impact rebooking are the nonmassaging touches of moving the client around and handling the drape.

Repositioning Clients. Moving or repositioning your client is a skill that often does not get the attention it deserves. Picking up a client's arm to do a range of motion exercise or move it under the drape can be a graceful and unnoticed motion, or a startling disruption depending on how it is carried out. Moving a leg onto a bolster or placing a pillow under the neck needs to be done with the same smoothness and speed as the rest of your work; otherwise, it can be a disturbing and disconcerting experience. It is one thing to have a massage therapist press into tissue; it is quite another to have limbs picked up and maneuvered. Many clients probably will be fine with being moved around, but it can be disconcerting to others for a host of reasons. Before you do much range of motion work or a significant amount of repositioning, ask permission to do so. Then at least your clients won't resist or reflexively try to help as much.

Even if you are given permission, move people with the same amount of caring and regard as the rest of your work. One client I spoke with had gone to see a massage therapist who used to be a nurse. The client was greeted brusquely, and as she soon discovered, was handled brusquely as well. Using maneuvers and efficiency no doubt developed with hospital patients, this ex-nurse whipped this client around like a rag doll, rolling her sideways in the sheet to get to a bolster and stuffing pillows around with such vigor that it was jolting. Never was the client asked if the pillows were comfortable or wanted. A hospital patient may not know that they have a say in being comfortable, but massage clients do, and, surprise, comfort matters. Need I say that the client didn't rebook?

Handling a Drape. Handling a drape is also a much bigger deal than many people would consider it to be. Clients are watching you for every sign of whether they can trust you, and if before the session you are jerking on the sheet edges, slapping on the blanket to smooth it, or jamming pillows around, you probably could see them involuntarily flinch. How you handle inanimate objects around you may not be how you touch your clients during the massage, but they don't know that. Once the massage has started, and the client is under the sheet or towel and you are adjusting it, handle the drape the way you would handle them. Don't toss aside blankets, yank off sheets, or drop pillows on the floor. Small but crucial bits of trust can get lost by mishandling a drape, so be conscious of how you move it.

For the sake of your clients' comfort, don't wad the drape up into a big lump and jam it under a thigh, shoulder, or as I once saw done by a new student, rolled up and neatly tucked into the gluteal cleft. Visually it looked quite neat and tidy to the therapist, but for the client who proceeded to reach up and extract it, it looked mighty uncomfy. Please, do not trade neatness that only you see for comfort that your client feels.

Draping is a topic with many varied and conflicting opinions, but what matters most is, does it work well for your clients? Some clients may love being wrapped mummy-like in a tight cocoon of blankets, but do that to a client with even mild claustrophobia and you've got a big problem on your hands. The purpose of the drape is to help the client stay warm, maintain modesty and privacy, and feel safe that they are not in any way exposed. That said, I have seen demonstrations of draping that were supposed to make the client feel safe, but the movements were so invasive that they bordered on indiscretion. Unless you are doing a lot of deep massage into the inner thigh and are going to be doing big ranges of motion, there is no reason in the world that your hand needs to come anywhere near the genitals to shove the sheet under the thigh or make some absurd version of a giant diaper. You must weigh which is of more concern to your client; that you are somehow peeking if you use a fairly loose drape, or that your hands are going way too close to places they shouldn't be.

Beyond these points, the mere act of disturbing a client floating in alpha state just to do a bunch of fancy sheet work does not seem a good tradeoff. On the financial side, I also would ask if lots of tight, neat draping is what your clients want to be spending their money on. If you charge $60 an hour, then at $1 per minute with one minute of futzing with the sheet per limb on both sides means you are blowing their money in ways they may eventually resent. Clients come to you for a good massage, not for good draping. The bottom line is that you keep your clients draped appropriately for modesty and warmth, and that you not disturb them or waste their time and money for what should be an invisible part of the massage.

Amount of Time in One Area.   Another hands-on variable to consider during the massage is the amount of time you spend working on one area of the body. Rebooking a client requires that you address the needs that they came in with, and how you spend your time affects how well you are able to address those needs. This may sound obvious, but I learned this lesson the hard way by making the mistake of taking too much time doing massage work in areas the client had not come to see me about. In particular, I remember a woman early in my career who had come to me because of her sore neck. Being a firm believer in the value of full body massage, I began my routine the usual way, starting at the feet and working my way up. Unfortunately, I kept finding trouble spots elsewhere, got involved in working those out, and by the time I got to her neck, oops, I was running out of time. Having booked my appointments too closely together since I hadn't quite learned that lesson yet, I had no extra time to do the work necessary on her neck. I had done good work, but not in the right place. The woman didn't feel like giving me a second shot, and frankly, I don't blame her.

Transitions

Regardless of your massage modality, you will have moments of transition, and how you handle those moments can make your massage a relaxing bliss or a disquieting experience. These moments of transition are:

- the beginning of each stroke.
- moving the length of the stroke.
- the ending of each stroke.
- staying in physical, energetic, or auditory contact when moving to new areas.

- rituals at the beginning and end of the massage.
- turning the client over.
- waking a person up with touch and voice.

From watching my many students practice, I would say the biggest difference between the good looking massages and those that seemed bumpy was the quality of the transitions. Easy transitions were modulated and flowing, with interludes for getting oil or moving from limb to limb as all part of a slow and rhythmic dance. Key moments of transition such as finishing a side, turning over, or ending the massage were given time and attention for flow and continuity, keeping the receiver relaxed and as undisturbed as possible. Each bodywork or massage modality has different ways of transitioning throughout the work, and the more you practice polished and seamless starts and stops, the more your client will let go. Moments of transition go more smoothly if there are finishing strokes that mark the completion of one area or side before going on to the next. If you can, do strokes to reintegrate the parts you have been working back into a cohesive whole, especially as you finish each limb and side. This teaches your clients to experience themselves as a whole, and gives a sense of satisfaction and completion as well.

Keeping Contact. During times of transition, you can use various forms of contact to keep your connection to the client. If your clients are nervous or tentative, lost contact can pop them out of a restful state to search for where you've gone. Even if you must lift both hands off to move around the table or change positions, you can maintain contact by letting your client subconsciously follow where you are. By using sounds such as breathing, pressing on the table where you are about to work, or leaving energetic "hand prints" where you lift off and land again, you can stay in touch even if you have lost physical contact. If you have taken your hands off during a time of transition, I recommend that you reapproach the body with a touch that starts a few inches away from the skin, moves gently through the energy field, and lands softly on the tissue.

If you get really good at using your intention to maintain contact, you can leave an area with an energetic sensation that you are still in physical contact even though you're getting a well-deserved sip of water. Some massage professionals place a high priority on always maintaining contact as well as keeping up a steady motion. However, over the years, I have found that when I stop or rest my movements, and leave my hands on them, that the clients also get a break from constant stimulation and relax even deeper.

EXERCISE: Approaching and Leaving the Skin Surface

- Approaching the Skin Surface
  Pair off, establish a Partner A and Partner B and sit so that you can touch.
  Partner A is the client and B is the massage therapist.
  Partner A uncovers and holds out his or her forearm, which has very sensitive skin.
  Partner B practices approaching the skin starting 10 to 12 inches away from the body, gradually moves through the energy field toward the skin, and lands gently. Practice this a number of times, focusing attention on how to create the feeling that the therapist is touching the arm even before physical contact.

■ Leaving the Skin Surface
Partner B then practices leaving an energetic hand print on the skin surface using the intention of creating the sensation that touch has not
been lost, even as the hand is being lifted. Focus on leaving a sensation
of warmth and pressure, and practice how far away the hand can move
before its absence is noticed. Try this a few times with Partner A watching, and then with Partner A keeping his or her eyes closed.
Then reverse roles and practice this valuable skill again.
If you are reading this book on your own, do this to yourself by practicing on your own forearms.

Client Participation

Keeping clients happy enough to have them rebook also means paying attention to what level of participation they want to have in the session. Some
people think that the ultimate massage means not moving a muscle and
wishing you had a giant pancake turner to flip them over. Others expect to
be fully engaged with range of motion work, muscle testing, and constant
feedback. Needs for rest and relaxation usually involve less participation,
while needs for injury recovery or performance enhancement require the
client to be awake and active. Mixing up these needs can leave clients frustrated. If a stressed out executive just got to the dozing stage and you insist
on rousing him with your regular routine of range of motion for the hips,
complete with the involved draping, he will resentfully change his state to
accommodate your routine, but he probably won't be happy. If a marathon
runner with tight hamstrings wants help with muscle lengthening and
strengthening, and your basic routine doesn't incorporate even passive range
of motion work, her needs will not be met and the odds of rebooking diminish greatly.

To know what level of participation your clients want, ask them. Tell
them during the intake time that you want to serve their needs, but you
need to know how awake or involved they want to be. Clients can participate at varying levels including:

Actively participating—ROM, resistance, involved feedback, working
with breath

Partially participating—giving feedback, maybe some passive ROM

Awake and talking—general conversation with minimal feedback

Awake and silent

Floating

Sleeping

If your clients want to actively participate, please be careful about how
you talk them through their exercises, breathing patterns, or ask for feedback. Be patient with people and give guidance, not commands. Instructions
on anything from taking a breath to assisted stretches can elicit resistance or
cooperation depending on how they are given. Old dictating-style communication models from football coaches and drill sergeants may work in other
settings, but I don't recommend them for most massage clients.

New clients who have never had massage before also may find that their
limbs and body don't cooperate the way they want them to. The more a

client participates, the more apparent it may become that range of motion has been lost, muscle control has diminished, and strength has evaporated. Tears of frustration or anger have been part of the process for a number of my clients trying to regain fine-motor control lost in an injury, especially the type of clients I have that are pretty much used to having their way in the world. Commanding someone to relax an arm they are holding stiffly rarely works; giving instructions to imagine it being warm and heavy or falling into your hand makes more sense, and creates less embarrassment at uncooperative limbs.

So what does this have to do with marketing? Everything. Clients who are given education, gently guided through stubborn holding patterns, and treated as the intelligent adults they are will appreciate and respect your methods of handling them, and they will be more likely to rebook and refer. Clients who are treated with exasperation because they won't relax on command like a dog being told to sit (and I've seen it!) will not be back. When clients don't come back, you have to go back to reaching new clients and the dream practice stays out of reach. Subtle points such as we have covered here matter a great deal to clients, and the more you consider and try them, the faster you will succeed.

Results of the Session

Ultimately, many clients rebook based on the results they get from your work. I've met clients who put up with their therapist having a pack of dogs lounging around the treatment table or bruising them with deep work because they got the results they went in for. Unraveling blankets and rooms reeking of patchouli oil may be a bit bothersome, but if you offer caring and compassion, and can fix that nagging knee problem, much may be forgiven.

Results of a session are measured a number of different ways, and understanding how clients measure success gives you a greater advantage in reaching it. The success of your work is evaluated based on your clients':

- experience during the session.
- short-term results of the session.
- long-term results of the session.
- cumulative results of multiple sessions.
- ability to maintain improvements by helping themselves.

For many people, getting a massage is about having an "experience." They just want a grand and royal pampering, and the stated purpose of their visit can seem rather vague. Massage has become a significant symbol for the good life, and some people just want the glitz and glamour of the moment, reveling in the thought that they are getting the treatment usually reserved for the rich and famous. Glamour massages are actually kind of fun to do. I enjoy creating the atmosphere and feeling that the client truly has arrived. Recognizing clients with this mindset is crucial; it means that their results are measured solely by the moments during the massage, and being king or queen for the day is what is expected. Pain relief, joint mobility, or open chakras are not the goal; bragging, and feeling smug and superior is.

Mixing up clients who want a glamour massage with clients who want real help can be frustrating to both client types. People who want pain relief, stress reduction, posture reeducation, or performance enhancement will be judging your results very quickly, and what they decide may bring them back or not. Fast food drive-up windows and Internet e-tailers have taught our culture that wants and needs can be met instantaneously, and drug companies make promises of pain relief in a matter of minutes with magical pills. However, the body, as marvelous as it is, sometimes takes a while to repair itself, and you will need to educate your results-oriented clients about what to expect from one session. Interviewing your clients during the intake session can reveal what their expectations are, and whether or not you can meet their desired results in one or more sessions, or at all.

Motivated clients who want to participate in their own healing will be wanting genuine help and guidance from you. Often, they are some of the most gratifying clients to work with because they will push you to learn more, work smarter, and be more effective with your time. Results-oriented clients will come back to you if they know that you are thinking and strategizing about how to help them. Patience is available for you if your clients know what to expect realistically. On-the-table education using pressure, stretches, or other feedback tools can demonstrate that you are making steps large or small toward helping them, and they can measure your success with valid sensations of improvement. Giving motivated clients at-home exercises, stretches, or self-massage routines also can put you up another notch in the trust and value columns, and if that homework increases the benefits of your work, rebookings are virtually assured.

What You Say During the Massage. The second primary element during the third moment of decision is what you say during the massage. It is a smart therapist who knows that what you say and talk about can have a great deal of impact on whether or not your clients come back. Since many of my interviews with massage clients across the country revealed that talking and poor communication skills were some of the main reasons they left their therapists, we are going to thoroughly, and some may think, exhaustively, cover the art of communication during your massage session. However, the purpose of this book is to help massage therapists be successful, and if what follows can help you keep one client coming back for one more session, then it will be worth the price of this book.

The Art of Conversation

Talking and conversation during a massage is a highly individual matter. I have found that some clients just grunt, get on the table, and that's the end of that whereas others want to talk the whole time. Some clients will talk only when they are face up and some will talk only when face down. Some talk for the first 10 minutes, then fall silent; others suddenly get chatty right before it is time to end the session. Clients talk out of nervousness, loneliness, interest, and curiosity about you and your work. They ask questions about their symptoms and many other topics. You can let them lead the conversation and respond, or you can let them know that they might relax more if they are quiet. Some clients are afraid of silence and being quiet might be more than they can bear, so keep chatting until you feel them drift.

Depending on your type of work and target market, your primary service may not be your massage, but your conversation or ability to listen. My contingency of elderly widows talked from the moment I got in the door to the time I closed my car door and drove away with them waving. I was offered, and accepted, more than my share of tuna casserole luncheons, knowing I was the only visitor coming by that week. Of course, I helped their aches and pains, but they rebooked to talk. And that was fine with me.

During the Massage

Although some massages may be totally quiet, if you and your client are going to talk, I recommend you take time during the massage to tell your clients what you are doing and why. This creates immense value for them in their impression of you and in their understanding of the benefits of massage. Once into a session, I tell my clients what I discover about tension or compensation patterns, temperature variations, muscle spasms, involuntary reflexes, or whatever else I notice. If they are open, I also say what I am picking up intuitively. I usually save intuition-based information until they are more familiar with me and have learned to trust me many sessions later, but in some cases, I go with my gut.

On-the-table education is one of the best forms of marketing you can do. I often tell new clients the purpose of the stroke I am using and how it affects their muscles, nervous system, blood flow, and the like. Since new clients often are nervous to some degree, this gives them something to focus on. However, once I feel them start to float away, I shut up. In addition to general education, I give specific information about their bodies, especially if anything my hands feel is unclear or confusing to me. I tell them what I notice including my thought processes, hunches, or suppositions. I explain how a stubbed toe can lead to low back pain or a tight neck can lead to tennis elbow. We cover holistic principles about how the body works as a whole, and together, we work as a team with me giving my observations, asking questions, and striving to solve the puzzle they came in with.

Managing Boundaries

Once your clients are relaxed and your work is underway, your responsibilities during the massage come down to two things: taking care of yourself and taking care of your clients. Taking care of yourself means protecting yourself physically, emotionally, and energetically. In this respect, your highest need is on yourself. Your boundaries of how much you will push yourself physically, how much you will reveal about yourself or allow your clients to reveal about themselves, and how connected you will allow yourself to become are of utmost importance for a long-term career. Poor boundary skills can lead to injuries, pain, and drained energy for you, and that, ultimately, doesn't serve your clients well.

Beyond these boundaries of self-protection, though, it is my opinion that the clients need to receive the highest priority. It is their turn to tell stories, to be silent if they choose, to set the temperature, choose the music, select the oil scent, give feedback on your work and pressure, and otherwise control the many elements of the massage they are paying for. They are not paying to listen to your problems, hear your stories, or offer you counsel, sympathy, or advice.

I remember a particular story during my crosscountry interviews from a woman who had gone into a spa for a dual massage where she and her husband were to receive simultaneous massages, side by side in the same room, to celebrate their anniversary. While this sounded wonderful and romantic in the fancy spa brochure, in reality, the two therapists talked between themselves the whole time they were working, chatting away as if the clients weren't even there. It wasn't quite the experience these poor clients were hoping for and their disappointment was evident. No rebooking there, that's for sure!

When I have worked in settings with other therapists in rooms close enough to overhear them, I have been appalled by the lack of boundaries, inappropriateness of subject topics brought up by the therapist, and barrage of monologue from the therapist to the poor client helplessly lying there trying to relax. This doesn't mean you don't talk while you work; I've had many enjoyable conversations with clients, but I let them lead the conversation, choose the topic, or just be silent. Depending on your target market, you may have formal relationships with your clients, or more informal interactions and conversations, but regardless, beyond your self-protection, put your clients first and have your time together be about them.

Listening

Much of your conversation during the massage will entail you listening, and if you are paying attention, you will pick up on information and insights not available during your intake time. What you hear can tell you a lot about your clients, and if you are facing a perplexing physical symptom, listen for clues to its source. The body is affected greatly by emotions, stress, and personal and professional problems, and more than a few times, I have figured out that the source of their physical pain was emotional. One client had an intractable problem that I just could not solve until her husband went out of town for a two-week vacation. Magically, her tight shoulders released and

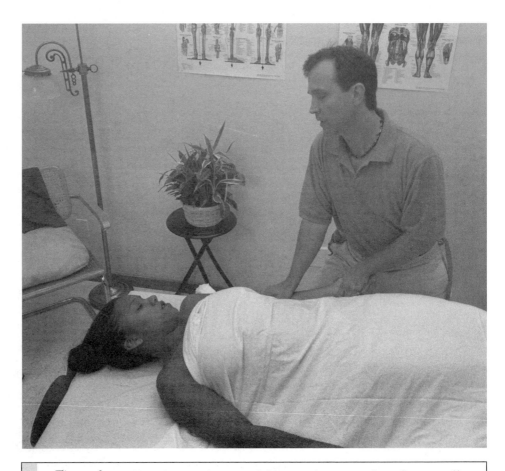

Figure 6–4 Listening can be one of the most important benefits you offer your clients.

stopped hurting, and we both were baffled but pleased. Then her husband came home and her shoulders resumed their usual tension and pain. When I pointed out that little correlation to her, she was mighty surprised, but it was like a light bulb going off in her head. I'm not a psychologist so I didn't take it any further, but my job is to help my clients' pain and help them understand more about it. By listening to her talk and correlating what she said about her life with what my hands felt, I at least helped her draw her own conclusions about her source of pain.

Responding During a Massage Conversation

When it is appropriate for you to join in the conversation, you will be responding to what your client has said or asked. When a person asks you a question about your day, your weekend, or some other facet of your life, you certainly can respond with an answer. However, questions such as these often are a polite way for others to get an opening to talk about themselves. If you don't want to talk about yourself or if you think the client is fishing, simply say, My day (weekend, boyfriend, girlfriend, children) is great. And how was your weekend? Then settle in for a long story while you get to work on that tight shoulder. In normal life, conversation is a give and take, but in a massage setting, let your client do most of the talking.

In addition, when you are responding to their stories, do not try to top them. If your client was stranded at the airport for four hours, don't launch into how you were stuck for eight hours. If your client is excited because of finally getting in a bike ride of 10 miles, don't cut off the story to talk about your bike ride across Canada. Turn over the spotlight, and let your clients revel in the horror or glory of it all. Remember, they are there to take care of themselves, and the more your responses turn the attention back to them, the more your value will increase as both a massage professional and a listening ear. When it comes time to rebook and multiple needs are met beyond the massage, the appointment book is much more likely to get filled in.

Verbal Check-ins

One of the most important things you can do during a session to ensure that you keep this client is to make sure that they are happy. During your first session, it is important to ask on a regular but not disruptive basis if this is what they had expected, if there is anything you should change, or any way you can make it better. Ask about sound, heat, pressure, or room scents. If they are squirming, ask if they need to change positions. Don't ask with a sense of fear or lack of confidence; your work is good; you just want it perfect. If they are not happy with something, you can change it instantly, circumventing the possibility of being surprised at the end of the massage. If your verbal check-in has demonstrated that something is amiss, you can't change it, and it's a big deal to the client, you can end the session and give a refund.

If your verbal check-ins frequently result in curt responses such as "I'm fine!" then take notice. Either everything is fine and they are annoyed at being disturbed from their reverie, or they don't know that they are allowed to have the massage the way they want it. Many clients make the wrong assumption that getting on a massage therapist's table is like getting on a doctor's table. They expect it to be uncomfortable and don't know they are "allowed" to ask you to change anything that may be causing them discomfort. Most of them have experienced hard, cold, paper-lined tables, cold doctor instruments, rooms that smell like rubbing alcohol, and scratchy paper dressing gowns. Why would they think that a massage session, especially if it's more therapeutic in nature, would be different than a doctor visit?

I talked with a woman who got a massage on a cruise ship and was so badly manhandled that she was bruised and hurting for days. When I asked her why she didn't tell the therapist that the pressure was too heavy, her response was, "I thought he knew what he was doing, so I let him do it." Her old programming was that you just put up with what the doctor does to you. Unfortunately it did not serve her well, and it meant a bad massage for her. For the therapist who wasn't paying enough attention to the fact that she was probably stiff and bracing, or flinching underhand, she would not be a repeat client. Unfortunately, this young man by now probably has mangled more than his share of one-time clients who don't know any better. When those clients come ashore, they probably will never get a massage from you or me, and they'll tell all their friends about how painful massage is when they show off their bruise-tinged tans. Verbal check-ins can prevent such stories, keep you on track, and let your clients know that you are paying attention and care about how they feel.

Creating Awareness, Especially of Improvements

Besides not hurting your clients, one of the other good reasons to pay close attention to them is so that you can point out their improvements. You can tell them when you feel muscles relaxing, energy releasing, and so on. Of all the ways for you to give directive yet unobtrusive feedback, the best word you can use is the word "good." Softly repeat to yourself "good, good, good," as you feel muscles let go. This focuses clients on where you are working and trains them to gain sensitivity to incremental improvement. The words "good, good" also serve another function. While there may be a few exceptions, most clients will want their massage therapists to like them. When you say "good," they know they are performing well, and your praise can give them the feeling you approve of them. I have been testing the effect of the word "good" for many years on my clients and students, and while it is a simple word, millions of people long to hear it and feel the approval that goes with it.

Creating awareness of improvements also can be done by asking questions, but be careful: how you ask is important. Always state your question in the positive. Don't ask, "Does that still hurt?" This question starts the mind on a search for pain, which it will most likely find, and since they are now noticing the pain, they will think your massage is not working, even if you have felt improvement. Instead, ask something simple such as, "Does that feel better?" The mind will now scan for improvements, and when they say "yes," they are recognizing benefits they hadn't noticed until you asked.

Another important reason for them to acknowledge improvement is that many people have a psychological belief that their problems are permanent and unchangeable. By admitting to you they feel better, they begin to break that psychological chain that often holds a pain pattern in place. If they say "no," tell them you are going to try a different technique. If you switch modalities, tell them what you're doing and why. Again there is nothing more fascinating to people than themselves, so talk about them and what you are doing to them.

Handling an Emotional Release During the Massage

Paying attention and doing verbal check-ins are important for emotional shifts as well as physical ones. If your clients feel the trust, silence, and safety to experience what is going on for them physically and emotionally, there is the possibility of them having some form of emotional release. While this may not happen often or at all, you should be prepared to handle it so that your client will feel secure enough to rebook a return visit. If clients suddenly start to cry, laugh, twitch, or release emotions, they may be afraid of what you will think; some people may think they should end the session and leave. If possible, let them know that the release is temporary, it will subside, and it's often a good thing to let go of built-up energy. Emotional release massage is a skill well beyond the scope of this book, but how you handle an emotional release can make the difference between whether clients stay and especially, whether they come back.

For example, if I notice that a client is crying and breathing in such a way it is apparent to both of us that I have recognized it, I will say something like "I can see that something has come up for you. If you want to talk about it, I'm here, but you don't have to. I can stop the massage if you'd like; otherwise, I'll just keep working." This simple statement is unobtrusive, gives her permission to experience whatever she is feeling, and lets her know she is in charge of the situation. It also removes the burden of feeling like she has to explain anything to me, and it prevents me from getting in over my head if the emotion is more properly handled by a trained psychologist or mental health professional.

Letting people cry can be very freeing for them. Don't make them stop so you can hand over a tissue or stop the massage in the middle of a stroke. If possible, shift your work down to more gentle and soothing strokes, send the powerful intention of your love and caring, and let the emotions release. Be present and caring, ride it out, and listen quietly. Your client most likely will be very grateful, and most likely will be back.

Music During the Massage

Sounds during the massage can be from conversation and also from music. We have discussed music chosen for 20 to 30 seconds of play time on your answering machine, but it becomes even more important during an hour-long massage. Many clients enjoy having music on in the background while you do your massage. While your preferences in music may be different from those of your clients, having music you enjoy and can work to with consistent volume, rhythm, and flow is important. That said, it can be a good idea to ask if your client is enjoying your selection or would prefer silence. Play different tapes or CDs, find out which ones they like, or show them your selection and let them choose one. Unless your music is the focal point of the massage, keep the volume down. This is especially helpful when the type of client who likes to talk in the face-down position decides to tell you about his weekend trip while his face is deep in the headrest.

Whatever music you choose, get feedback on it, and please, leave out the spoken word tapes. I talked with a woman whose new therapist was playing a talking tape by Deepak Chopra when she first arrived for her appointment. The client didn't think much of it at first, but throughout the intake time and the first few minutes of the session, Deepak's voice and words permeated their conversation. Finally, after lying there listening to him talk while she was trying to relax, she asked the therapist to please turn off the tape. The therapist was greatly surprised that the tape was bothering her client, and even though she immediately turned it off, that minor incident made the client wary about other ways the therapist wasn't paying attention or considering her needs. A precedent had been set with a simple oversight. And you guessed it, no rebooking followed. So let me tell you right now. Don't play talking tapes during your session unless they are a strategic part of your work. If worst comes to worst, you can get a white noise machine and play a babbling brook or rainy day sounds. Just make sure it is a sound your client likes.

Silence

Finally, in the art of conversation there is time for silence. Sometimes, silence truly is golden, both for your client and yourself. I let my new clients know up front that I don't expect them to talk, and that they can relax better when they focus on the work being done and how they feel. It is almost as if you have to give some people permission to be still. One of the harder things to do in the course of a conversation with a client during a massage is to just let it die when they suddenly fall silent. I have had to bite my tongue more than a few times when I was responding to a question and I suddenly felt them drift off into sleep. I have had clients stop talking in mid-word or sentence when their energy suddenly shifted, and talking to them after that can be quite jarring.

You also will have to weigh constantly the value of the silence and the need to give instructions, ask for feedback, or ask background information about what your hands are picking up in the muscles. If a client is coming to you primarily to relax, then silence is the better choice. However, if you are working on a specific problem or need that is the main reason for the appointment, get feedback or give instructions when necessary. Interrupting the silence to have a client turn over is probably my least favorite thing to do, and if you are going to break the silence, do so gently. If I need to wake a client to turn over, I go through my wake-up ritual by covering them with the sheet, running my hands the length of the body, stopping my movements, resting my hands, and gently rocking. The stillness usually wakens them. If that fails, I quietly ask, "How are you doing?" and take it from there.

Even at the end of the massage, I am careful how I break the silence. During the premassage spiel, I tell all my new clients that I have a closing ritual at the end of the massage. When they hear the words "ta da" somewhere in the far reaches of their alpha state, they will know I'm done. There is nothing worse than doing a great session, then having your client look up, confused and say, "Is that it?" This closing ritual lets them know they can drift away, and that you will take care of them while they are gone and will bring them back safely.

Waking Up a Sleeping Client

A predetermined ritual also lessens the number of times you have to go through the process of trying to awaken people gently without scaring them. If you do have to wake them, stand near the waist and shoulder, gently rock them, and ask "How are you doing?" This wakes them up but it also lets them be in charge. It may sound odd but when I used to ask, "Are you awake?" or say, "Time to wake up," I noticed my clients had a tendency to deny immediately that they were asleep, even if they had rattled the windows with their snoring. If they don't want to admit that they dozed off, fine, but I have learned from vehement denials that some people think there's something wrong with falling asleep. Maybe it has something to do with thinking they were vulnerable or out of control, but whatever the reason, I have found repeatedly that people don't like to be told they were asleep. I now get past this hurdle by saying, "How are you doing?" During this time, be in view so they can focus on you easily. Don't put your face down close to theirs because when they come to, they may not know where they are or who that stranger is towering over them. It will startle them and they may reflexively crack you upside the head.

I have a client who sometimes falls asleep at the end of the session. When he doesn't rouse with my usual closing ritual, I leave him snoring peacefully, wash up, read a magazine, or look out the window until he comes to on his own. Since I don't book my sessions close together, especially around his session, I can do this. That extra time for snoozing seems quite valuable to him, and not only does he always rebook but he also keeps giving me raises without my asking. In this case, silence truly is golden.

Moment 4: At the End of the Massage

Once the hands-on part of the session is over, and your clients are up and dressed, take a moment to ask them how they are, listen to their responses, and answer any questions they may have. If they set any specific goals or had clear expectations, review those and point out improvements you have noticed. Graciously accept their compliments, which may take some practice for you, and let them bask in the glow of their massage.

I also use this time to prepare them for the next few days. If they have never had a massage before, they will not know how to interpret how they feel and may think something is wrong. Depending on the kind of work you do, if they are going to be sore, spacey, emotional, or anything like that in the next day or two, let them know what to expect without setting them up for self-fulfilling prophecies. To talk safely during this impressionable time, use qualifying words such as "may," "might," "can," "some people experience," or "if you notice," then describe the symptom they may experience. In that way, if they do experience soreness or tenderness, they won't think something is wrong or that you didn't know what you were doing. If they don't experience those symptoms, they won't think anything is wrong since you said they might have those symptoms.

Trust needs to be maintained even when they are not in your presence, and giving them appropriate expectations for the days following their massage will let them maintain that trust. You may even go so far as to give them a sheet of paper with instructions for the next day. You can tell them to drink more water than usual, give them instructions on how to apply ice or heat, or give them stretches, exercises, or self-applied massage techniques to do to gain the most benefit from their investment. Even if they never do any of what you suggest, going this extra step continues to build their perception of your professional skills and your personal caring. Of course, if you're a smart marketer, you'll have all your contact information on that piece of paper so if they lose your card but have kept this instruction form, they can rebook or refer later.

Last Impressions

Your last few minutes with your clients are critical to rebooking. Your clients now have been connected to you closely for the last hour or so, and if you did good work, they will be warm and open. Besides being hazy and relaxed, they are looking at you with new eyes, and you can see them almost looking at you for the first time as they reevaluate their first impressions of you. They are watching you closely now that the session is over, to create their next impression of you.

It is important that you maintain the loving spirit you demonstrated during the massage throughout the rest of your experience with them. In essence, your client is in a hypnotic trance. If you have studied hypnosis, you know that the person who induces the trance must maintain the personality they used to put the person into a trance to get them out of the trance. If you suddenly start moving faster and talking noticeably louder during the close of the session in a way that is markedly different than what was used during the session, it is both jarring and confusing. Your goal is to maintain a sense of safety, trust, and connection from the moment they walk in the door until they walk out, so how you handle yourself between the end of the massage and when they leave needs to be given just as much import as when they arrive for the first time.

I remember the first time I really saw this concept in action. I had a student who was a large, muscular man trained in the martial arts and who dressed like a biker, complete with large tattoos decorating both of his arms from his shoulders to his wrists. He was intimidating to most people, but when he centered himself using his martial arts background to prepare to do massage, a marvelous, gentle spirit emerged and his work was like a beautiful dance. However, the second he was done working, he would pop out of that gentle state, smack his fellow student on the back, and announce loudly, "You're done!" I am happy to say that after a few coaching sessions, he realized the importance of maintaining his state throughout his entire contact time, and he did so with a grace and power that became his more permanent persona.

Handling the Separation Stage

In addition to good feelings created by maintaining the spirit of the massage throughout your contact time, your last few minutes are important for a number of other reasons. Whether spoken aloud or not, some clients go through split seconds of separation anxiety, fear of abandonment, and pain of loss. I have heard everything from "Don't stop," "Don't leave," "Can't this go on forever," all the way up to, "If I won the lottery, I'd build you a house out back so you wouldn't have to go." While I realize that these are ways people give compliments, there is a grain of truth in what they say. After all, who else has lavished such love and attention on them in recent years? If they had loving, touching parents, you are now linked to their happy memories, and your leaving is, for some, a moment of betrayal.

How you handle this moment is critical. If you briskly pack up, whip sheets off the table while they are dressing, move much more rapidly than during your massage, talk louder and faster, and look at the clock, you indicate nonverbally that the client is "dismissed." The ensuing feelings can seem irrational but some people will leap to the conclusion that you really don't care, you're just in this for the money, you're abandoning them, or that this isn't really a relationship, it's just another job for you. After all, their unconscious reasoning goes, you felt so loving and caring just a moment before and now you're giving them the brush off.

While this mental/emotional scenario may sound rather overanalytical or overblown, I think it must be given credence. Massage is different from just about any other profession or service. Because of the amount of touch, type of touch, extent of touch, nudity, and length of contact time, massage can create an intimate practitioner/client connection. Due to this, your clients may feel incredibly vulnerable at this point for a host of reasons. Some clients have been feeling their body, maybe for the first time in years, and others may have been going through a whole host of emotions and old memories. Maybe no one touches them this way anymore, or if ever, and their massage experience exposes the lack of this most basic of human needs. If your client is a single, working mother, the odds are high that it has been years since anyone has devoted time and energy to her. If your clients have had negative experiences with touch, a whole range of emotions may be swirling. If your clients think they are unattractive or unlovely, which millions in our country do, having someone touch them with caring and compassion can be emotionally wrenching.

Since you don't know what is going on in your clients' heads at the end of the massage, treat them as you did during your session to help them transition back into their "real world." Keep your voice and movements close to your massage level, act as if they're the only person in the world (even if you are running late), and keep your energy open to them until you or they are out the door. No one wants to be treated like that next sheep down the chute. During those last few minutes when your clients are most vulnerable, be gentle, be present, and keep your energy consistent. This is so subtle but so important, especially at the beginning of your relationship, for keeping and rebooking clients.

Booking the Next Appointment

During this final time together, you have your best opportunity to rebook your new clients. They are happy, feel good, and have immediate experience of your work. I usually say something like, "If you'd like another massage, we can book one now, or if you're not sure right now, you can call me later." This relieves the pressure they may have been expecting and removes resistance. The last thing you want to do is make them feel awkward, guilty, or pressured into rebooking.

Even if you don't have full confidence in your work, you must not let that show at this time. Give no excuse for yourself or demonstrate any lack of confidence. Don't undermine yourself by saying something like, "Well, I'm still pretty new at massage and don't know if it helped, but I hope it was okay. Would you like to rebook?" If you have misgivings about your work, keep them to yourself. Don't ruin their enjoyment of the moment by telling them how you could have done a better massage or any other such comment. Swallow your self-doubt, listen to their compliments, and offer them the opportunity to rebook. If they liked your work, they'll be back.

Rebooking

People have one of three responses when you ask them to rebook. They can say "yes," "maybe," or "no." If they say "yes," you can open your calendar or fire up your electronic appointment gizmo, and figure out the next time you can get together.

If a client seems hesitant to rebook, you have a number of options. The first question is whether or not you want to rebook them. There are some people I have worked on that I don't want to see again or retaining them isn't worth it to me financially, and I don't rebook them. However, if you want to rebook your new but hesitant clients, you will have to find out what is in the way.

The most common obstacles cited are lack of time and/or money. If time and money get in the way, do what you can justify to your business to remove these obstacles. You can deal with the obstacle presented to you but be apprised that the obstacles people bring up may or may not be the real problem. Time and money often are an easily constructed front for another issue, so before you give a discount, see if you can find out what that issue really is. If you don't want to push and just take them at their word, you can make a number of offers. You can offer a financial incentive such as a New Client Special of three massages for $99, a two-for-one deal, or a prepaid package series at a lower rate. A note of warning: Research in marketing has begun to show that the practice of giving discounts and coupons to current clients undermines the value of the service and dramatically cuts profits in the long haul. You have to evaluate whether or not giving a special like a three for $99 would cement long-term relationships or diminish the value of your work. If you decide to go with a one-time special, be very clear about its purpose. Tell your clients that your regular price is X, but you are making a one-time special deal so they can better experience and understand the value of the cumulative effects of massage. If they still balk at that, they either don't value your work, really can't afford you, or the underlying reason for not rebooking is not financial.

If your financial incentives have not led to a rebooking, you can be upfront and say, "It sounds like you're not sure about rebooking. If you don't want to, that's fine, but if I did something wrong I'd like to know about it so I can be more helpful to my future clients." Then be still and listen. If you are lucky, they will be honest and give feedback you can use the rest of your career. Once they've said what was bothering them and you handle their dissatisfaction professionally, they actually may reconsider and rebook.

They might have liked your touch but your fingernails kept scratching them, the room was too cold, or they didn't like feeling greasy. Issues that mundane can keep a client from coming back. Another phrase to use to dig out such obstacles is, "My goal was to give you the best massage you've ever had, and if anything was less than perfect, I want to know about it. I'm here for you, so what could I have done to make it perfect for you?" Very few massage clients ever hear those words from their therapists, and if you want to be head and shoulders above your competition, the things your clients will tell you at this point will set you a world apart.

Even if you never see them again, you have done major damage control. Because they have been able to articulate to you what they disliked, they will be less likely to complain to others. If they were personal referrals from other clients or mutual marketers, appeasing them is even more important because they could damage your other relationships. It may not be comfortable in the moment, but the moment passes. You can either integrate what they said into your work or know that some people will be unhappy no matter what. If they are really unhappy, insist on giving them their money back. It's one of the best investments you can make because it helps protect your reputation. After all, if someone complains about your work but concludes by saying, "she gave me my money back" you at least come across as an honest professional. In addition, money is an exchange of energy, and some people's energy I would just rather not keep.

Get Them on the Books

Once you get over the hump of booking your clients for a second session, you have passed all the first tests and are on your way to creating a long-term relationship. That doesn't mean that you don't have to do any follow-up or improve your work on a regular basis, but the skills you now get to focus on move primarily from marketing to customer service. At some point in your relationship with your client, instead of booking a new appointment at the end of each session, it can be advantageous for both of you to consider booking appointments months in advance. This gives them the opportunity to get your best time slots on a regular basis and it lets you predict your income more clearly.

If your practice is not the type to have ongoing, returning clients but has fast turnover, many direct referrals, or new clients from ongoing marketing projects or referrals, the prior material is still valid. However, instead of doing your usual great work with the knowledge that your services will be re-booked, you can practice with the knowledge that good massage therapists are hard to find and word will spread about you. Again, most long-term success stories have the common factor of happily rampant, positive word-of-mouth referrals, and the same elements that get people to rebook are what get them to refer.

Your Cancellation Policy

For my clients who book months in advance, I understand that things happen in life and sometimes clients need to change appointment times. If you have a 24-hour cancellation policy, let your clients know up front so they know what your rules are and that you value your time. However, if your steady clients have emergencies, which they will, don't damage your good relationship by being a boundary thug and demanding payment. Your relationship and their client net worth are too precious to risk because of an isolated incident. Instead, tell them you usually have to enforce your 24-hour cancellation policy because there are other people you could have booked and you've lost the salable hour, but you understand, are letting them off the hook since they are such a good client, and you hope the business meeting, funeral, interview, whatever goes well. Some of my clients have paid me for the canceled time anyway and others have not; they just rebooked within a few days so I really didn't lose the money.

In one case, I had a client who was "very important." The first time I showed up at his house and he wasn't there, I went ahead and billed him for that time because I had a suspicion that this was going to be a trend. I was right. However, from then on, whenever I went to his house and he had left for some reason, his maid came to the door with a check already made out for my full fee, complete with apologies that he had to leave suddenly. I would have preferred him to call me ahead and not waste my time to drive out, and after a number of times of getting paid for a drive, I chose not to rebook him.

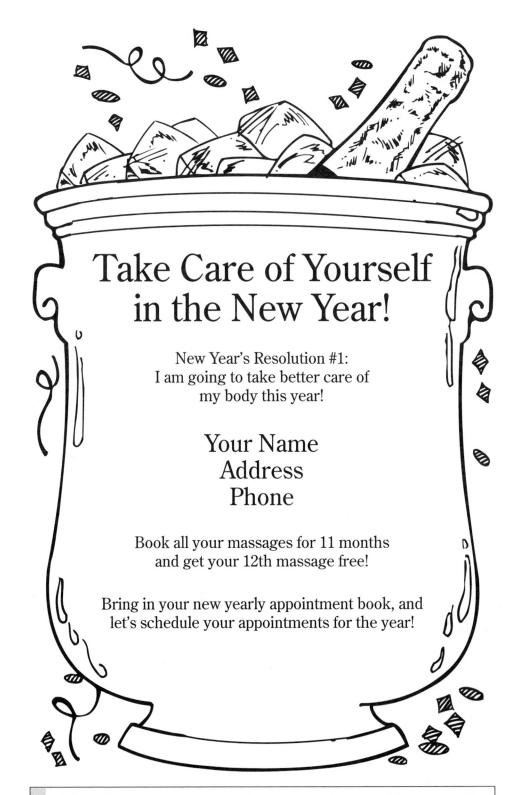

Take Care of Yourself in the New Year!

New Year's Resolution #1:
I am going to take better care of
my body this year!

Your Name
Address
Phone

Book all your massages for 11 months
and get your 12th massage free!

Bring in your new yearly appointment book, and
let's schedule your appointments for the year!

Figure 6–5 Booking clients far in advance can be done with a special offer as well. One of the best times to run a special can be at the beginning of the year.

If you are working with a few clients who regularly cancel out at the last minute or have to constantly rebook, I suggest you do yourself a favor and take them off your client list, and not lose your valuable time and energy. I practice massage because I enjoy it and it is fulfilling for me. In the case of my very important client, I was genuinely disappointed not to work with him, and it was a feeling I didn't enjoy. In the early days of my practice, it took a lot of energy to prepare for my clients and it was too hard on me when they canceled at the last minute.

SATISFACTION SURVEY

Dear (Client):

Thank you for taking care of yourself and your health by booking a massage with me. I hope you had a good experience, and I look forward to seeing you again soon.

It is very important to me that my clients are happy with their massage experience, and I ask that you take a few minutes to complete this survey and return it in the enclosed envelope.

Thank you,
(Your Name)

What did you like about your massage? _____
_____
_____

Did you feel your needs were met? _____
_____
_____

Did you feel your expectations were met? _____
_____
_____

If you could change anything about your massage experience, what would it be?
_____
_____

What else could I have done to make your experience even better?
_____
_____

Please rate the following: Excellent   Good   Fair   Poor   Comment
   Quality of massage
   Professionalism
   Attitude
   General Atmosphere
   Environment

Figure 6–6   Follow up with new clients to constatly improve customer service . . . and your success.

Handling a Dissatisfied Client

Beyond the answers of "yes," "maybe," or other various excuses, the word that is hard to hear during rescheduling is "no." If for some reason some of your clients just flat out tell you that they don't want to rebook, it may hurt but take it in stride. Massage is an art and the odds are good that somewhere during your practice, you will encounter a client who doesn't like your art. Just as some people think Picasso was brilliant and some people think their four-year-old could draw better than he did, so you will have mixed reviews to your art. Sift the reviews for ways to improve, and leave out the input from people who are perpetually negative or whose advice you think would not help your practice grow. I once had a client who was an esthetician tell me I would get more clients if I wore peasant skirts, open-toed shoes, and painted my toenails. It took everything I had not to laugh out loud at the absurdity of her sincerely offered opinion, and while I have had many chuckles over that client suggestion, I still have not painted my toenails.

Making the Most of a Dissatisfied Client

If you are like the many successful therapists I interviewed who have a hunger for learning and growing, then losing a client can spur you to continue to work on yourself and your skills. As with the esthetician's peasant skirt suggestion, I decided to just accept myself and my work, and be myself, even if that meant that I wouldn't draw clients who had a penchant for layered outfits. However, when I got feedback that was valuable, I would do what I could to improve. Studying anatomy, and going to seminars and conventions to learn new techniques and trading with other therapists gave me new skills and have absolutely improved my retention levels.

I love the title of a book by Janelle Barlow entitled *A Complaint is a Gift*. Her view is that customer and client complaints are what you can use to improve yourself and your business, and I agree with her. If clients complain with any consistency about a certain topic, pay attention. If your room is too cold, get a better heater; if you are hard to reach, get a cell phone; and if your work is too light, then get some weights, go to the gym, get stronger, or learn better body mechanics. In the case of pressure complaints, if you can't or won't increase your strength for whatever reason, have a list of other therapists you can send clients to. Your job is to serve your clients, even if it means referring them out. If you need to do this more than once, create a partnership with another therapist for a referral fee or cut of the work. You did the work of getting the client and should get some reward for it, even if it's just good will.

Getting Professional Feedback

Finally, if you have done all that we have covered and clients are not rebooking, get professional feedback. Call the best therapists you can access locally and ask if they will help you figure out what is keeping people from rebooking. Even if you have to pay for their time to get the chance to work on them, do so. Book appointments with as many therapists as possible, take them through your whole intake process and massage routine, do what you normally do, and see what they say. We all have our blind spots, and sometimes the only way to see ourselves clearly is to have others help us where we can't see ourselves. Part of the commitment to succeed is to get help and support, especially around an aspect as important to your business as rebooking.

Moment 5: After the Client is Gone

Once your clients have left, there are still moments of decision they will go through. If they said "yes" to rebooking, they may question their decision or even have a touch of buyer's remorse. People are funny about doing things to take care of themselves, and what may have sounded like a good idea at the moment can come under review. You can help them remember why they rebooked by giving a follow-up call in the next day or two. Ask how they are feeling, remind them of the problem you were working on and what their goals were, and ask if they have any questions. Tell them you look forward to seeing them and that you enjoyed working with them. This seems so simple to do, but it can greatly help your new clients in the moments of decision they face about whether or not to keep the appointments they booked. You can even send a "thank-you" card as an additional follow up.

Clients who left with a "maybe" answer to rebooking most likely will be harder to rebook, but you can stay in touch in numerous ways if you got the sense that they would rebook at a later date. You can always call, or if you have a newsletter you do yourself or buy preprinted by someone else, send one on a regular basis. Promotional projects you are engaged in, either on your own or with a marketing partner, can be announced through the mail by means of flyers, letters, or postcards. Basically, you will need to go back to the marketing methods you used for reaching new clients, only this time, your target market already has the experience of your work. Even a satisfaction survey, mailed off to be done in the privacy of their own home, can be a great way to stay in touch with clients and keep you as a conscious part of their mental process. Just be sure to include a self-addressed stamped envelope so it is easy for them to get back to you.

Conclusion

In the end, rebooking is one of the most overlooked aspects of marketing. As you can see, it takes more than just getting a client in the door to build a practice. I have talked with hundreds of massage clients over many years about their experiences, and their tales—good and bad—are what have gone into this chapter. What makes these clients leave a therapist, or want to go back for a second session or a lifetime of regular massage are no great mystery, at least not anymore for you. Their stories of what works and doesn't work are what you really need to know about how to market to build a dream practice. I hope the general principles and minute details they shared can help you toward success.

Finally, I encourage you to keep learning by talking to as many people as you can about massage. You may be surprised at how many people have received massage or know someone who has, and vivid stories are sure to follow if you simply ask. The best people to help you continue to learn what it really takes to rebook clients are the clients themselves, so start talking about massage to everyone, then be still and listen.

Rebooking Tools

CHAPTER OBJECTIVES

After reading this chapter, you should be able to:

- explain the value of a welcome letter and suggestion lists.
- create a client file.
- describe how to use various marketing tools to manage or encourage a rebooking.
- describe ways to stay in contact with clients on a regular basis.

Once your new clients have booked a first appointment, you move from the reaching function of marketing to the next stage; rebooking. Your goal at the rebooking stage is to make sure your new clients show up for their first appointment and have a great experience with you during the session. The more you can reassure them that they made a wise choice ahead of time, the better the session will go. And the better the session goes, the easier it will be to get a rebooking when it comes time to ask, if you even need to. Satisfaction from having your new clients tell you that they want to rebook before you even have to ask is sweet indeed. I recommend that you enjoy a few visualizations of clients initiating the rebooking process just to get in some practice.

The process of rebooking can begin before your clients show up for the appointment if you have enough lead time. If there is a short turnaround time between making the appointment and doing the massage, you can start the process once they show up for their first session. Remember, your marketing isn't over just because you booked the client. The process of creating trust, establishing value, and shaping their perceptions needs to continue at every step of the way.

Tools to Use Before Your Clients Arrive

If you can, send your clients the rebooking tools of a welcome letter, your policy forms, and a suggestion list before their first session. These tools tell them about you, prepare them to make the most of their session and your time together, and let them know how you plan to comport yourself as a professional.

Welcome Letter

Policy Forms

Suggestion Lists

The Welcome Letter

Acknowledging and thanking a new client for making an appointment can give the feeling of reassurance that a good decision was made. Your welcome letter can be a short card saying that you are looking forward to the appointment at the set date and time, or it can be a letter with background information about you and your practice, and what to expect from the session. Clients who book with you over the telephone based on a referral or ad will be curious about you, and you can tell a lot about yourself in a welcoming letter. You can include your brochure and background information about yourself that you may not be able to get to when you are focusing on the client on arrival. Think about what your clients should know, what they might be curious about, and what you can say to make sure they come to their appointment with the best expectations and anticipations for seeing you. Consider also what they might be worried about and alleviate those worries. Let them know that you keep strict privacy standards, cover them with a drape, maintain their modesty, keep them warm, or anything else that can reassure them all the way in your door.

Policy Forms

Policy forms can be anything from a legally binding document that you and your client both sign agreeing on codes of conduct, to a simple list of requests such as that the client not wear perfumes. Legalistic documents can be helpful if you have a large or full practice where it matters that clients are on time, give 24-hour cancellation notice, or abide by other rules that let you run your practice smoothly and efficiently. Policy forms can contain requests or demands regarding client cleanliness, sexual harassment, revealing medical conditions, giving accurate feedback during the session, or anything else that you anticipate may become an issue during or after a session.

Suggestion Lists

A suggestion list lets your clients know what they can do before, during, and after the session to make the most of their investment and experience. You can take some of the elements from the policy form and put it into a suggestion form. Suggestions for before the massage can be to shower, wear comfortable clothes, or bring a change of clothes. Suggesting places to park or creating a space where you can set up in their homes before you get there can save both of you time and frustration.

Making-the-most-of-the-massage suggestions can cover topics such as breathing into the work, not needing to talk, and showing up on time so they get in all their minutes. Somehow, it seems less punitive to encourage promptness for the session so they maximize their time with you than to have a legalistic looking policy that states the session begins and ends at the predetermined time whether the client is late or not. The end result is the same, but the tone of a suggestion is a lot friendlier and more welcoming than a statement. After-the-massage suggestion lists can include topics such as the value of drinking water, stretching exercises, what to expect the next day, and how to call you if they have questions later.

Tools to Use During the Appointment

Once you and your client are together, you can go over your policies and suggestion lists, either to reiterate your points if you mailed the forms previously or to talk about them for the first time. These forms and the rebooking tools you bring out during the intake process to go over together will make up what will go into your client files.

Client Files

Your client files can range from a single piece of paper with basic contact information and initial session intake notes to 3-D computer graphic images of stress and compensation patterns, full medical history, fragrance and music preferences, referral source, and demographic profile. Receptionists in your fancy office can make computerized files with back-up forms in snappy folders with color-coordinated tabs. Or you can have some rumpled papers that get jammed into your portable expanding folder that are left to alternately bake and freeze through the seasons in their permanent position in the trunk of your car, right beside your portable outcall table or chair. Basically, whatever you need to remember about your clients, write it down. Sophisticated or simple, your files should include at least your clients' contact information, emergency contact information, reason for seeing you, basic medical history, observation notes from your initial and subsequent sessions, and the ever-popular birthday notation so you can send a card.

Beyond that, you can add SOAP forms, photographs of postural changes, information from their referring medical practitioners, or astrological charts, depending on the kind of work you do. Sources for more standard preprinted forms with the generic bodies in the various positions can provide you with whatever you need depending on the information you want to gather on your clients, and they are included in the Reference section in the back of the book.

Tools to Use After the Massage

After the massage session is over, you face the moment where your clients let you know whether or not they are going to rebook immediately. As stated in the last chapter, they can say "yes," "maybe," or "no" to rebooking. If the answer is "yes," get out your primary rebooking tool, your appointment book.

Appointment Book

If you have already filled in your calendar with preestablished time slots for massage, open up your appointment book and schedule a time that works for both of you. If you have not set up your calendar ahead of time, be careful not to overbook yourself or schedule appointments too close together. It is exciting to get a rebooking, but remember to protect your time boundaries.

Even if your new client doesn't say "yes" but gives you a "maybe," you can still use your appointment book. Look up at the person, let him know that you understand he doesn't want to rebook at the moment, and ask if you may call him in a week to follow up with him. If he says "yes," make a notation in your appointment book. By writing this down, he knows you will be calling, and he now expects you to since you said you would. Later, even though you may feel like you're taking an ego hit if he says "no," you still will call because you said you would. When you call, he once again can say "yes," "maybe," or "no," and you take it from there, either rebooking or bravely asking if he would be willing to tell you how you could have made it a better experience for him.

Business/Reminder Cards

Whatever happens at the moment of rebooking, be sure to have your cards close by. If you have a happy client who rebooks, write down the next appointment time on the back of your card, first as a reference, and second so your card can find its way, once again, to the bottom of your client's purse where it can be retrieved after she loses your first card. Really happy clients can take a stack of your cards with them to hand out to family, friends, coworkers, and others. Even your "maybe" clients can take cards with them as they leave. After all, they may not be rebooking because they can't afford another massage, but they know lots of other people who would love your work. If that is the case, leap ahead to the referral section and read about how to help your less financially endowed clients accrue free time by referring others to you.

One-time Specials

Sealing a deal to get a waffling client to rebook may spur you to make a one-time deal to prove the value of your work over a number of sessions. We covered this concept in the last chapter, but if you decide to use specials to rebook, make sure you write down the details that you both agree on. For example, if you do the two-for-one special, give a coupon for use later, or take a check then and book both sessions in your appointment book. If they don't want to schedule that moment, book a deadline time to call to follow up on their decision as to whether or not they will use the special offer.

Frequent Buyer Cards

Creating customer loyalty is a big deal to a lot of big businesses and it is to you, too. Of all the big businesses to succeed by creating customer loyalty, the airlines have one of the best records around. Smart marketers copy great ideas from other industries, one of which is the frequent buyer card. Quite simply, you can have a card that keeps track of how often your clients get a massage. When they reach a certain number, especially by a certain date, they get a reward. Rewards can range from extra time or a free session to a free dinner cooked in their home by your friend who does home meal preparations for busy people. Be creative, think outside the box, and do what you can to have your new clients signing up for multiple sessions.

WELCOME TO (YOUR BUSINESS NAME)

I am pleased you have chosen me as your massage therapist!
I appreciate your business and your commitment to
taking care of yourself with massage.

To help introduce you to the many other services I offer, please bring these
coupons to future visits and discover the many ways you can improve and
enjoy your health.

COUPON OPTIONS

$10 off next visit
30 minutes extra on next visit
Free aromatherapy treatment ($20 value) with next visit
Buy two massages, get one free
Three massages for $99
Free reflexology with next visit

Figure 7–1   Coupons with a variety of incentives can encourage a new client to rebook another session or to try different services.

FREQUENT BUYER CARD

1	2	3	4	5

Your Name
Frequent Buyer Club
Buy 10, get your 11th massage FREE!

6	7	8	9	10

Figure 7–2   The Frequent Buyer Card encourages clients to consider multiple bookings.

Tools to Use Once Your Clients Are Gone

After your clients have left, you can stay in touch in numerous ways. Reminders of you that show up in the mail, come over the Internet, or through the telephone keep your clients aware of you on whatever basis you choose. You can send a premade monthly newsletter with informative articles, post e-mails announcing a seminar or class you are giving, or mail out notices about a birthday special you are offering that features an in-home gourmet meal (made by your friend) and massage (by you) on their birthday. Satisfaction surveys also are a good way to reconnect with clients. You can send a form for them to fill in about what they liked or didn't like about their session, and then offer a bonus of time or a gift they will receive when they come in for their next appointment. "Thank-you" notes are a great way to make a thoughtful contact after a first session, and they are a rare treat in these days of impersonal e-mails and people who haven't read Ann Landers.

Birthday cards are a nice touch, even for clients you have seen only once. I remember sitting on my back porch by the golf course where I used to live, and as I often did, I got into a conversation with the golfers waiting around to tee off. I was working on this book, and a golfer asked me what it was about. When I told him it was about marketing massage, he launched into an enthusiastic tale about a local therapist. As he raved about how wonderful the therapist was, I finally figured out that what brought on such a response was that the therapist had sent him a birthday card. And he had only been there once! I got a high-decibel referral, not because of a great massage but because of a card. If you are going to send a card, send a nice one, and sign it. In this day and age, a card you send through snail mail may be quite memorable.

HAPPY BIRTHDAY!

Enjoy This Gift:
A <u>FREE</u> Aromatherapy Treatment
With Your Next
Massage Appointment

Happy Birthday to my treasured client. I enjoy working with you and look forward to making your next visit even more special with an aromatherapy treatment.

YOUR NAME
Phone
Address

Figure 7–3   Make even better use of a birthday card by including a coupon with a special offer.

Telephoning

If you are comfortable with the telephone, you can use it to stay in touch with clients, especially the infrequent, special-occasion types. I have called clients I haven't heard from in a while only to hear, "We lost your card and wanted a massage but didn't know how to reach you," or "We were just talking about getting a massage but we got busy and forgot to call. Let me get my calendar." If new clients don't rebook but say something such as, "I should do this more often," ask permission to call them if you haven't heard from them in a while. If they say "no," don't, but if they say "yes," provide good customer service and call them yourself. Most people would love to get more massage but may have a hard time rationalizing it to themselves. One call from you gently taking them by the hand and leading them to book an appointment can restart your relationship.

CHAPTER 8   *Referral Skills*

CHAPTER
OBJECTIVES

After reading this chapter, you should be able to:

- identify communities you can target for referral marketing.
- gain referrals from formal and informal referral sources.
- use marketing tools for gaining referrals.
- create incentives for those who give referrals.
- explain the benefits and drawbacks to networking groups.
- explain the benefits of joining professional associations for gaining referrals.
- explain the benefits and drawbacks of working for someone else.

Building Your Dream Practice with Referrals

Building your dream practice can be a faster, easier, and fun process if you know what it takes to get clients through direct referrals. Word-of-mouth or direct referrals are how most successful therapists have built their practices, so if you want a successful career in massage, pay close attention to these simple but valuable concepts.

People who refer you to others do so for a whole variety of reasons but basically, people refer because it helps them in some way or another. If other businesses such as your mutual marketing partners refer you, it may be because you have the ability to help their businesses succeed by bringing in new clients, building their customer loyalty, or growing their businesses through joint projects. If your referral sources are your clients, they will refer because they like you and want you to succeed. Bonuses of time, special treatment, and "thank-you" gifts may motivate some clients, but most clients refer you because they have other people they care about that you can help. Medical practitioners can be a source of referrals because they know you can help their patients with soft tissue needs that will respond to massage. Giving referrals back to them also may be motivation for medical doctors or other professionals. Friends, family, and the checkout lady at the grocery store you go to every week just may give you referrals because, well, because you asked them to.

Building Referrals within Communities

Before you start going out and getting referrals, first think about what you want for your life and your work. You can go through the same process you did when planning to reach new clients. Think about what kind of clients you want, who knows them, and what you need to do to get their referrals. Go through the same mental steps of working with small businesses as mutual marketing partners except this time, think about community groups you want to serve. Community groups can be formal or informal in their composition, and while they may seem less definable than your marketing partners' customers, whole client pools are right in front of you, waiting for an introduction, if only you could see they were there.

Figure 8–1   Look for groups that need massage and that you would enjoy working with.

Do you want active, living-life-to-the-fullest kind of clients? One woman active at the local tennis club near you can be the doorway into a large enough pool of potential clients to build your whole practice. Do you enjoy the elderly and like hearing some interesting stories? One happy client in a large retirement community could be a fountain of referrals for you. Do you want more aware people who already take care of themselves? One enthusiastic yoga student can talk about you to her classmates, teacher, friends, and coworkers. Look around at the types of communities you want to reach. If you know people in that community already, talk with them about what you can do to get yourself into the group.

If you don't know anyone in that group yet, use the material on reaching new clients. Do a marketing outreach into that community, get a client or two, and you're in. A flyer up at the tennis club, a one-hour class on foot reflexology at the senior center, and you're on your way. If need be, join the yoga class yourself and get to know your fellow classmates. Even informal networking can be specific and strategic.

As you did with the mutual marketing material, think about what kinds of people you want to work with. Then think about where they work, play, shop, recreate, socialize, congregate, or worship. Whether they are hanging out at bowling alleys, coffee shops, bookstores, the gardening club, or the city swimming pool, people gather because they are social animals. If you spot a herd of them that interests you, figure out your best way into the group, wander over, and just be yourself. So many people are looking for a good massage therapist that even just introducing yourself and talking about what you do for a living can be enough to get you started. One person in that community who becomes a client can then become your leverage with the whole group.

This informal and unstructured marketing is by far the cheapest, safest, and easiest way to reach your target market directly. The successful therapists I interviewed who have built their practices from one or two well-connected clients got started with seemingly lucky breaks, but they were out there talking to people when those breaks came. The benefit you have over the therapists before you is that you don't have to wait as long for the lucky breaks or coincidental encounters that got many of them going. You now have the tools and skills to make your own luck, and you can be much more proactive and specific in reaching target markets earlier in your career.

EXERCISE: Identifying Communities You Want to Work With

- Think about the kinds of clients you would enjoy working with. You can look back at the work you did on describing your ideal client in the first section of the book, or think about it with thoughts a little different from the ones you might have had when you started this book.
- Get out a blank piece of paper and write My Referral Communities at the top. Then write down answers to these questions.
  Who is my ideal client?
  What 10 communities might my client be in?
  What can I do to get into those communities informally?
  What can I do to formally market to those communities to get my first clients?

If you are in a group, share your ideas so that others can expand their thinking.

A Note About the Exercise. If you found yourself not wanting to share because someone might "steal" your idea, take note. Scarcity will block your thinking and squelch creativity. And if you find yourself viewing your classmates or colleagues as competition, you need to reread this book. There are more clients out there than you can ever reach, and there are enough methods and ideas in this book to reach clients to keep you busy for as long as you choose.

I bring up this issue because of an incident at one of my seminars. Being a golfer and having many clients who play golf, I use golf examples frequently in my seminars. During a break at a class I was giving at a massage school I was visiting, a young man stormed up to me, glaring and indignant. "Stop talking about golfers!" he scowled. "You're giving away my secret!" Then he leaned in conspiratorially, jerking his thumb at his classmates behind him. "I'm the one who thought of working with golfers first, so quit putting ideas into their heads, okay?"

I could tell by looking at his face, hearing his attitude, and watching him sulk in his seat as I continued to give more golf examples that he wasn't going to last in massage for more than a couple of years. His arrogance, small-mindedness, and aggression were going to be spewed all over his clients just as they were at me, and somehow, at least from what I gathered, the all-important desire to serve just didn't seem to be present. Even if he did get a golfer or two as clients, I'd bet you a set of golf clubs that they weren't going to be referring him to their golfing buddies. Getting into a community is one thing; staying in and getting referrals requires all the other things we have talked about so far.

Informal Referral Sources

Many successful practices have gotten their start from the referrals of family and friends who believed in and supported the new therapist. My father kindly referred an elderly widow from his congregation to me, and though I was quaky and unconfident, and almost irritated at him for getting me a client before I felt "ready," she became an integral part of my practice and stayed with me for years. Thanks, Dad! If you are going to ask for referrals from family and friends, be prepared for them. Even if you don't feel ready, are unsure of your abilities, or don't have your cards, or matching sheets yet, get started anyway. Readiness is a feeling many people get long after they have gotten started, so don't wait until you feel ready to take on your first clients referred by family and friends.

Once again, the clearer you know what you want, the more you can tell your friends and family how to help you reach your target market. Tell them—or better yet, show them—what your work is about so they can talk about you more enthusiastically. Then tell them what kind of clients you want, what kind of work you want to do, days you plan to work, and other details to focus on. Being specific about what you want will help them know who to talk to and what to say in their circle of familiars. Making your dreams clear lets others help you make them a reality.

Referrals from Your Current Clients

Much advice about building a massage practice trumpets the glories of getting word-of-mouth referrals from current clients. The Catch-22 to that advice is, how do I get my first clients so that they can refer me? I hope by now you've seen many ways to reach new clients, and if you use those methods and tools, you will then have a pool of clients of your own from whom to get referrals. In all likelihood, your current clients will be some of your best sources of new clients. So, why will your clients refer you? Mostly because they are pleased with you and your work, and will talk to everyone about how much better they feel.

Since a lot of people are out there looking for a good therapist, even an off-the-cuff mention of you from a current client can turn into a direct referral. One of my clients found me in this manner. He was looking for a therapist, and while at a dinner table at a social function, he overheard one of my clients about four seats down say the word "massage." He subsequently went over and asked her if she had a therapist she liked. She said "yes," gave him my number, and that was that.

Many of your clients will be happy to help you, and if you need more clients, let them know and ask for referrals. Be forewarned though. One mistake I made was to talk to my clients when we were booking our appointments about how busy I had gotten and how hard it was becoming to schedule everybody. Little did I realize that this made a number of my clients get protective of their staked claim to me until one client said something like, "Well, just don't get any more new clients because then you won't have time for me." Oops. If you are going to ask for referrals, realize that you are often a significant touchstone in your clients' lives, and some will have a fear of abandonment that you will leave them if you get too successful or busy. Minimize talk about how busy you are, but if they know you are busy, allay their fears of losing access to you because that guarantees those clients won't refer you.

Making It Easy to Refer You

Give your clients and others ways that make it easy to share you. Give them your business cards to pass out, invite them to your promotional events, or better yet, give them gift certificates to give away to people they know who would be likely to convert to regular clients. You will gain a great deal of good will from your clients, and you will get a prescreened client, most likely in your target market, who has the trust of a personal referral with the decision to buy removed. If a full session is more than you can bear to give, give away a half-hour session but don't be cheap. This can be an invaluable way to safely and easily reach new clients, so make the most of it.

Making It Beneficial to Refer You

If you can't believe that clients will refer you just because you ask, come up with incentives that offer additional motivation. You can offer your clients extra time in each session or build up the minutes to a full free massage for a set number of referrals who become full-paying clients. "Thank-you" cards, flowers, or one of your promotional items or crossselling bonuses are nice touches as appreciation for new referrals. Clients have different needs, so pay attention. If money is tight, give them a "thank-you" discount instead of extra time. If they need flexible scheduling or forgiveness for having to change their appointment times, give that. If they want your most coveted time slot, use it as a "thank you" for their referrals. Some people just want gratitude and that is easy to give. Whatever it is that your referring clients want—within reason, of course—offer it. Just recognize their referral in some way.

Networking

In addition to your formal and informal referral sources is a well-structured source of referrals which comes in the form of networking groups. A marketing book would not be complete without some mention of networking groups, so here it is. Since my goal is to create pinpoint accurate, proactive marketing, I prefer mutual marketing to traditional networking, but it can be effective if used correctly. I don't mean to be down on networking groups, but they can be time-consuming with meetings, expensive to join, not reach members who interact with your target market, and take a long time before they are worth the investment.

I went to my first networking group in 1986, but it was not worth the time because at that point, the California market was still at the product acceptance stage. No one looking for a massage therapist because then most people associated massage with prostitution, and the members of my networking group were uncomfortable talking about it to other people. In 1998, I went to a networking meeting to promote my business as a speaking consultant, but when I happened to mention I was also a massage therapist, people became very excited because many of them knew someone who was looking for a massage therapist. My, how times have changed.

If nothing else, networking groups can serve as a social group of colleagues and peers dealing with business matters, and if you find yourself lonely in your practice, join a group for the support as well as referrals. Loneliness is a big drawback for working alone, and since sleepy clients and boundary issues keep your source of human contact during your working hours at arms' length, get your needs met through structured channels on which you can rely.

If you are going to join a formal networking group, go in knowing what you want. Say that you want 10 new clients or three on-site contracts with local businesses. Have specific needs that people can help you with or bring up specific problems that people can give you advice about. Remember, Americans are problem-solvers, so use that to your best advantage. Also, stay with the group long enough for it to pay off. People I have talked to who use networking groups have said that it takes time and persistence and showing up, as well as giving good referrals to other members. If your local area is still in the product acceptance phase, you will have to educate your fellow network members on what to expect from people's reactions and give them advice on how to refer you. Finally, read books on how to network. This is an art and science unto itself, and if you're going to do it, do it right.

Networking with Other Massage Professionals

I highly recommend joining an association of your peers. You can sign up for association referrals through printed and online directories, or through 800 number referrals. For example, the California Chapter of the American

Massage Therapy Association started its own 800 number so that the public can call for member referrals in their area. For clients who want therapists but don't know who to trust, seeing an ad, article, or bumper sticker for the AMTA-CA's 800 number gives them somewhere to start. Not every state chapter has this benefit, but large national organizations such as AMTA or Associated Bodywork and Massage Professionals (ABMP) do offer various forms of referral.

If you are new at massage, don't be alone. Go to association meetings or have your own get-togethers with classmates or massage professionals listed in the telephone book. If you want to get involved with your new profession, I highly recommend that you become active on an association committee. You will learn a lot about your profession, meet people who have already gone down the path you are walking, and you can learn a lot from them. You also can learn a lot about yourself as a practitioner and get a sense of just how broad this field is. When you are volunteering with your colleagues toward a higher mission or project, barriers come down and you often can get help, advice, and a host of other rewards that only show up when you are "on the same team" together. Dreams die in solitude. If your dream is to have a successful, long-term private practice or a hundred-acre healing center, or to work with movie stars, surround yourself with others who will help you keep your dream alive. The more you know what you want and tell others about it, the more someone who knows someone who knows just the person you want to meet can make your dreams come true magically.

Colleagues also are a possible source of referrals. I have met more than my share of scarcity-minded therapists who view other therapists with suspicion and competitive animosity (probably because they don't know how to market!). However, colleagues can offer many new clients through crossreferrals. I have given away numerous client leads to other therapists I knew from my association work because I didn't work in that person's neck of the woods or I was too busy. Having qualified therapists to refer my clients to when I did my crosscountry research and this book was easier for me because I knew my clients were in hands that I personally trusted. Get to know massage professionals with other specialties or modalities. I know the benefits and limitations of my work, and if I am faced with a client who needs help beyond my abilities and training, I refer them to the professionals that I know. As often happens, what you give comes back to you. That's how cross-referrals work.

Nonpersonal Referral Sources

Massage therapists who are willing to build their practices by referrals from nonpersonal sources have a growing list of referral sources available to them. If you want to grow your practice, especially in the medical direction, you can conceivably get referrals from Internet referral services, insurance companies, HMOs, and alternative medicine networks.

Referrals from Health Professionals

Working in close conjunction with health professionals—whether alternative, complementary, or traditional—can be a rich source of satisfaction and referrals. Across America, medical practitioners and massage therapists are creating positive working relationships, and crossreferring patients and clients in ways that could not have been imagined even a few short years ago. Even if this form of medical mutual marketing is not prevalent in your area yet, it is a growing trend that ultimately can be a great assistance to doctors, massage therapists, and their shared clients. Doctors, psychologists, acupuncturists, chiropractors, homeopathists, naturopaths, and other mental or physical health professionals are all becoming viable sources of referrals.

Knowing these professionals is something you should consider, even if you don't want or expect referrals from them. Over the course of your career, it is virtually guaranteed that someone will come to you with a problem that needs medical treatment. Many people are afraid of going to the doctor for whatever reason and may come to you seeking help because you feel safe. It is part of your ethical duty not to take clients who need medical care and not to work beyond your scope of practice. Having a list of doctors and other practitioners to suggest to them will allow you to rest easier knowing that your client is more likely to seek additional help since the referral came from you.

Working for Someone Else

While much of this book is geared toward owning a private practice, more and more new therapists are getting their starts working for someone else. Whether you are an employee, contractor, or renting space in a gym, salon, day spa, or doctor's office, you can get wonderful referrals and clients from those you work for and with. Usually, you give up a significant amount of your income for these referrals, but when you are starting out or doing side work in addition to your practice, it may be worth it. If or when you leave such a setting, if you have signed a contract not to take clients with you, keep your word and leave their clients in place. You have many marketing methods from this book to reach and get new clients, so you don't have to harm your reputation by taking clients against your word.

Even if you are working for someone else, the material in this book can help you build your practice in someone else's establishment. You can make an agreement that new clients that you bring in yourself have the option to go with you when you leave, or you can ask for a higher percentage or hourly rate for clients that you bring in the door. Working as an employee or contractor in a group setting can alleviate some of the loneliness, boredom, and risk of building your own practice right away, but be the marketing guru anyway since you now know how.

Conclusion

If you have the Bare Bones attributes and skills, and use a few Muscle Marketing techniques for getting and keeping clients, you will probably find that referrals will be all you need to round out and sustain your practice. Know what you want, think about who you want to work with, do what it takes to get a few clients, do good work, give excellent customer service, and watch your practice grow. In a service such as massage, the people who want your services are looking for a personal referral, so talk with all your sources about how to help spread the good word about you and your massage.

CHAPTER 9 · *Referral Tools*

CHAPTER OBJECTIVES

After reading this chapter, you should be able to:

- identify the seven basic tools for getting referrals.
- describe the three steps for using marketing tools to get referrals.
- explain the purpose of a referral tracking system.
- describe the key elements of a referral tracking system.

How to Build Your Practice Using Referral Tools

The marketing function of getting referrals is crucial to the long-term success of your practice, but in many ways, it can be the easiest function with the simplest tools. Compared to the possible complexities of getting new clients through the reaching skills and tools, getting referrals can be fairly straightforward, especially with personal referrals from family, friends, and clients. The primary tool you will need for getting basic referrals is your business card because it is small, easy to carry, and a socially acceptable tool for your family, friends, clients, and others to hand out without hesitation.

That said, getting referrals also can be involved and creative undertakings, and you can use every tool you have at your disposal to get into the communities or markets you want to reach. Once you are in, you can use your tools to inform, educate, and motivate those in your target community to book with you and give you referrals. The tools you can use for getting direct referrals are the same you use for reaching clients through other means, but with some interesting twists. From earlier chapters, you now are familiar with these tools, but now let's look at *new* ways to use your basic referral tools.

- business cards
- brochures
- gift certificates
- coupons
- flyers
- special offers
- promotional items

As you think about the people you want to work with in your targeted communities, consider which of your tools can get you into that community

235

quickly and easily. Think back to the ladies in the tennis club, for example, and ponder how each of these tools can be used to:

1. Market to get in the door of the club.

2. Reach and book a client who plays there.

3. Then have her refer you to her friends.

First, getting in. You can ask the club manager if you can put up a flyer, do a demonstration massage class, put brochures at the cashier's counter, leave a stack of cards by the towel pile, raffle off a few gift certificates at a fund-raiser for getting new tennis nets, or leave out a basket of free wooden massage tools with your name and number on them under the tournament schedule. You can ask to include a two-for-one discount coupon in the quarterly members dues envelope, take out an ad in their monthly club newsletter, or write a short article for the newsletter about massage for tennis elbow. One of those ideas should get you in the door!

Second, once you're in the door, you meet Loraine, the one with the tennis elbow who decides to give you a try. How do you use your tools to get her to refer you to the rest of her foursome? You give her a great massage; help her tennis elbow; give her exercises, stretches, or recommendations for heat and ice; and, of course, check the range of motion in her neck since she is probably chopping at the ball because she can't fully turn her neck, and, therefore, turns her torso and shortens her stroke to compensate.

Thoroughly impressed, Loraine goes to her friends with great stories and a few of your tools. She has a pile of your cards, gift certificates for a free half-hour massage, brochures that go with the gift certificates, and a deal for that group only that states if all the ladies come in for their free half-hour massage, or full hour for half price, Loraine gets a free massage. Of course, once this group of gals goes out and beats everyone's socks off, the losers will want to know how they got that spring back in their step. Surprise! The answer is you! Better get some more sheets and oil because here they come! Any questions? Now you try it!

EXERCISE: How to Use Your Marketing Tools for Referrals

- Go back to the exercise you did in the last chapter and choose one of the communities your ideal client is already in. Then look at the basic tools listed on page 235 and think about how you can use them to get into the community, get one first-time client, and get referrals from that one person.

- Take three minutes to think about how to use these tools and write down some of your ideas. If you are in a group setting, break up into groups of five and share your ideas.

ATTENTION: TENNIS FANS

> *You are cordially*
> *invited*
> *to our*
> *First Annual*
> WIMBLEDON
> SPECIAL

Just tell us the scores from the previous day's match and you will receive a **10% discount** on a tennis-oriented **sports massage** session.

YOUR NAME

ADDRESS   PHONE

Figure 9–1   Use events important to your community to introduce them to massage.

The Referral Tracking System

If you are going to be doing a lot of marketing using referrals where the incentive is more than just good will and gratitude, you will need a tracking system to keep tabs on your various referral projects. Contact management software may be necessary if you have a lot of irons in the fire, but if you like systems that don't crash, pen and paper work fine, too. Basically, your system needs to record information about your:

Client's name

Date you started the referral project

Terms of agreement

Method of accruement

Referral names

Referral usage

Referral rebooking status

Referral follow up

Deadline of the project

Status of the project

Termination of the project

Let's go back to Loraine and the tennis ladies as an example.

Client's name—Loraine Tennison

Date you started the referral project—10/6/01

Terms of agreement—one free massage for Loraine

Method of accruement—three tennis partners come in for half-price hour massages

Referral names—Susan Swing, Chris Chopper, and Nancy Netgame

Referral usage—10/9/01, Susan in; 10/13/01, Chris in; 11/01, Nancy not in yet

Referral rebooking status—Susan rebooks, Chris considering after vacation

Referral follow up—call Chris 11/01 evening

Deadline of the project—none

Status of the project—waiting for Nancy

Termination of the project—when all three have first massage and Loraine has her free hour

Obviously, this is a pretty simplistic system but you get the idea. There are so many types of projects with both mutual marketing partners and informal communities that no one project management form would be right for all of them. However, the basics used here are what you need most. They can help you keep track of your projects so that you can keep your current clients happy, stay on top of how well or often they are referring, and make the most of the referrals you get. After all, the purpose of such projects is to get the referred clients to rebook because, you guessed it, that's how you build your dream practice.

Conclusion

When I first started giving seminars about marketing, the title I chose for the class was Marketing: The Grand Adventure. I named it that because I truly believe that the process of marketing, including all we have just been through in this book, is one of the grandest adventures a human can take. Successful marketing takes knowing yourself, understanding the many facets of human nature, and being in touch with and observant of the world around you. When you are aware of yourself, others, and your environment, you grow as a person and succeed as a professional. The study of psychology, anthropology, history, philosophy, health, business, and more all go into understanding what drives human beings into getting their many needs met with the art and science of massage. I find it utterly fascinating, and I hope you have developed a healthy curiosity about why humans do what they do and why they come to you to be touched.

Grand adventures don't have any maps, road signs, or beginning and end points. An adventure is a journey, and journeys can begin anywhere and lead anywhere. Where you are today on your journey—with your skills, experiences, training, beliefs, and values—got started a long time ago, and your road will take many twists and turns as long as you live. My purpose for this book is to walk with you for the brief moment in time that our paths have crossed, and give you some skills and tools to build your dream practice. I hope this conversation will help to sustain you along the time of the journey that massage is part of your path, and I wish you well on your way. Very few people in the world have the privilege we have to live such lives and journey on such adventures, and I hope our time together here will make the rest of your adventure that much more enjoyable.

The Skill of Reevaluation

Before we part ways, there is one last marketing skill that I want to tell you about. It is the skill of reevaluation. It is, if you look closely at the word, the skill of reviewing your values. Grand adventures take many unforeseen paths, and who you become along the way and how you change must be evaluated on a regular basis if you are going to sustain your success. You can reevaluate yourself daily, once a month, or once a year, but to me this fundamental step is the secret to a long and happy massage career. So, what do you need to reevaluate? Yourself, your goals, your dreams, your skills, your practice, your beliefs, your values, and even your vision or mission statement.

Being a massage and touch professional changes you. Interactions with clients, conversations with colleagues, observations about bodies, talking to people about yourself, touching people, learning about the body, and all that goes into a practice shapes you into an ever-evolving and maturing person. Over time, you will discover there are certain skills that you enjoy more than others and you will notice that there are certain clients you prefer. You will notice that there are some things you are really good at and some things that you're not. Even better, you'll notice that there are some things that you're not good at and it doesn't bother you anymore. Or, you may discover that there are things you're good at, but you no longer enjoy doing them.

Massage practices succeed when you pay attention to the latest terrain you are in on your adventure, then adapt to it by learning more about yourself, studying more about your work, and otherwise growing and changing as a person and a professional. Massage practices fail when you stop paying attention to yourself, your clients, and the world around you. Without regular reevaluation, and the growth and change that comes with it, therapists get bored, frustrated, or burned out. It may feel secure to play it safe year after year doing what you've always known, but over time, the stagnation that comes with not keeping up with yourself and the world around you can ruin what was once a thriving practice. The goal of this book is to help you succeed at making a living with massage, but if you no longer enjoy your work, what's the point?

To get and stay successful and happy, I strongly suggest that you do a regular reevaluation of yourself and your business. The more frequently you ask yourself questions of reevaluation, the sooner you can make corrections on your course, and the less time, money, and energy you will spend spinning your wheels or getting lost on bumpy side roads. At the very least, do an annual review at the beginning of each year to help you see if you are still doing the right kind of work and still aiming for the right kind of clients. There are thousands of questions you can ask yourself to see if you are on the right path in your journey, but I am including here some of the questions I ask myself when I face times of transition and change.

The Questions of Reevaluation

How have I changed recently?

Are my goals different?

How am I handling success and setbacks?

Am I happy and fulfilled with my work?

Is my life balanced, do I need to unbalance it for a while for a big growth spurt, or do I need to stop pushing and let myself recover for a while?

Am I reaching my financial goals?

What new skills have I learned, or would I like to learn and incorporate into my practice?

Am I doing the kind of massage I want to do?

Is my level of skill still serving my clients?

Do I still enjoy working with my target market or current clients, or do I want a new market?

Am I ready to change my work status (e.g., part-time to full-time, employee to owner)?

Do I want to expand, get a business partner, or hire employees?

Do I want to sell my practice and move?

Do I want to narrow my practice and become a specialist?

Do I still want to be in the massage profession?

In answer to that final question, I hope the answer is "yes" for you. Millions of people are in need of healing and loving touch, and massage and touch professionals can help people around the world in ways we are just beginning to understand. You can have great success and satisfaction in this field, and if I have been able to help you learn how to reach and keep the clients that you need to make a living and build your dream practice, then you will be able to continue to change others lives with touch, and we all will leave this world a better place.

Resources

MARKETING MASSAGE RESOURCE GUIDE

The following guide is a compilation of books, magazines, businesses, associations, organizations, and Internet connections that can help the reader continue to learn how to build a dream practice.

The topics are alphabetized and include Business Management, Communication Skills, Customer Service, Financial Planning, Insurance Reimbursement, Internet Connections, Life Planning and Goal Setting, Marketing Books, Marketing Tools for Massage Therapists, Massage and Bodywork Associations, Massage Products, Massage Publications, Massage Resources, Networking, Public Speaking, Referral Sources, Resumes, Software for Massage Practices, Spa and Day Spa, and Visualization.

BUSINESS MANAGEMENT

Steve Capellini, *Massage Therapy Career Guide for Hands-On Success*. Albany, NY: Milady/SalonOvations Publishing, 1999.

Michael E. Gerber, *The E-Myth Revisited—Why Most Small Businesses Don't Work and What to Do About It*. New York: HarperCollins Publishers, Inc., 1995.

Anita Roddick, *Body and Soul - Profits with Principles*. New York: Crown Publishers, Inc., 1991.

Mark H. McCormack, *What They Don't Teach You At Harvard Business School*. New York: Bantam Books, 1984.

Paul Hawken, *Growing A Business*. New York: A Fireside Book Published by Simon & Schuster, 1987.

Cherie M. Sohnen-Moe, *Business Mastery—A Guide for Creating a Fulfilling, Thriving Business and Keeping It Successful*, Third Edition. Tucson, AZ: Sohnen-Moe Associates, Inc., 1997.

David A. Palmer, *The Bodywork Entrepreneur*. San Francisco: Thumb Press, 1990.

Roger E. Allen and Stephen D. Allen, *Winnie-the-Pooh on Problem Solving*. New York: A Dutton Book, 1995.

Bernard Kamoroff, *Small-Time Operator—How To Start Your Own Small Business, Keep Your Books, Pay Your Taxes, and Stay Out of Trouble!*. Laytonville, CA: Bell Springs Publishing.

Business Touch
29 Charlotte Street #2
Lombard, IL 60148

(630) 691-8141
E-mail: BizTouch@aol.com

Rick Vrenios—*Preventative Care and Maintenance for the Health of Your Practice*, a 118-page book for business success.

COMMUNICATION SKILLS

Dale Carnegie, *How to Win Friends and Influence People*. New York: Pocket Books, 1956.

Larry King, *How to Talk to Anyone, Anytime, Anywhere—The Secrets of Good Communication*. New York: Crown Trade Paperbacks, 1994.

Sam Horn, *Tongue Fu! How to Deflect, Disarm, and Defuse any Verbal Conflict*. New York: St. Martin's Griffin, 1996.

Dawna Markova, *The Art of the Possible—A Compassionate Approach to Understanding the Way People, Think, Learn & Communicate*. Berkeley, CA: Conari Press, 1991.

Anne Katherine, *Boundaries: Where You End and I Begin*. St. Louis, MO: Fireside Parkside Books, 1993.

Nina McIntosh, *The Educated Heart: Professional Guidelines for Massage Therapists, Bodyworkers & Movement Teachers*. Decator Bainbridge Press, 1999.

CUSTOMER SERVICE

Leonard L. Berry, *Discovering the Soul of Service—The Nine Drivers of Sustainable Business Success*. New York: The Free Press, 1999.

Ken Blanchard and Sheldon Bowles, *Raving Fans—A Revolutionary Approach to Customer Service*. New York: William Morrow and Company, Inc., 1993.

Carl Sewell, *Customers for Life—How to Turn That Onetime Buyer into a Lifetime Customer*. New York: Pocket Books, 1998.

FINANCIAL PLANNING / MONEY MATTERS

Napoleon Hill, *Think and Grow Rich*. New York: Fawcett Crest Books, 1960.

Suze Orman, *The 9 Steps to Financial Freedom—Practical and Spiritual Steps So You Can Stop Worrying*. New York: Three Rivers Press/Random House, 2000.

Suze Orman, *The Courage to be Rich—Creating a Life of Material & Spiritual Abundance*. New York: Riverhead Books/ Penguin Putnam, 1999.

Diane Kennedy, *Loop-Holes of the Rich—How the Rich Legally Make More Money & Pay Less Tax*. Warner Business Books, 2001.

Paula Ann Monroe, *Left-Brain Finance for Right-Brain People—A Money Guide for the Creatively Inclined*. Naperville, IL: Sourcebooks, Inc. 1998.

Mark E. Battersby, *SalonOvation's Tax & Financial Primer*, Albany, NY: Milady Publishing, an imprint of Delmar, a division of Thomson Learning, 1996.

David Bach, *Smart Women Finish Rich: 7 Steps to Achieving Financial Security and Funding Your Dreams*. Broadway Books, 1998.

Shakti Gawain, *Creating True Prosperity*. New World Library, 1997.

Sanaya Roman and Duane Packer, *Creating Money*. Tiburon, CA: H J Kramer Inc., 1988.

Jerry Gillies, *Moneylove, How to Get the Money You Deserve for Whatever You Want*. Warner Books.

Stuart Wilde, *The Trick to Money is Having Some*. Carlsbad, CA: Hay House, 1995.

Phil Laut, *Money is My Friend*. New York: Ivy Books, 1990.

George S. Clason, *The Richest Man in Babylon*. New York: A Signet Book, 1955.

Peter Lynch and John Rothchild, *Learn & Earn—A Beginner's Guide to the Basics of Investing and Business*. New York: A Fireside Book, 1995.

Susan Laubach, *The Whole Kitt & Caboodle—A Painless Journey to Investment Enlightenment*. Baltimore, MD: 1996.

INSURANCE REIMBURSEMENT AND DOCUMENTATION

Diana L. Thompson, *Hands Heal: Communication, Documentation, and Insurance Billing for Manual Therapists*, Second Edition. Baltimore, MD: Lippincott, Williams, and Wilkins, 2001.

Bodytherapy Business Institute
Christine Rosche
4157 El Camino Way, Suite C
Palo Alto, CA 94306
(650) 856-3151 or (800) 888-1516
Insurance reimbursement specialist.

Christine Rosche, M.P.H., *The Insurance Reimbursement Manual for America's Bodyworkers, Body Therapists, and Massage Professionals*. Palo Alto, CA: Bodytherapy Business Institute, 1998.
Insurance reimbursement for massage therapists.

Jo Ann C. Rowell, *Understanding Health Insurance: A Guide to Professional Billing*. Albany, NY: Delmar Publishing, 1999.

Ed Denning and Deborah Hecht, *The Medical Code Manual for Massage Practitioners*.
(800) 843-8607

Ea$y Billing
Marla Productions
524 Don Gaspar
Santa Fe, NM 87501
(800) 618-6136
www.easybillingsoftware.com
Insurance billing software.

Bodyworker Business Forms
P.O. Box 1016
Gainseville, GA 30503
(800) 295-7085
Intake forms, charts, insurance billing statement kit.

CompMed Billing
(303) 840-7500
CompMed offers a billing guide, kits, software, camera-ready forms, and a code summary with evaluation charts. They also do billing, bookkeeping, and secretarial services.

Professional Salon
3375 Motor Avenue
Los Angeles, CA 90034
(800) 710-3879
www.prosalon.com

INTERNET CONNECTIONS

Bodywork Mailing List
Join in on the conversation of hundreds of massage therapists from around the world.
Send an email to LIST-PROC@listproc.echomyc.com and in the body of the message write Subscribe Bodywork followed by your name.

www.realtouchmarketing.com
The "in-touch marketing specialists" sends out mailers every month for a year and can help you with a professional massage website.

www.massagetherapy.com
Massage Therapist Listing, Massage Therapy Schools, Employment Opportunities, Products, Associations, Links, etc.

www.massagetherapynetwork.com
Site offering therapist and client services, support and information. Offers client screening, 24-hour answering service with massage coordinators, and lots of links.

www.timetrade.com/mt1
To get connected on the net with your own webpage, and put your massage menu of services and appointment schedule online. Let clients schedule instantly or forward calls to phone operators to make appointments for you. (877) 884-9224

www.myreceptionist.com
My Receptionist offers the only answering service designed just for massage therapists, and provides Internet scheduling, messages, and more.

www.massageclothing.com
Order massage clothes online.

Massage Therapy Web Central
www.mtwc.com or www.qwl.com/mts.html
Information about massage therapy, including bookstore, massage school guide, training, products, and more.

National Certification Board for Therapeutic Massage and Bodywork
www.ncbtmb.com
(703) 610-9015

TimeTrade Systems, Inc.
(877) 884-9224
www.timetrade.com/mt1
Web-based appointment book, home page, e-scheduling, phone service for appointments.

LIFE PLANNING AND GOAL SETTING

Barbara Sher, *Wishcraft—How to Get What You Really Want.* New York: Ballantine Books, 1979.

Barbara Sher, *I Could Do Anything If I Only Knew What It Was—How to Discover What You Really Want and How to Get It.* New York: Delacorte Press, 1994.

Laurence G. Boldt, *Zen and the Art of Making a Living —A Practical Guide to Creative Career Design.* Arkana Penguin, 1999.

Paul and Sarah Edwards, *The Practical Dreamer's Handbook—Finding the Time, Money and Energy to Live the Life You Want to Live.* New York: Tarcher/Putnam, 2000.

Stephen R. Covey, *The 7 Habits of Highly Effective People.* Fireside, 1990.

Claude M. Bristol, *The Magic of Believing—The Science of Reaching Your Goal.* New York: Prentice Hall Press, 1985.

MARKETING BOOKS

Jay Conrad Levinson, *Guerilla Marketing—Secrets for Making Big Profits From Your Small Busines.* Third Edition. New York: Houghton Mifflin Company, 1998.

Seth Godin, *Permission Marketing—Turning Strangers into Friends and Friends into Customers.* New York: Simon & Schuster, 1999.

Marilyn Ross, *Shameless Marketing for Brazen Hussies—307 Awesome Money-Making Strategies for Savvy Entrepreneurs.* Buena Vista, CO: Communication Creativity, 2000.

Jay Conrad Levinson and Seth Godin, *The Guerilla Marketing Handbook.* New York: Houghton Mifflin, 1994.

Emanuel Rosen, *The Anatomy of Buzz—How to Create Word of Mouth Marketing.* New York: Doubleday/Currency, 2000.

Al Ries and Jack Trout, *The 22 Immutable Laws of Marketing—Violate Them at Your Own Risk!* HarperBusiness, 1994.

Al Ries and Jack Trout, *Positioning: The Battle for Your Mind*—20th Anniversary Edition. New York: McGraw-Hill, 2001.

Al Ries and Jack Trout, *Marketing Warfare.* New York: McGraw-Hill, 1986.

Sam Hill and Glenn Rifkin, *Radical Marketing—From Harvard to Harley, Lessons From Ten That Broke The Rules And Made It Big.* New York: HarperBusiness, 1999.

Rick Crandall, *1001 Ways to Market Your Services—Even if You Hate to Sell.* Lincolnwood, IL: Contemporary Books, 1998.

Roger Ailes, *You Are the Message.* Homewood, IL: Dow Jones-Irwin, 1998.

Joseph Aldrich, *Gentle Persuasion.* Portland, OR: Multnomah Press, 1988.

Jay Conrad Levinson and Seth Godin, *Guerilla Marketing for the Home-Based Business.* New York: 1995.

Jay Conrad Levinson with Charles Rubin, *Guerilla Marketing Online.* New York: Houghton Mifflin Company, 1995.

Elaine Floyd, *Marketing With Newsletters.* St. Louis, MO: Newsletter Resources, 1997.

Kenneth J. Cook, *AMA Complete Guide to Small Business Marketing.* Lincolnwood, IL: NTC Business Books, 1992.

Kevin J. Clancy & Robert S. Shulman, *Marketing Myths That Are Killing Business—The Cure For Death Wish Marketing.* New York: McGraw-Hill, Inc., 1994.

Harry Beckwith, *Selling the Invisible—A Field Guide to Modern Marketing.* New York: A Time Warner Company, 1997.

Guy Kawasaki, *Selling the Dream—How to Promote Your Product, Company, or Ideas—and Make a Difference Using Everyday Evangelism.* New York: HarperCollins Publishers, 1991.

Anthony O. Putman, *Marketing Your Services—A Step-by-Step Guide for Small Businesses and Professionals.* New York: John Wiley & Sons, Inc., 1990.

Stewart W. Husted, Dale Varble, James R. Lowry, *Marketing Fundamentals.* Albany, NY: Delmar Publishers, Inc., 1993.

Eric Yaverbaum, *Public Relations for Dummies.* Foster City, CA: IDG Books Worldwide, Inc.

Kay Borden, *Bulletproof News Releases: Help at Last for the Publicity Deficient.* Franklin Sarrett Press, 1994.

William Parkhurst, *How to Get Publicity and Make the Most of It When You've Got It.* HarperBusiness, 2000.

MARKETING TOOLS FOR MASSAGE THERAPISTS

TOUCH, Ink
225 Harrison
Oak Park, IL 60304
800-296-3968
www.touchink.com
Quarterly Newsletter sent straight to clients in your name, brochures, gift certificates.

Staying in Touch
(877) 634-1010
www.stayingintouch.net
Massage client newsletters typeset with your name, address, phone number.

Hemingway Publications
P.O. Box 4575
Rockford, IL 61110-4575
(815) 877-5590
www.hemingwaymassageproducts.com
Hemingway offers a full line of brochures for massage therapists.

Information For People
P.O. Box 1038
Olympia, WA 98507-1038
(800) 754-9790 or (360) 754-9799
www.info4people.com
Marketing brochures, videos, greeting cards, display cases, brochures, gift certificates, post cards, software, all designed for helping massage therapists build their practices.

G.E.T. A CARD
P.O. Box 66060
Downsview, Ontario
Canada M3M 1G7
Greeting cards for massage clients.

WaterColors Printers
P.O. Box 6269
Navarre, FL 32566-0269
(800) 804-2019
www.watercolorscards.com
A full line of greeting cards, posters, postcards, special occasion cards, gift certificates with a massage theme.

MASSAGE AND BODYWORK ASSOCIATIONS

American Massage Therapy Association
820 Davis Street, Suite 100
Evanston, IL 60201-4444
(847) 864-0123
www.amtamassage.org

Associated Bodywork & Massage Professionals, Inc.
1271 Sugarbush Dr.
Evergreen, CO 80439-9766
800-458-2267
www.abmp.com
expectmore@abmp.com

International Massage Association, Inc.
92 Main Street, P.O. Drawer 421
Warrenton, VA 20188-0421
(540) 351-0800
www.imagroup.com
www.internationalmassage.com

American Organization for Bodywork Therapies of Asia
1010 Haddonfield-Berlin Road, Suite 408
Vorhees, NJ 08043
(856) 782-1616
www.aobta.com

American Oriental Bodywork Therapy Association
Suite 510, Glendale Executive Park
1000 White Horse Road
Vorhees, NJ 08043
(609) 782-1616

National Certification Board for Therapeutic Massage and Bodywork
8201 Greensboro Drive, Suite 300
McLean, VA 22102
(800) 296-0664
(703) 610-9015
www.ncbtmb.com

The Touch Research Institute
Department of Pediatrics (D-820)
University of Miami School of Medicine
P.O. Box 016820-MM
Miami, FL 33101
(305) 243-6781
www.tri.com or www.miami.edu/touch-research

MASSAGE PRODUCTS

The Massage Company
1714 Lombard Street
San Francisco, CA 94105
(415) 346-7828

The Massage Company
1533 Shattuck Ave., Suite A
Berkeley, CA 94709
(510) 704-2970
Both Massage Company stores carry an extensive line of many different products for the massage professional.

Massage Warehouse
(800) 910-9955
www.massagewarehouse.com
Over 4,000 products for massage therapists.

Bodywork Emporium
(800) TABLE-4-U
www.bodywork-emporium.com
One of the largest retailers of massage supplies and tables.

Educating Hands Bookstore
120 SW 8th Street
Miami, FL 33130

(305) 285-0651 or (800) 999-6691
A large selection of books, videos, tables, chairs, and accessories.

Downeast School of Massage Bookstore
99 Moose Meadow Lane
Waldoboro, ME 04572
(207) 832-5531
A good selection of books, study aids, charts, videos, and accessories.

Utah College of Massage Therapy Bodywork Mall
25 South 300 East
Salt Lake City, UT 84111
(888) 354-6348
www.bodyworkmall.com
A large selection of massage tools, tables, and accessories.

Best of Nature
176 Broadway
Long Branch, NJ 07740
(800) 228-6457
www.monmouth.com/~bestofnature
Best of Nature calls themselves "the largest massage supply superstore."

Massage Warehouse
Atlanta, GA
(800) 910-9955
www.massagewarehouse.com
A large selection of massage and spa products.

MASSAGE PUBLICATIONS

Massage Magazine (bimonthly)
1636 W. 1st Ave., Ste. 100
Spokane, WA 99204
(800) 533-4263
(509) 326-3955 (Int'l.)
www.massagemag.com

Massage Therapy Journal (quarterly publication of the AMTA)
820 Davis Street, Suite 100, MTJ subscription
Evanston, IL 60201-4444
(847) 864-0123
www.amtamassage.org

Massage & Bodywork Quarterly (publication of ABMP)
1271 Sugarbush Dr.
Evergreen, CO 80439-9766
(800) 458-2267
www.abmp.com

The Touch Training Directory (publication of ABMP)
(800) 458-2267
Features over 700 somatic training institutions and massage schools.

Journal of Bodywork and Movement Therapies
Editor: Leon K. Chaitow, ND DO
For a free sample copy, fax a request with name and address to 011 44 131 558 1278.

Massage Today
P.O. Box 4139
Huntington Beach, CA 92605
www.massagetoday.com

MASSAGE RESOURCES

Books that can help you succeed as a massage therapist.

Steve Capellini, *Massage Therapy Career Guide for Hands-On Success*. Albany, NY: Milady/SalonOvations Publishing, 1999.

Mirka Knaster, *Discovering the Body's Wisdom*. New York: Bantam New Age Books, 1996.

Deane Juhan, Job's Body: A Handbook for Bodywork. Barrytown, NY: Station Hill Press, 1987.

Carolyn Myss, *The Anatomy of Spirit*, New York: Three Rivers Press

Thomas Claire, *Bodywork—What Type of Massage to Get—And How to Make the Most of It*. New York: Quill/William Morrow & Company, Inc.

Martin Ashley, *Massage—a Career at Your Fingertips*, 3rd Edition. Mahopac Falls, NY: Enterprise Publishing.

Cherie M. Sohnen-Moe, *Business Mastery—A Guide for Creating a Fulfilling, Thriving Business and Keeping It Successful*, Third Edition. Tucson, AZ: Sohnen-Moe Associates, Inc., 1997.

Successful Business Handbook, Associated Bodywork & Massage Professionals publication, 2001.

MOTIVATIONAL

Anthony Robbins, *Unlimited Power—The Way to Peak Personal Achievement*. New York: Fawcett Columbine/Ballantine Books, 1986.

Anthony Robbins, *Awaken the Giant Within—How to Take Immediate Control of Your Mental, Emotional, Physical & Financial Destiny!* New York: Summit Books, 1991.

John-Roger and Peter McWilliams, *DO IT! Let's Get Off Our Buts*. Los Angeles, CA: Prelude Press, 1991.

Crockett Johnson, *Harold and the Purple Crayon*. Harper & Row, Publishers, 1955.

Richard Branson, *Losing My Virginity—How I've Survived, Had Fun, and Made a Fortune Doing Business My Way*. New York: Times Books, 1998.

Patricia Fripp, *Get What You Want!* Bookcrafters, 1996.

Susan Schenkel, *Giving Away Success—Why Women Get Stuck and What To Do About It*. New York: Random House, 1991.

NETWORKING

Susan Roane, *How to Work a Room: A Guide to Successfully Managing the Mingling.* 1992

Susan Roane, *How to Work a Room: The Ultimate Guide to Savvy Socializing in Person and Online.* 2001

Donna Fisher, *Power Networking Second Edition : 59 Secrets for Personal & Professional Success.* Bard Press, 2000.

Jeanne Martinet, *Getting Beyond "Hello."* New York: A Citadel Press Book, 1996.

PUBLIC SPEAKING

Cherie Sohnen-Moe
Sohnen-Moe Associates
(520) 743-3936 or (800) 786-4774
www.sohnen-moe.com
Presentation skills workshops and consultations

Sharing Ideas—The International Newsmagazine for Speakers, Meeting Planners, Agents, Bureaus, Consultants, Trainers, Seminar Leaders. Royal Publishing, Walters Speaker Services, P.O. Box 398, Glendora, CA 91740 626-335-8069.

Lee Glickstein, *Be Heard NOW!—End Your Fear of Public Speaking Forever—Tap Into Your Inner Speaker and Communicate with Ease.* New York: Broadway Books/Bantam Doubleday Dell Publishing Gorup, Inc., 1998.

Dale Carnegie, *How to Develop Self-Confidence & Influence People by Public Speaking.* New York: Pocket Books, 1956.

Dottie and Lilly Walters, *Speak and Grow Rich.* Englewood Cliffs, NJ: Prentice Hall, 1989.

REFERRAL SOURCES

Massage Today Locator Service
(800) 359-2289
www.MassageToday.com
Website you can put your information on to get referrals.

Alternative Health Insurance Services, Inc. (AHIS)
Thousand Oaks, CA
(800) 996-8467
Network of health care providers.

The WellTouch Corporation
Dallas, Texas
(800) WELLTOUCH
Enrolling 7,500 massage therapists for referrals.

Bienestar
Network of alternative health care practitioners.
(888) 692-4363

Oxford Health Plans Inc.
800 Connecticut Ave.
Norwalk, CT 06854
New Jersey, New York, Connecticut referrals.

The Portable Practitioner: Opportunities in the Healing Arts
P.O. Box 2095
Petoskey, MI 49770
616-347-8591
(800) 868-2877
www.cybersytes.com/portprac
Newsletter with employment opportunities.

RESUMES

Yana Parker, *The Damn Good Resume Guide.* Berkeley, CA: Ten Speed Press.

SOFTWARE FOR MASSAGE PRACTICES

Professional Salon from Select Computer Inc.
(800) 710-3879
www.prosalon.com

Elite Software, Inc.
(800) 662-ELITE
www.elite-usa.com

Software to manage sales, inventory, client files, marketing, appointments, and payroll.

Land Software
(202) 237-2733
www.landsw.com
Hands on business management software for massage therapists. Includes client manager, session manager, financial reports, track referrals, session history, medical history, etc.

Island Software Co.
Massage Office Version 2.2
Business Software for Massage Therapists
www.islandsoftwareco.com
(877) 384-0295

SPAS AND DAY SPAS

International Spa Association (ISPA)
2365 Harrodsburg Road, Suite A325
Lexington, KY 40504
888-651-4772
www.experienceispa.com

The Day Spa Association
P.O. Box 5232
West New York, NJ 07093
www.dayspaassociation.com

Steve Capellini, *The Royal Treatment: How You Can Take Home the Pleasures of the Great Luxury Spas,* New York: Dell, 1998.

Mark E. Battersby, *SalonOvation's Tax & Financial Primer,* Albany, NY: Milady Publishing, an imprint of Delmar, a

division of Thomson Learning 1996.
Financial advice for salon owners setting up a day spa.

Erica Miller, *Day Spa Operations*. Albany, NY: Milady Publishing, an imprint of Delmar, a division of Thomson Learning, 1996.

Erica Miller, *Day Spa Techniques*. Albany, NY: Milady Publishing, an imprint of Delmar, a division of Thomson Learning, 1996.

SPA Magazine
www.spamagazine.com
(877) 745-7195

American Spa magazine
(800) 225-4569, extension 743
(218) 723-9477

DAYSPA magazine
P.O. Box 10566
Riverton, NJ 08076-0566
(800) 624-4196
www.dayspamagazine.com

Healing Retreats & Spas magazine
(805) 962-7107
www.healingretreats.com

Spa Finder magazine
(888) 763-6409
www.spafinder.com

Spa Management Journal
P.O. Box 2699
Champlain, NY 12919-2699
www.spamanagement.com

Premier Spas magazine
(218) 723-9200
www.premierspa.com

Tara Spa Therapy
P.O. Box 222639
Carmel, CA 93922
(800) 552-0779
Tara Grodjesk offers consulting services for individuals or corporations opening new spa properties.

MCM International
2190 SE 17th Street Causeway, Suite 308
Ft. Lauderdale, FL 33316
(954) 525-3922
Michael McCaffrey of MCM is one of the top spa strategists and planners in North America.

SpaMassage Alliance
www.spamassagealliance.com
An alliance created to strengthen the working relationship between spa leaders and touch therapy professionals.

Universal Companies
(540) 466-9110
(800) 558-5571
www.universalcompanies.com
Billed as the one-source spa solution with information on thousands of spa products and services.

Day Spa Warehouse
(800) 910-9955
www.dayspawarehouse.com
Over 5,000 products for spas and day spas.

TAXES / BARTERING

IRS
www.irs.ustreas.gov/cover.html

Barter Age magazine
(503) 245-0748

Bartering News
P.O. Box 3024
Mission Viejo, CA 92690

BarterNet
http//barter.net

Gregory L. Dent and Jeffrey Johnson, *Tax Planning and Preparation Made Easy for the Self-Employed*, John Wiley & Sons, 1995.

VISUALIZATION

Richard Bandler, *Using Your Brain—for a Change—Neuro-Linguistic Programming*. Moab, UT: Real People Press, 1985.

Shakti Gawain, *Creative Visualization—Use the Power of Your Imagination to Create What You Want in Your Life*. Mill Valley, CA: Whatever Publishing, Inc., 1978.

Index

(An f following page number indicates figure.)